The Book of Fishes

Trophy of a 3-hour Battle: A 53-pound King Salmon

Discovery of pay dirt brings no greater thrill to a miner than the conquest of a game fish to an angler. This male king, bound upstream to spawning grounds, wears the characteristic outthrust lower jaw of the breeding salmon. The catch was made by Erne St. Claire, Portland, Oregon, with a 6-pound test line on a 3½-ounce spinning rod.

THE BOOK OF FISHES

*1952 Edition, Revised and Enlarged, Presenting the Better-known
Food and Game Fishes and the Aquatic Life of the
Coastal and Inland Waters of the United States*

Edited by

John Oliver La Gorce, Litt.D., D.Sc.

Vice President, National Geographic Society

With 236 Species in Color with Biographies, 67 Other Color
Photographs, and 170 Monochrome Photographs

Narratives by John Oliver La Gorce; Charles Haskins Townsend, *Former Director,
New York Aquarium;* Leonard P. Schultz, *Curator of Fishes, United States National
Musuem;* John T. Nichols, *Curator of Recent Fishes, American Museum of Natural
History;* Paul A. Zahl, *Associate Director, Haskins Laboratories;* Louis L. Mowbray,
Former Curator, Bermuda Government Aquarium and Museum;* David Hellyer, *As-
sistant Director, School of Inter-American Studies, University of Florida;* Van Campen
Heilner, *Field Representative, Department of Ichthyology, American Museum of
Natural History;* Hilary B. Moore, *Professor of Marine Biology, University of Miami;*
Roy Waldo Miner, *Curator Emeritus of Marine Life, American Museum of Natural
History;* Luis Marden, *Editorial Staff, National Geographic Magazine;* Jacques-Yves
Cousteau; Gilbert Grosvenor La Gorce; Alan Villiers. Original paintings by Hashime
Murayama, Walter A. Weber, Maynard Reece, Craig Phillips, and Jacqueline Hutton.

NATIONAL GEOGRAPHIC SOCIETY
Washington, D. C.

Table of Contents

List of Species

Portrayed in Color, with Biographies

List of Species

The Book of Fishes

FOREWORD

FISH have played a vital part in the economy of our Nation ever since the first settlers came to America. In writing a description of New England in 1616, Capt. John Smith sought to attract people to Jamestown by writing: "And what sport doth yeeld a more pleasing content, and less hurt and charge than angling with a hooke!" The *Mayflower* Pilgrims planted fish as fertilizer with the seeds they sowed in the meager, rockbound soil of Plymouth. From far-off France, brave fishermen-explorers in their little ships sailed some 2,000 miles as early as 1525 to the then mysterious and often dangerous Grand Banks, which lie east and south of Newfoundland and are crossed by the cold Labrador Current and edged by the warm Gulf Stream, there to reap the rich harvest from the world's greatest codfish area.

The seemingly inexhaustible North American salt- and fresh-water reservoirs of fish life continue to provide not only delectable and necessary food to the ever-growing millions but healthful out-of-door recreation and wholesome sport to millions of young and old in every walk of life. Whether the angler fishes with bent pin or barbed hook of steel from a creek bank or a palatial yacht, he experiences a thrill that has few equals in sports, for the joy of battle with fighting fish calls to legions in all seasons throughout our continent.

It is hoped *The Book of Fishes* will interest and reward the experienced big-game sport fisherman and the novice alike. Presenting the life stories of many of the important fishes and other forms of aquatic life to be found in teeming American waters, it should aid the angler in deciding where to seek his game and to identify the species when caught.

So rich and varied is the fish life of North America's vast coastal waters and of its rivers, bays, lakes, and brooks, and so vital is it to our national economy, that to describe all the nearly 5,000 known species would necessitate a "five-foot shelf" of encyclopedic volumes, far too costly for general ownership. Therefore, out of the treasure of ichthyological material gathered by the National Geographic Society through the years, selections have been made of those deemed important to the army of sport-loving fishermen of both sexes. These are presented and described in nontechnical terms in the chapters, biographies, and legends and shown in the photographic illustrations and color reproductions illuminating this volume. In this 1952 volume readers will find much added material not included in the previous editions.

The Editor desires to acknowledge with appreciation the valued cooperation of Dr. Leonard P. Schultz, Curator of Fishes, United States National Museum, Messrs. Andrew Poggenpohl, S. E. Jones, and others of the *National Geographic Magazine's* editorial staff.

JOHN OLIVER LA GORCE

Washington, D. C., 1952

Water Seethes. A Rainbow Trout Leaps Out of the Depths

Not the catch in the frying pan so much as the excitement of the strike and the fight at opposite end of a line lures some 22,000,000 Americans to fishing waters each year (page 101). A broad iridescent band along the side identifies this trout as a resident of the Pacific slopes.

America's Rich Harvest of the Sea

By John Oliver La Gorce

Vice-President, National Geographic Society

FOR comparison, let us imagine a race living somewhere on tablelands towering into the stratosphere and possessing ships lighter than swan's down. Imagine them launching out on the surface of the oceans of air, with clouds forever screening the earth far below.

Now and then one of their exploring craft might drop a dredge into the unknown. The sounding tube, reaching the earth perchance, might sink into the soil of a cornfield or the mud of a riverbank.

The dredge net might capture a bumblebee or a butterfly. It might conceivably suck in a field mouse or a pine cone. But, whatever it got, how little that would be compared with the vast number of things that would escape its sightless groping!

And so it is with our knowledge of the sea and the vast numbers of creatures that inhabit its depths. Even on the floor of the deepest trench in the abyssal region of the sea's bottom, where no ray of light ever reaches, where Stygian darkness is perpetual, where temperatures are all but freezing, where inconceivable pressures prevail, the miracle of life still goes on.

In some ocean depths the pressure exerted would be equal to that of a block of limestone three feet square and six feet high resting on a square inch of surface. A creature five feet long with an average girth of four feet would have to sustain a pressure of some 20,000 tons.

Mysterious Hulks Washed Ashore

Denizens of the deep seas range in size from microscopic to mammoth. Occasionally huge hulks of tough, fibrous flesh, unlike that of any known creatures, have been washed ashore. One such hulk, 20 feet long and 40 feet around, weighed many tons.

The sea covers almost three times as much area as the land. Its average depth is more than two miles. The sea has 138 times as much territory lying 12,000 feet below sea level as the land has rising to 12,000 feet above. To bring about an even division of the areas available for life of marine and terrestrial faunas, the water level of the oceans would have to be lowered 10,000 feet.

With the great existing disproportion in area between the land and the sea, it is likely that the human race, with its seemingly insatiable mass appetite, will have to look more and more to the sea for its food.

The story of the fishes and fisheries of the United States, which cover only a small part of the great world ocean, has the fascination of a romance. Whether we consider the biology of the species sought by fishing fleets, the methods of reaping the harvest, or the stern battle against depletion of the supply, there are stirring chapters at every turn.

From the seven seas man annually gathers an enormous and valuable crop of living creatures, useful not only as food but for a multitude of other purposes. The latest estimate of the United Nations' Food and Agriculture Organization places the total world catch at 25,000,000 tons, with a value of about $3,000,000,000 at the fishermen's level.

San Pedro, the Leading Port

The Fish and Wildlife Service, Department of the Interior, estimates that fisheries of the United States and Alaska account for approximately 2,200,000 tons of the annual world haul. The value of that portion is placed at about $365,000,000 at the fishermen's level and approximately $1,119,273,000 at the retail level.

Government figures for 1948, the latest year for which a complete compilation was available, designated San Pedro, California, as the leading fishing center of the United States. Landings there in that year totaled almost 481,000,000 pounds, with a value of nearly $31,000,000. Gloucester, Massachusetts, ranked second nationally and first on the Atlantic coast, with a catch of more than 251,000,000 pounds valued at $11,200,000. San Diego, California, occupied third place with a 213,000,000-pound catch valued at $37,400,000.

According to the National Fisheries Institute, the task of meeting America's ever-increasing demand for the sea's products gave direct employment to 170,000 fishermen in 1950. Four thousand more were employed as transporters, and 110,000 as shore workers.

Nova Scotia Fishermen Race World's Highest Tide as They Pick Netted Shad Like Apples

Catching fish in mid-air during five summer months is the business of the hardy fisherfolk of Minudie, on the Bay of Fundy where Nova Scotia joins the rest of Canada. As the tremendous tide ebbs, they drive their horses and wagons three miles out on Cumberland flats to set 1,000-foot nets. When the tide sweeps in, it fills the nets with shad and salmon. When it rolls out a second time, it leaves the fishes high and dry. Fish retrieved and nets repaired, men and horses rush for higher ground before the tidal bore returns.

Another 300,000 were given employment in allied industries, such as boatbuilding and the manufacture of fishing gear and processing equipment.

The Institute also reported that 94,000 craft of all sorts were employed in the fisheries in 1950, and 4,275 fishery shore establishments were in operation. The 1950 replacement value of fishing craft, gear, and wholesale and processing plants was estimated at $890,000,000.

From an economic standpoint, one of the most striking fishery developments in recent years has been the growth of the southern shrimp industry from toddling youngster to lusty giant. Gone are the small boats with their crude rope rigs, which formerly made one-day trips to trawl the shallows of bays and inlets. The modern 75-foot Diesel trawler travels to fishing grounds 500 miles distant, makes its catch with 100-foot nets handled by power winches, and returns to port with tons of iced shrimp that, within a few days, will appear on tables throughout the Nation.

Revolution in Shrimp Industry

Several factors have brought about this revolution in shrimp catching and marketing.

3

Casting the Bait Can Be as Satisfying as Catching the Fish

A skillful caster, choosing a wave-washed rock like this southern California angler or venturing knee-deep into the surf of a flat beach, can hurl his hook more than 400 feet to sea. Patient devotees of surf fishing are an increasingly common sight along the ocean coasts of the United States. Highways along the 1,190 miles of the California coast today are dotted with bait and tackle stands to serve the surf anglers. In less than 15 years the number of fishermen in the United States has trebled.

Equipped with larger craft and more efficient gear, fishermen explore ceaselessly for more productive grounds. Electronic fathometers serve as eyes for the crews, recording the depth and charting the contour and substance of the ocean bottom.

Modern packaging and freezing methods are afforded by shore plants. Railroad and truck lines furnish fast, dependable refrigerated transportation.

A few years ago shrimp were not sought in waters deeper than 10 or 12 fathoms. Seasonal fishing was the practice; the off-season was accepted as a time when the boats remained in port and crews sought other means of livelihood. Today shrimping is a year-round, deep-water proposition, interrupted only by extremely bad weather. Operations extend from the Carolinas southward around the tip of Florida and the curving shore line of the Gulf of Mexico.

Scientific and exploratory information furnished by the Fish and Wildlife Service has aided the industry immensely. White shrimp (*Penaeus setiferus*), for years the only species fished commercially, is now joined on the market by brown shrimp (*Penaeus aztecus*) and by pink shrimp (*Penaeus durorarum*).

John Mahony

The First Boat on the Fishing Grounds May Get the First Fish

At the start of the tuna tournament at Bimini, British West Indies, contestants' boats race out to sea to find the fish and drop the lures. These boats push through Gun Cay Cut toward the Gulf Stream and its migrating tuna, a quarter-mile away. All powered fishing boats in excess of 16 feet operating in United States federally controlled waters are carefully regulated by the Coast Guard for safety.

Recently Fish and Wildlife announced discovery of still another species, red shrimp (*Hymenopenaeus robustus*), in large quantities off the Texas and Louisiana coasts in waters of 190 to 220 fathoms. Because of the great depth of its habitat, this shrimp has not yet been fished commercially.

Seven thousand vessels, valued at $150,000,-000, fished for shrimp in 1950, according to the Shrimp Association of the Americas. An estimated additional $50,000,000 is invested in shore plants and equipment. Their catch totaled 180,000,000 pounds, valued at $60,-000,000 at the wholesale level. Industry employment is estimated at 50,000 directly and a like number indirectly.

Menhaden First in Volume

In the United States' Atlantic and Gulf of Mexico fisheries as a whole, the menhaden takes first rank in the weight of the catch, with the enormous total of more than one billion pounds in a recent year.

The wealth of the United States and the high per-capita income of the people have enabled them to indulge their whims rather than their needs for food. They select their food, from both land and sea, more for flavor than for nourishment. Thus, in prosperous years, choice cuts of meats and the choice species of fish are taken, and all too frequently the remainder are not properly appreciated.

We have been particularly slow to adopt new salt-water fishes into our diet. Still, tastes change, even if only gradually. What was ignored yesterday comes into the market today, and tomorrow acquires a vogue.

Not so long ago the pollock (page 24) was in such small demand that it was scarcely worth the taking. So also with the tuna (pages 212, 213). Today, both find ready sale. On the Pacific coast tuna has been canned extensively for years. Beginning in 1937, quantities of Atlantic tuna have been packed in response to a growing demand.

The flounder (page 23), too, used to be

National Geographic Photographer Robert F. Sisson

Each Thrust of the Dipper Transfers 2,000 Menhaden to Ship's Hold

The big purse net, drawn around part of a menhaden school, has been tightened until it is solidly massed with the fish. The giant dipper hangs from a boom operated by a deck engine on the mother ship. Horizontal motion is controlled and steered with the hickory handle (right) by a crewman. Below it a chain opens and closes the dipper. By law, food fish caught in the menhaden nets must be thrown back or consumed by the crew.

eaten only by the initiated few; now it is one of the best sellers. So it has been with the haddock (page 24) and certain salmons, principally the pink (page 88). New England's rosefish, or ocean perch, is popular everywhere.

The growing popularity of sea mussels and tilefish (page 27) shows how the public taste can be trained under proper guidance. As the population of the country grows, we shall follow Europe in the utilization of marine resources to supplement our land crops. Today we eat only about half as much fish per capita as the people of Europe and have only scratched the surface in promoting the utilization of our food-fish resources.

Some Handicaps Are Overcome

Until recently, three basic handicaps—perishability of the product, instability of supply, and unsteady consumer demand—have hindered large-scale development of the fresh-fish industry.

Other products have one or two of these handicaps: milk is perishable, but considered imperative; canned goods have an uneven demand and supply; but only fish suffer from all three conditions.

But lately ways have been discovered to overcome the perishability of fish. These include quick-freezing and the use of dry ice. Fish are frozen in low-temperature brine as soon as they are taken from the sea.

A fresh fish bought in a market stall is seldom as fresh as a frozen fish precooled when caught. Now that this type of frozen fish has become widely available, the zone in which marine fishes are eaten fresh reaches far back from the coasts into the American hinterland.

That fish from the sea will help solve the food problem of America whenever it becomes acute is shown by the fact that analyses reveal how readily fish can be used as a substitute for meat.

Fresh salmon, for instance, has more nutrients in it than round steak; shad, more than chicken.

6

Oregon Indians Take Salmon from Celilo Falls as Did Their Forefathers

Perched precariously over the turbulent Columbia River, Yakima and other tribesmen use dipnets to snare migrating salmon. Perpetual fishing rights were guaranteed to them by treaty. Here, in 1805, explorers Lewis and Clark noted stacks of salmon "neatly preserved" by the Indians.

Men, Women, and Children, from the Atlantic to the Pacific, Fish from Every Vantage Point

Hopeful anglers line the Rickenbacker Causeway against a backdrop of Miami Beach, Florida, hotels. Below, diggers for butter clams at Kalaloch, Washington, assume a characteristic posture.

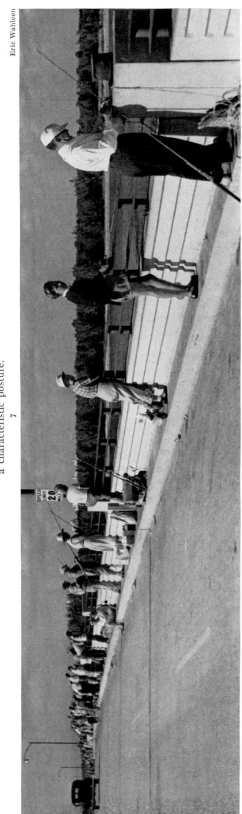

Eric Wahleen

7

The Fish and Wildlife Service has foreseen the day when exact knowledge of the marine and fresh-water conditions that make for an abundant fish supply will be one of our major concerns.

Knowledge of All Phases Needed

It recognizes that, without such knowledge, efforts to utilize fully the sea's food resources must be so handicapped that species which might render rich returns will be neglected, while others that have met with great favor may be all but exterminated.

The Service's introduction of the shad (page 29) into Pacific waters and making it abundant through 2,000 miles of coastline has been of first importance. Its success in saving the Atlantic salmon (page 34) and the shad from extermination in eastern rivers not in the critical stage of pollution is of similar value. Its rescue of the fur seal fishery from destruction and its protection of the Alaskan salmon fishery from inordinate depletion have earned wide appreciation.

Thanks to the achievements of scientists like G. Brown Goode, David Starr Jordan, B. W. Evermann, J. T. Nichols, E. W. Gudger, H. B. Bigelow, Thomas Barbour, G. H. Parker, C. H. Eigenmann, C. H. Townsend, C. M. Breder, S. F. Hildebrand, and many others, ichthyology today can make a correct appraisal of the problems remaining to be solved to develop for an ever-expanding race all the potential treasures of the sea.

Much Still to Be Learned

Despite these efforts, the things yet to be learned about marine creatures are vastly more numerous than the things already discovered. The list of fishes fit for food is inestimably longer than the list of food fishes.

Yet on every hand one already sees the results of overfishing on many of the species now entering the fish markets. Anadromous fishes, so called because they go up the rivers from the sea to spawn, such as the shad and the Atlantic salmon, become scarcer with each passing year, because they are so easily taken. Between overfishing and stream pollution, the fresh and brackish coastal waters are seeing their fisheries depleted rapidly toward the vanishing point.

The Atlantic salmon has disappeared from many rivers. Along the Maine coast the catch has dwindled to less than one-tenth of what it was in 1880, and there was an even greater decline before that year. Connecticut's Housatonic, Thames, and Saugatuck Rivers, once nationally famous for their salmon, now yield none.

The story of the shad is one of steady decline. Early decades of abundance were fol-lowed by a period of increasing scarcity in the Potomac, the Susquehanna, the Hudson, and the Connecticut Rivers. So hardy is the fish, however, that enough shad annually ascend the streams to support modest commercial fisheries.

Shellfish Steadily Disappearing

A condition of diminishing supply also prevails in the shellfish fisheries. Oysters, in spite of Federal and State watchfulness, are disappearing from beds where once they were plentiful.

In colonial times, lobsters (page 36) were so plentiful that even the poorest people ate them commonly.

Even as late as 1889 the lobster catch in the United States reached a total of 30,000,000 pounds, which sold for $800,000—less than three cents a pound. Ten years later the catch dropped to 15,000,000 pounds, and the price more than doubled.

By 1937, Maine's lobster catch had dropped to a low of 7,348,500 pounds.

But, aided by an enlightened conservation program, its annual lobster catch had climbed in 1949 to 19,272,700 pounds, valued at $6,-696,961.

Where stream pollution is the chief cause of the decline of the fisheries, nothing except radical protective legislation to save the streams will avail. The Government has found that a pound of bark to 30 gallons of water will kill bass in one day, and that even a pound of chips to seven gallons of water is fatal to salmon fry.

Stern Safeguards Required

If such simple pollutions as these destroy fish wholesale, what destruction is wrought by oil and tar, sludge and bilge!

Overfishing may be combated in two ways —by artificial propagation and by restricting the catch, either as to season or as to size of fish—in short, applying common sense.

Artificial propagation has proved its value in the case of fresh-water and anadromous fishes. The shad fishery has been bolstered by the artificial propagation activities of the Fish and Wildlife Service. The same is true of the salmon.

For sea fishes, authorities differ as to the value of methods at present employed. As new knowledge of the sea is gathered, however, there is reason to believe that conditions may be established under which artificial propagation can be made a success.

One Lives as Hundreds Die

It has been found lately that there is a dangerous age for the fry of fish, just as there is for the children of men. We know that the

9

"O Wad Some Pow'r the Giftie Gie Us To See Oursels as Ithers See Us!"

Three-year-old Mike Loughmiller of New Albany, Indiana, takes Robert Burns at his word as he presses nose and lips against aquarium glass at the Indianapolis State Fair to let some bluegills see us as we see them.

death rate for children between the day of their birth and their first birthday exceeds the combined rate for all other age groups up to 54. The reason is the greater vulnerability of infants and their consequent relatively high number of deaths.

Likewise, the first few weeks of a fish's life constitute a high mortality period, in which hundreds die where one survives.

If safe artificial methods could be devised to bring the fry past the critical period, their chances of survival would be vastly improved. Usually this period of wholesale decimation is reached about the time of the absorption of the yolk sac.

Apparently at or before this stage, minute forms of plankton—the mass of drifting plant and animal life near the surface of the sea—are needed as food by the fry that can no longer draw on the yolk sac for nourishment. Without this plankton they die.

The supply of plankton probably depends upon weather conditions generally, and an examination of the scales of the fish reveals that in any school of adults there is a great pre-ponderance of some particular age. Study of case histories reveals that this class coincides with the year most favorable to the development of plankton.

This affords a clue to the discovery of a method by which marine hatcheries may bring their salt-water fry past the dangerous age before releasing them.

This line of investigation shows how important the study of marine life is, what invaluable revelations it may yield, and the splendid character of the results that may be attained.

Lobsters Now Better Protected

To meet the alarming decline of the lobster fishery, the several States interested in its protection enacted various laws. Some have provisions for a closed season, in which the taking of lobsters is forbidden. Laws also prohibit the destruction of female lobsters "in berry"—that is, carrying their eggs after laying them.

In addition to this protection, attempts have been made to propagate lobsters artificially, by hatching and liberating the fry.

11   John Alexander, Pix

A Lean and Hungry Pike Stalks a Small Carp

In the seas, big fish prey on smaller ones. Here a pike (page 96) on the prowl first samples a fin (top left). Satisfied with the appetizer, he follows as the carp dives frantically for bottom gravel. The marauder's razor teeth get a good hold (top right) and the headfirst meal begins (middle right). Fat and happy (bottom right), the pike looks for dessert. The pike is a notoriously greedy fish and prefers a solitary life as it prowls around for food. It will also gulp down field mice and frogs if the pike can catch them along the shore.

Annual Winter Carnival Contest Provides Sport for Thousands

Some 5,200 enthusiasts braved near zero weather to fish through holes chopped in the ice of Minnesota's White Bear Lake in the 1952 competition. The tournament design is the four-leaf clover of the 4-H clubs.

E. L. Martin, St. Paul Pioneer Press

Lake Fishermen Vie for Prizes in White Bear Lake, near St. Paul

Hundreds of anglers spilled outside the cloverleaves to compete with fish caught through outlying holes which they chopped themselves. A five-pound, 3¼-ounce northern pike took first prize.

Men and Gulls Vie for "Fatback" Trapped at Sea

Small boats from five North Carolina mother ships have laid two purse nets and drawn them about portions of a big school of menhaden. Taking aboard sections of the seine, they constrict the fish into a smaller area. Once the fish are massed, a mother ship will load the harvest. "Fatback" along the Carolinas' coast means menhaden, a fish yielding oil used in soaps, paints, varnishes, waterproofings, and in tempering steel.

Although present policies have somewhat checked the decline, new forms of protection and propagation must be adopted if the fishery is to be saved.

The late Dr. Francis H. Herrick, America's foremost student of the lobster problem, proposed the abolition of the closed season, which he considered a futile practice. He suggested adoption of a double gauge for traps to permit the escape of all lobsters under 9 inches and to make the entrance of all over 11 inches impossible. He also would have forbidden the capture of all outside those limits and would have protected the "berried" lobsters, fixing a bounty for each one delivered to authorities. He proposed rearing young lobsters to the bottom-seeking stage in hatcheries, liberating them only when the perils of infancy are past.

Maine, which produces the bulk of the United States' catch of American lobsters, has adopted the double gauge for traps, protecting both the young lobsters and the extremely fertile, largest individuals.

Fish Dating from 360,000,000 B. C.

Jordan observes that, when a fish dies, it leaves no friends. Its body is promptly attacked by scores of scavengers, ranging from the one-celled protozoa and bacteria to members of its own species. The flesh is soon devoured, the gelatinous substance of the bones decays, leaving the phosphate of lime content to be absorbed by the water. Hence the multitudes die without leaving any trace behind. Once in a great while a few teeth, or a fin spine, or a bone buried in clay may endure, but the exceptions are notably rare.

It is because of this condition that few traces of the earliest fishes of the geologic past have been left. An expedition from the Smithsonian Institution some years ago unearthed near Canon City, Colorado, what are believed to be the oldest fish remains known

National Geographic Photographer Robert F. Sisson

Purse Strings Tighten Around Some 200,000 Menhaden

Single catches of half a million fish have been made. Menhaden nets, costing up to $6,000, require constant repairs. Sharks, trapped inadvertently, frequently rip the netting to shreds. Despite intensive fishing, menhaden numbers do not seem to decrease. Catches of this Atlantic and Gulf coast fish have exceeded one billion pounds annually in recent years and represent about one-fourth of United States ocean fisheries poundage.

to science. They come down from the Lower Silurian age, a time when neither man nor other mammal, nor reptile, nor any other living land animal with a backbone had yet appeared—a time, indeed, when some of the deepest sandstones we know were being laid down.

From early geologic times, many elements have played important roles in determining the distribution of the several species of fish. We see those same forces at work today.

Biologically, perhaps the most interesting of all species that figure in the returns are the flatfish—halibuts and flounders (pages 22, 23)—with their changing forms and migrating eyes. By what quirk of Nature the left eyes of species inhabiting cold water usually migrate to the right side of their heads, whereas the right eyes of most species inhabiting warm water journey to the left, no scientist will venture a guess.

When they are hatched, all flatfish are of orthodox symmetrical shape, with conventionally placed mouths and eyes; but after they swim around in ordinary fashion for a little while, they exhibit a tendency to turn to one side or the other.

Immediately after this peculiar tendency begins to develop, the eye on the lower side seems to be seized by wanderlust. Stephen R. Williams, who studied this change, says that the optic nerves are so placed in the youngling as to provide for the migration.

The first sign of the transformation is a rapid change in the cartilage bar lying in the path of the eye that is to migrate. Then comes an increase of the distance between the eye and the brain, caused by the growth of facial cartilages. In the winter flounder, three-fourths of the 120-degree migration takes place in three days. What if that should become a human habit!

The extent of the eye migration and of the flatness of the species is closely related to its

16   National Geographic Photographer J. Baylor Roberts

Stacked Like Lumber, Stiffly Frozen Salmon Await Shipment Inland

Modern quick freezing has brought fresh fish to interior areas where less than a decade ago its delicacy was rare or unknown. Both commercial and more recently home freezers have revolutionized fish marketing. Here in the vaults of a California cold-storage company, half a million pounds of Sacramento River salmon share space with ten million pounds of frozen fruits, meats, and vegetables.

The growth of the California fishing industry has been one of the most phenomenal stories in American economic history. Today it ranks first among all the states, and one of its cities, San Pedro, has nosed out Gloucester, Massachusetts, as the fishing capital of the Nation (page 1). During the most recent year for which total figures are available, California produced a catch of 895,492,500 pounds, valued at about $80,000,000.

Symbols of the Shrimp Industry's Jumbo-ing Size

Big shrimps like these have long been taken from shallow bays and bayous of the Gulf of Mexico. Until 1937, however, commercial shrimp fishing was largely limited to the white species taken in shallow Gulf waters in the autumn. Operations now range from the Carolinas southward to the Key West area and extend to the new species, deep waters, and all seasons of the year.

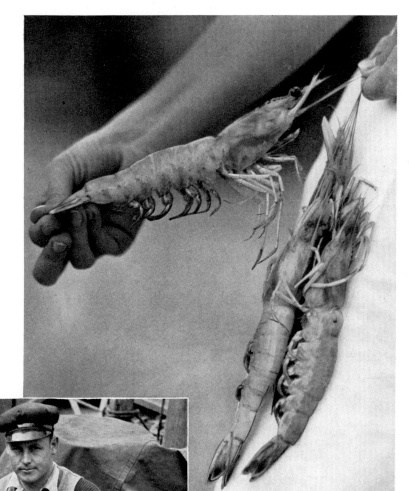

National Geographic Photographer
J. Baylor Roberts

Luis Marden, National Geographic Staff

"Have 'Em Grilled, Steamed, or in Jambalaya?"

White shrimp now share the market with brown and pink species. Red shrimp have recently been discovered in large quantities in south Florida waters, and 200 fathoms deep off the Texas and Louisiana coasts. Greatly improved refrigeration and motorization of trawlers contribute to growth of the industry, which directly employs 50,000 people and 7,000 vessels.

17

18

Hook Strikes Water, and—Wham! Tuna Strikes Hook

From San Diego and San Pedro, tuna boats roam west-coast waters the year around, ranging as far south as Peru. Churning the surface into boiling white patches, tuna in Panama waters gorge on small fry showered to them by a "chummer." Hooks, disguised to resemble live squids, are seized eagerly. The fishing pace is hard and fast until the school moves on. Now and then a man is pulled overboard when a very large tuna strikes the one-man rigs.

Four Men Hoist One Hook as a Giant-sized Tuna Is Hurtled Aboard

Off South America a school of giant tuna was lured to the ship's side by chumming with live sardines. Four strong men with four stout poles respond to a "strike" on their single, barbless hook. Their concerted, well-timed heave lifts the big fish over the guardrail onto the deck. Seconds later their short line is back in the ocean and they are set for another strike.

habits. The sole and the shore flounder, which keep close to the bottom, are more twisted than the halibut, the sand dab, and the summer flounder, which are more given to free swimming.

Cause Remains a Mystery

How this deviation from the conventional bilateral shape arose is a mystery. Whether there came a "sport" in the family tree at some stage of its history, or whether the deviation grew from a gradual modification of the adults under the influence of their environment cannot be said. If it came from the latter, selection naturally favored its appearance earlier

and earlier in the development of the fish, until it reached the larval stage. Earlier transformation would be disadvantageous, since there is a lack of plankton—that imperative, if almost microscopic, food supply of the newly hatched—at the sea bottom, and the transformed fishlings would find a scarcity of provender at a critical period in their lives.

Some species that help constitute the fisheries of the North Atlantic are anadromous—that is, they spend most of their lives in the sea but come into fresh water to spawn. Among these are the salmon (page 34), the shad (page 29), the alewife (page 28), and the sturgeon (page 64). On the Pacific coast, the most striking instance of this is the chinook salmon (page 91), which may ascend the Columbia River as far as 1,000 miles, and the Yukon as much as 2,000, to find its spawning ground.

How acute the instinct is in some species to return to the streams of their infancy was proved by a Canadian experiment. Salmon were accustomed to swim up both branches of a Nova Scotia river to spawn. Fish from one of the streams were tagged. The next year it was found that marked male fish returned to the same pool in which they had been tagged before they began their journeys.

How Did Landlocked Species Evolve?

The origin of such landlocked species as the alewife and the fresh-water salmon is a theoretical question. One explanation is that the anadromous relatives of these fishes found their way into waters from which they were unable to escape because of the blocking of outlets by geological forces in past ages. In time their changed habits led gradually to variations from their ancestors. Thus many new species have developed.

The eel (page 59) has habits of spawning which are the reverse of those of the anadromous species and is thus called a catadromous fish. It spawns in salt water but always seeks out fresh-water streams in which to pass part of its life.

Until recent years, the location of the eels' spawning ground was an unsolved mystery of the sea. Finally a Danish scientific expedition succeeded in locating it in the region between Bermuda and the Leeward Islands, where the water reaches the depth of a mile.

Although they are so nearly alike that the layman cannot recognize the difference between them, and although their breeding grounds partly overlap, the European and American species neither cross nor visit one another's shores—truly a biological mystery.

A Question Still Unanswered

The eggs are laid at depths of about 650 to 1,000 feet, and the larvae slowly rise toward the surface as they grow. At this stage, and until they reach their respective shores, they are mere bits of ribbon, so transparent that the vertebrae of their backbones may be counted without difficulty. The only difference yet found between the European and American species is that the European has a few more vertebrae.

Both species start out, mayhap together, over a route neither has traveled before. But when they come to the parting of the ways, the European elver, with a three years' journey ahead of it, says good-bye to its American cousin, which has only a year's swim to get

to its future home. By what means this unerring homing instinct is transferred from the parents, which never return, to the offspring, which must travel a road they have never been over, is also a mystery that will probably long await a scientific solution.

The spawning habits of fishes differ as greatly in other respects as in those just mentioned. Some eggs are laid at the surface and left to their fate, with no responsibilities of any kind for the parents; others are heavy enough to sink to the bottom. Some fishes, like the chinook salmon, lay their eggs on the stream bed, where they are covered with gravel, after which male and female drift helplessly down the stream, tail first, and die.

Some species, like the sticklebacks (page 92) and the lumpfish, guard their eggs until they are hatched. The courage of the male lumpfish and his devotion to the task have often been noted. He eats nothing while guarding the eggs, but constantly fans the egg mass to keep it free from silt and bathed in flowing water. He never deserts his post save to drive away some intruder, and finally, when the eggs are hatched, he is a picture of exhaustion and hunger.

The males of other species, including some of the sea catfishes, carry the eggs in their mouths until they hatch. The females of still other species, following the example of the lobster, glue their eggs to the undersurface of their bodies. The male sea horse (page 228) opens up a little pocket beneath its body, takes in the eggs from its mate, and carries them in the tiny pouch Nature provided until they hatch. Hundreds of sea horses are thus liberated at a hatching, so tiny in size that the human eye can hardly distinguish them, yet perfectly formed.

Some Fishes Bear Young Alive

Not all fishes lay eggs. Some give birth to their young alive. Among these are most sharks, the sawfishes, the rosefishes, the rockfishes, the surf fishes, and many species of top minnows.

The number of eggs laid varies widely in different species. Scientific census takers report that the herring (page 28) lays about 30,000. The sturgeon (page 64) may produce as many as 2,400,000, the halibut (page 22) more than 2,000,000. The cod (page 24) has been known to lay more than 9,000,000.

By the number of eggs spawned, one can gauge the perils through which the several species of fish pass from the egg state to maturity. It is demonstrable mathematically that if all the eggs of a single female herring were to produce similarly productive generations, in ten years the oceans would be overflowing with herring, and all the other creatures of the

21 Painting by Hashime Murayama

The Atlantic Mackerel Is Familiar to the Markets of Three Continents

THE Atlantic mackerel (*Scomber scombrus*) is a member of the family Scombridae, which includes also the tuna, the bonito, the kingfishes, the Spanish mackerel, and the wahoo. The muscular, cigar-shaped body of the mackerel has made it capable of great speed.

Although a maximum length of 22 inches has been attained, the usual length is from 12 to 16 inches. A mackerel a foot long weighs 12 to 16 ounces, and the longer ones weigh between three and four pounds.

Often called the northern or Boston mackerel to distinguish it from the southern or Spanish mackerel, this species inhabits both coasts of the North Atlantic. On the European coast, it ranges southward to Spain, and on the American coast to Cape Lookout. Although the Atlantic mackerel can scarcely be classed as a shore species, it is not taken very far out at sea.

The Atlantic mackerel congregate in schools, some of which comprise a great number of fish. Huge schools 20 miles long and a half mile wide have been sighted. By actual measurement it has been found that the fish in a school do not vary more than an inch in length, a fact indicating that they are all of the same age.

No other important commercial fish has fluctuated so much in abundance as the Atlantic mackerel. The fishery has yielded as high as 120,000,000 pounds and an all-time low of only 4,000,000 pounds.

Within a single year (1922–23), the total catch for the United States has varied as much as three hundred percent. Recent investigations have shown that fluctuations are caused in large part by temperature and the abundance of microorganisms available as food for the young fish.

The food of the Atlantic mackerel throughout life consists of free-swimming organisms, chiefly small animals. The diet includes copepods, small shrimps, molluscan larvae, annelids, squids, fish eggs, and small fish.

The most recent annual catch for New England was 13,969,400 pounds. South of New England the catch was 24,154,000 pounds. The fish are caught principally with purse seines, with drifting gill nets, and with pound nets, weirs, and traps, and to a limited extent with lines.

Spawning occurs from about May to July. When the fish are ready to spawn, they come to the surface. The Atlantic mackerel has no particular breeding ground. The fish merely cast their eggs wherever their wandering habits have chanced to lead them. Thus the eggs generally occur over a wide area.

Probably the Atlantic mackerel is as well known as any other species on the market. Salted mackerel are widely exported, and are to be found in grocery stores in European, North American, and South American countries. Not only are large quantities salted, but the fish is also sold fresh and smoked.

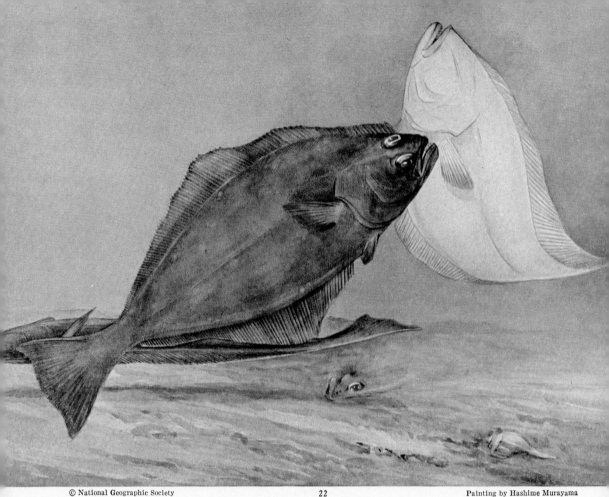

22 Painting by Hashime Murayama

The Twisted Eyes of the Halibut Search for Any Kind of Food

ONLY a few fishes, such as the largest sharks, swordfish, tuna, and sturgeon, exceed in size the **Atlantic halibut** (*Hippoglossus hippoglossus*), the largest fish of the flounder family. Though "large" halibut landed in New England ports range in length from only about four feet to six feet, and in weight from 50 to 200 pounds, some weighing 300 and 400 pounds are taken. A 9-foot 2-inch giant, weighing 625 pounds when dressed, was caught 50 miles off Thatcher Island, Massachusetts, in 1917.

The halibut is a cold-water fish inhabiting all northern seas, ranging southward on the European coast to France, on the Atlantic coast of America to New Jersey, and on the Pacific coast to northern California, where it is known as *H. stenolepis*.

The Atlantic halibut, like the winter flounder, has the eyes and color on the right side. In this large fish the left eye does not complete its "migration over the head" until the animal has attained a length of close to two inches. In this migration the eye carries its socket with it. In fact, the whole skull is twisted.

The Atlantic halibut is very voracious, feeding chiefly on fishes. Crabs, lobsters, clams, and mussels also are eaten. Even sea birds occasionally are taken, as well as refuse from vessels. The halibut is a good example of the assertion that fish live to eat, and the very large halibut, weighing 300 pounds and more, probably have also attained a high age.

In recent years, both Atlantic and Pacific hali-

but have declined sharply in abundance. New England landings for 1949 totaled only 472,200 pounds, compared with catches of nearly 3,300,-000 pounds in former years.

On the Pacific coast, a recent annual catch was 14,242,400 pounds; formerly the figure approached 25,000,000 pounds. The fish are taken principally with long set lines.

Contrary to what one might expect, very little was known about the breeding habits and the early life of this common and important food fish until very recently when the investigators of the International Fisheries Commission succeeded in finding the eggs and larvae on the Pacific coast of America. It is believed to spawn in February in Iceland and Europe.

On the New England coast, it apparently continues to spawn throughout spring and summer, as shown by ripe fish taken, for naturally spawned eggs have not been reported from there.

On the Pacific coast of North America, the eggs and larvae have been taken from December to June.

The age of halibut may be determined from a study of the otoliths, or ear stones. A European investigator has determined that in the vicinity of Iceland fish one year old range from 3.1 to 5.9 inches in length. At five years of age they were 16.1 to 59.5 inches.

The wide range in length of fish at these different ages indicates very unequal growth, which is not unusual among fishes.

The Flounder's Eye Migrates Topside, Causes It to Dwell Bottomside

WINTER, or **blackback, flounder** (upper left—*Pseudopleuronectes americanus americanus*) inhabits shallow water and occurs from northern Labrador to Cape Lookout, where it is found only during the coldest winters.

In Chesapeake Bay, though absent during the summer, it is an important food fish during the winter, when almost all other species sought commercially are missing.

The most obvious feature of all flatfishes is their literal flatness. They swim and rest on one side, some species on the right and others on the left side, and both eyes are on one side of the head.

The young start life quite normally, for at first they swim in an upright position, and, like most other fishes, have one eye on each side of the head. However, very early in life the eye that happens to be on the lower side of the head begins to migrate to the upper side. In the various species studied, the migration is completed before the young fish reach a length of one inch.

The winter flounder almost invariably rests on its left side, which causes the right or top side to become pigmented, whereas the other side, being away from the light and generally on the bottom, remains pale. Because it is the left eye that migrates to the upper or right side of the head, this fish rests on the left side.

The meat of this fish, which reaches 15 to 17 inches, is of good flavor. The catch of the winter flounder in the New England States alone exceeded 20,000,000 pounds in a recent year.

The **summer flounder,** or **fluke** (center— *Paralichthys dentatus*) lives in the shallow shore waters from Cape Cod to South Carolina and probably to Florida, being most numerous, however, from New York to North Carolina. It frequents both sandy and muddy bottoms and often is taken in muddy estuaries where the water is only moderately brackish.

The summer flounder has its eyes and color on the left side, whereas the winter flounder has them on the right side.

This fish is remarkable for its ability to mimic or to simulate the color and pattern of the ground upon which it lives. If placed on a red background, it becomes red; on blue it turns blue; and so on through all colors one may care to use in the bottom of an aquarium.

Although the flesh of this flounder is rather dry, it has good flavor, brought out best when baked. A recent annual catch in New England and the Middle Atlantic area exceeded 9,000,000 pounds.

Because it has a larger mouth, taking larger bait, and because it grows larger, and wages a harder fight than the winter flounder, it is a better sport fish. Though the usual length of fish seen in the markets is only about 15 to 20 inches, 24-inch fish are not rare, and giants three feet long and weighing 25 pounds have been reported.

Painting by Hashime Murayama

24

Cod, Pollock, and Haddock Help Feed the World

THREE of America's most important food fishes (top to bottom), the pollock (*Pollachius virens*), the **Atlantic cod** (*Gadus morhua*), and the **haddock** (*Melanogrammus aeglefinus*), belong to one family, which includes also the hakes and cusks (page 25).

The pollock ranges both sides of the Atlantic, reaching our shores as far south as Cape Henry. It attains a weight of more than 40 pounds and a length of four feet.

A glutonous eater, it preys on young fish and is very destructive of young cod. Though bottom feeders, pollock also frequent the surface and intermediate depths.

Pollock appear about Cape Cod early in May. A favorite spawning ground is off Cape Ann, where they stay from early May to late January. The annual New England catch is some 28,789,400 pounds.

The Atlantic cod, usually weighing from 10 to 35 pounds, owes its value as food to its flavor, size, comparatively few bones, year-round abundance, and adaptability to dry-salting. It is taken in commercial quantities in the Atlantic States from New Jersey northward. A recent annual New England catch was 58,794,800 pounds.

A cold-water fish, the Atlantic cod is generally taken at depths of from eight to 40 fathoms, but is known to inhabit much deeper water. It is found on our Atlantic coast from Cape Hatteras northward and also on the European coast.

Spawning takes place along the New England coast from October to June. Nature has rendered the cod very prolific, and a good-sized fish contains a few million eggs.

So important were the cod fisheries in early America that a pine effigy of the cod was authorized for a permanent place of honor in the Massachusetts State House in 1784, and still hangs opposite the Speaker's chair (page 39).

The haddock resembles the Atlantic cod both in appearance and as food. A distinguishing mark is the black lateral line from head to tail. The finnan haddie of commerce, said to take its name from Findon or Findhorn, both towns in Scotland, is smoked haddock.

Among Atlantic food fishes, the haddock has a big lead in annual catch, with 134,970,400 pounds.

Hake and Cusk Frequent Deep Water off America's Atlantic Coast

COMMERCIALLY important members of the cod family, along with a near relative, are pictured here. Top to bottom, they are the **squirrel hake** (*Urophycis chuss*), the **cusk** (*Brosme brosme*), and the **silver hake** (*Merluccius bilinearis*).

Squirrel hake has six near relatives on the Atlantic coast of America, and several others more distantly related, all belonging to the large cod clan. It seldom exceeds a length of 30 inches. Squirrel hake ranges from the Gulf of St. Lawrence to North Carolina. Strictly a bottom fish, it is found on both sand and mud. Though squirrel hake's meat is soft, it has good flavor and finds a ready market. The latest recorded annual catch for New England was 55,879,100 pounds. Middle Atlantic and Chesapeake Bay fisheries accounted for 1,060,000 more pounds.

Cusk, also of the cod group, resembles the squirrel hake in body form, but differs in having only one, instead of two, fins on the back. It occurs in the Arctic polar region and ranges south on the American coast regularly to Cape Cod and occasionally to New Jersey. A recent annual catch was 3,620,200 pounds. The cusk is taken chiefly on rough bottom where there are rocks, ledges, and gravel.

Usually 18 to 24 inches long, the cusk is among the most prolific fish. A medium-sized female may deposit as many as 2,000,000 eggs in one season.

Silver hake, or whiting, formerly was bracketed with cod, but is now regarded as sufficiently different to require, with certain near relatives, a separate family. It lacks the cod's barbel, or chin whisker. Pelvic fins are of ordinary form, rather than long and filamentous as in the hakes.

Silver hake's range extends from Newfoundland to the Bahamas, but it is most common between Cape Sable and Cape Cod. In New England it is taken from shoreline to 300-fathom depths. Southward it is found only in deep, cold water.

The usual length of the silver hake is from 12 to 20 inches. Its food consists chiefly of fish of suitable size, squids, crabs and other crustaceans.

Painting by Hashime Murayama

25

Butterfish and Northern Scup Have Many Aliases

BOTH the flat, silvery **butterfish** (upper — *Poronotus triacanthus*) and the fat, prickly-finned **northern scup** (*Stenotomus chrysops*) are popular food fishes, and each appears in markets under names which vary according to locality.

The butterfish, so called by consumers in Massachusetts, the Chesapeake Bay States, and along the southern coast, is known as dollarfish in Maine and pumpkinseed in Connecticut. Other popular names are shiner, skipjack, and harvest fish, the latter more widely used for *Peprilus paru*, a member of the butterfish family.

Scup, as it is called in New England, is porgy in New York; maiden, fair maid, and ironsides in Chesapeake Bay; and porgy again in South Carolina.

Butterfish, ranging from Nova Scotia to Florida, live along the shores during the summer and disappear in winter. They attain an average length of 7 to 9 inches. In Chesapeake Bay they are caught from May to November. They have also been taken in the winter trawl fishery off the Virginia capes, indicating that the fish make their cold-weather home in these offshore depths. The most recent annual catch in the United States was 6,889,500 pounds.

Scup, averaging 8 to 10 inches, belong to the porgy family, which includes also the sheepshead porgy, the pinfish, and the southern porgies. They range between Maine and South Carolina, and are common from Cape Cod to the Virginia capes, occurring along the shores only during the summer. In Chesapeake Bay, scup are taken from April to October. Northward they appear in the shore waters somewhat later and depart earlier. Upon the approach of the Virginia capes takes place.

© National Geographic Society

Scup live principally on the bottom, preferring smooth, hard sand and feeding largely on small crustaceous mollusks, worms, and small fish. They bite greedily, and furnish sport for a large number of anglers, particularly along the coasts of New Jersey and New York.

Though the scup has been an important food fish along the Atlantic coast since colonial days, the annual catch during recent years has increased greatly. The total catch for a recent year was 28,959,100 pounds, nearly six times the take of twenty-three years earlier.

Painting by Hashime Murayama

Bright Tilefish More Valuable than Tough Tautog

FEW commercial species have had a more interesting history than the **tilefish** (upper). Unknown prior to 1879, the tilefish (*Lopholatilus chamaeleonticeps*) was first taken off Nantucket that year and introduced in markets. Averaging from 18 to 24 inches in length, they were an instant success.

Three years later, calamity struck the great schools that range from New England to the Virginia capes. Ships reported seeing myriads of dead tilefish. One vessel sailed through 150 miles of them. The estimated toll was a billion and a half fish.

The explanation of the catastrophe was that Arctic gales, driving ice down to the border of the Gulf Stream slope, had made the water too cold for the tilefish.

Scientists predicted that the tilefish would return when the water returned to its normal temperature. Nature took her time, and not until 1892 were any more tilefish caught—then only eight. But succeeding years brought increasing catches, and a recent catch was 1,238,500 pounds.

The **tautog** (*Tautoga onitis*) is a member of the family Labridae, consisting of about 450 species mostly living in tropical and subtropical regions. Of the western Atlantic species, only the tautog and the cunner regularly range north of North Carolina.

Nature has equipped the tautog with very strong teeth in the jaws and powerful conical teeth far back in its mouth. With this double set, the tautog feeds on the hardest of crustaceans and shellfish.

The tautog is a good game fish and provides extensive sport. Commercially it is among the less important species. Landings one recent year totaled 189,200 pounds.

© National Geographic Society
Paintings by Hashime Murayama

28 Painting by Hashime Murayama

The Atlantic Herring (Lower Pair) Is the World's Most Important Food Fish

ATLANTIC herring (*Clupea harengus*) is strictly a sea fish, for unlike the other herrings, the shad (opposite) and alewife (top), it does not enter fresh water. A North Atlantic fish, it occurs on the American coast from Cape Hatteras northward to Labrador and Greenland, and on the European coast from the Strait of Gibraltar to Norway.

In America it is most numerous north of Cape Cod, though taken commercially as far south as Virginia. According to the latest statistics available, the annual yield in the United States alone was 170,680,000 pounds.

The herring schools along the shore during the warmer part of the year, though some schools, presumably consisting of immature fish, remain offshore. When cold weather comes, the fish supposedly withdraws to deep water.

During the time they are near the shore, the spawning activities take place. The reproductive season is a long one. In some localities, at least, spawning takes place in spring, summer, and fall, spring and fall being the chief seasons.

The newly hatched fish are extremely slender, and about one fourth of an inch long. Growth is rapid, fish at one year of age sometimes reaching a length of three and a half to five inches. At this size they are utilized as "sardines." The large ones are used fresh, salted or smoked. Herring also are used as bait in line fishing for cod, haddock, and other fishes.

Aside from the herring's usefulness as food for man, it is of much indirect economic importance as food for other fishes, including such important species as the cod, haddock, halibut and bluefish, all of which feed on them extensively.

The **alewife** (top—*Pomolobus pseudoharengus*) is a relative of the herring and the shad. The greatest length attained is about 15 inches, and the usual length only about 11 inches. The female apparently grows a little larger than the male.

This fish is anadromous—that is, it runs up streams to spawn, from North Carolina to Nova Scotia. It has become landlocked in some lakes in New York, and in Lake Ontario, where it multiplies rapidly, but has become so dwarfed that it has little or no value.

This fish, unlike the Atlantic herring, has declined in abundance. The chief causes evidently are overfishing, obstructing of streams used as spawning grounds, and especially polluting of the rivers.

The catch for the United States declined from 52,061,000 pounds in 1908 to 32,179,000 pounds in 20 years. Much of the catch is salted, and a considerable portion of the roe is canned.

The alewife is prolific, for it has been determined that the average yield of eggs by a female is near 100,000. The young grow fast and are about 2½ inches long in November, at about six months old when they begin their journey to their home in the sea.

29 Painting by Hashime Murayama

The Popular American Shad Cannot Be Tempted with Bait

LARGEST member of the herring family in American waters is the **American shad** (*Alosa sapidissima*). Individuals weighing 12 and 14 pounds have been reported, the larger fish being always females, or roe shad.

The American shad is an anadromous fish, ascending fresh-water streams only to spawn. Almost immediately after the reproductive products have been cast, the fish return to the sea, where they spend most of their lives. All suitable streams from the St. Johns River in Florida to the tributaries of the Gulf of St. Lawrence are entered, progressively late from November to May.

Because the shad was highly esteemed on the Atlantic, its introduction on the Pacific coast was undertaken in the 1870's. From these early plantings shad soon became common from the Columbia River to Monterey.

It was long believed that the shad migrated northward along the coast as the temperature of the water increased. That seems not to be true, for it now appears much more likely that the migrations are inshore and offshore. In any case, the shad always returns to fresh water for spawning.

During the last 40 years, the Atlantic yield has declined steadily from 48,500,000 pounds in 1897 to 5,569,000 pounds.

On the Pacific, the catches declined from between 4,175,000 and 7,478,000 pounds to some 2,199,700.

Because shad can be taken only during the spawning season, there is danger of overfishing, which has contributed to the decline. Further factors are the obstruction and the extensive pollution of our streams.

The shad was one of the first fishes in America to receive the attention of fishculturists. As early as 1867 a successful hatching apparatus had been invented, and in 1872 the U. S. Fish Commission began artificial cultivation. Many millions of shad fry have been hatched and liberated. But artificial cultivation has not re-established the shad in its former abundance.

Since the shad rarely feed while in reach of man—that is, while in or near the mouths of streams, bays, or sounds—they cannot be tempted with bait. While rushing upstream to spawn, however, they occasionally strike at flies or spoons. The fish are taken chiefly with three kinds of gear: gill net, pound net, and haul seine.

Spawning occurs shortly after the shad enter fresh water. It has been estimated that the average number of eggs produced by a female is about 25,000 to 30,000, though exceptional individuals may have 100,000 or even 156,000.

In the lower Potomac the newly hatched fish reach a length of three inches at the age of about six months. At that time they migrate to the sea, where they remain until mature, at the age of probably about three or four years. At maturity many presumably return to the rivers in which they were born.

30

Sensitive to Temperature Changes, the King Whiting Acts as a Thermometer

THE range of the **king whiting** (*Menticirrhus saxatilis*) varies with the weather. Popularly called the kingfish (not to be confused with the much larger pelagic kingfish—page 211), the common king whiting ranges from Maine to Florida but frequents the northern extent only in the summer.

From North Carolina southward it withdraws from the shallow shore waters only during cold snaps and reappears as soon as the weather gets somewhat warmer. In North Carolina this species, and at least one other, are taken in considerable abundance along the shores in four fathoms or more of water in late winter and early spring. South of North Carolina the common king whiting is commercially unimportant. In fact, in Chesapeake Bay and North Carolina it is greatly outnumbered by one of the other species (*Menticirrhus americanus*). A third species (*Menticirrhus littoralis*) ranges from Chesapeake Bay to or beyond Texas.

These relatives are so close that fishermen generally do not distinguish the three, and therefore they have no distinctive common names. The group as a whole is well supplied with local or common names. Besides kingfish and king whiting, they are called whiting, surf whiting, shore whiting, silver whiting, roundheads, sea minks, and sea mullets. Wherever the three species occur together, the local names apply alike to each.

The king whiting feeds on shrimps (probably its chief food), crabs, and other crustaceans. It also eats small mollusks, worms, and small fish. In some localities the fish takes the hook readily and is a favorite game fish for anglers with rod and reel.

The king whitings, usually 12 to 18 inches long, rate high as food fishes wherever they are well known, and there they are in demand and bring a good price. For some reason they are not so well known generally as some other species they far surpass in quality. By far the greater numbers of these fish are now taken from North Carolina southward.

The fish are caught principally with haul seines, gill nets, pound nets, and otter trawls. Few if any of the fish taken on lines enter the commercial catches. Virtually the entire catch is consumed in the fresh state.

The spawning period in New Jersey begins in June and continues until August. On the coast of North Carolina spawning begins in March or April and continues probably into June.

The early fry of this species floats on its back for a few days while it is still living on the yolk sac it has retained from the egg. When the larvae right themselves, their mouths are open and they must have food. In case microscopic organisms are not available, the fish will soon die. This is a critical stage in life, and no doubt many of the larvae perish at this time.

The Versatile Smelt Has Furnished Both Food and Candlelight

THE American smelt *(Osmerus mordax)* is structurally akin to the salmon, except in size. The usual length is 7 to 9 inches.

All smelt species are small, and most of them stick strictly to the sea, although a few go up rivers to spawn, after the fashion of the salmons. All the abundant species are edible, the flesh being extremely delicate and often full of a fragrant digestion-aiding oil.

The American smelt ranges along the coast from the Virginia capes to the St. Lawrence Gulf, and enters the streams and brackish bays to spawn during the winter months, when it is taken in great numbers with hook and line and in nets.

In going up streams, some of the smelts have lost their way and become landlocked in numerous lakes, such as Champlain and Memphremagog.

This fish has been introduced into several lakes in the Middle West during recent years. In some of the lakes it has become very numerous, showing that the species is able to perpetuate itself without making an annual migration to salt water, as it does along the Atlantic coast. It has become so numerous in some places that it is causing some concern.

The food of the smelt in the Great Lakes, as in the Atlantic, consists largely of invertebrates, though some fish are included. The species is particularly fond of shrimp and other small crustaceans. On the other hand, many smelts are eaten by commercially important fishes. This probably more than counterbalances the damage done by smelts.

The fishermen take vast quantities of smelts during the winter, and most of those caught are frozen and sent to the larger cities. Those that are not frozen are termed green smelts, rated very high as a finely flavored fish.

The annual catch in New England was 162,000 pounds recently, whereas in the same year 1,556,000 pounds were taken in the Great Lakes region.

The smelts in the lakes run into the lower parts of streams very early in the spring to spawn, just as their ancestors along the Atlantic coast have always done. Females yield from 25,000 to 70,000 eggs.

Growth seems to be fairly rapid, since a length of about six to eight inches is attained in two years. At the age of two years, at least some of the fish are sexually mature and spawn for the first time. Small wonder that a fish so highly fertile has no difficulty maintaining itself.

The smelt is remarkable for its extreme oiliness, which is so great that, when a fish is dried and a wick put into its body, it can serve as a candle. It is from this possible use that the species derives its common name of candlefish. The oil is sometimes extracted and used as a substitute for cod-liver oil. At ordinary temperatures it is lardlike in consistency.

A Bottom Feeder, the Sea Bass Frequents Wrecks

OFTEN known as black will in the Chesapeake region and almost always as blackfish in the southern States, **black sea bass** (*Centropristes striatus*) ranges from Massachusetts to the Atlantic coast of Florida.

It is found on rocky or rough bottom, and among piles, along breakwaters, and around old wrecks. The chief fishing grounds are off the coasts of North Carolina, Delaware, New Jersey, and Long Island.

The important grounds of North Carolina, some 20 to 30 miles off the coast, in 20 to 30 fathoms of water, have a hard rough bottom, composed principally of dead and broken coral. As long as the fishing vessel is over this kind of bottom, fish are taken in abundance.

In fact, the commercial fisherman, who always operates two hand lines simultaneously, each line being provided with three hooks, is kept very busy drawing in one line, removing the fish, and rebaiting it, while the other is overboard. Often two hooks, and sometimes all three, hold a fish. However, as soon as the vessel drifts beyond rough bottom, biting ceases.

A voracious biter, the black sea bass is nearly always ready to take any bait offered. Off North Carolina the fishermen provide themselves only with enough bait to start the catch. When that supply of bait is used up, they continue fishing with pieces of sea bass already caught. For inshore fishing, as along breakwaters, where the fish are less numerous and apparently less greedy, fiddler crabs and hermit crabs are excellent bait.

Black sea bass are caught extensively for sport also. It is a favorite diversion at Atlantic summer resorts to fish for black bass. Along the New Jersey coast, where the sea bass is taken from May to November, the sport is of great magnitude. Seagoing power boats carrying as many as 4,000 persons, principally from New York City, visit the fishing banks daily during the season.

A maximum weight of eight pounds has been attained, but fish weighing more than five pounds are rare. Southward the fish run smaller in size, the majority from Chesapeake Bay southward probably weighing less than a pound.

The meat of the sea bass is white, of fine flavor, and always in demand. Taken commercially from Cape Cod to Florida, the latest annual catch was more than 10,000,000 pounds. The game fish record was made in Nantucket sound with an 8-pound bass, measuring 1 foot, 10 inches.

32

Painting by Hashime Murayama

Hashime Murayama

Sea Trout and Bass Are Favorite Dinner Dishes on Our Atlantic Coast

Painting by Hashime Murayama

33

© National Geographic Society

THOUGH nearly always listed in books as **gray squeteague** (*Cynoscion regalis*), this species (upper left) is much more widely known in the field as **weakfish**, or as **sea trout**. Its wide range extends from Massachusetts Bay to Mobile Bay, Alabama.

The squeteague is an excellent food fish, always in demand. The gray squeteague is said to reach a maximum weight of 30 pounds. However, the usual weight of market fish is only about one to three pounds, and the usual length, 16 to 24 inches.

This fish enters bays, sounds, and estuaries from March to May and remains until late fall, when it withdraws to deep water to escape the low winter temperature of shallow water. The best fishing seasons are spring and fall, when large quantities are caught along the shores in haul seines. A recent total annual catch was 17,196,200 pounds.

The principal spawning period begins in the spring and continues into the summer. Most of the eggs are cast out at sea, though some spawning takes place in the larger bays and sounds.

The rate of growth during the first year of life is fairly rapid. When about 14 months old, the fish average eight inches in length, and it seems quite certain that many of them reach a length of 12 inches or more.

The **striped bass** (*Roccus saxatilis*), also known as rockfish (middle right and below), has a wide range, from the St. Lawrence River to Louisiana. It is able to endure both high and low temperatures. Introduced into California in 1879, it now ranges on the Pacific coast from southern Washington to southern California.

The striped bass stays near shore in salt, brackish, and fresh water. Very few have been taken out at sea, and they spawn only in fresh water, preferring streams with swift currents.

A great size sometimes is attained, a maximum weight of 125 pounds being recorded. However, the great majority of the fish sent to market weigh less than 15 pounds. The striped bass is a strong fighter and an excellent food fish, and can be taken in summer or winter. The total annual catch recently was 5,629,800 pounds. The fish are caught with pound nets, gill nets, haul seines, and other sorts of traps.

Painting by Hashime Murayama

34

© National Geographic Society

The Atlantic Salmon, Now Almost Historic in the United States

WHEN the white man first came, he found the **Atlantic salmon** (*Salmo salar*) common in every river in New England not barred by impassable falls. But as industrial developments progressed, one stream after another was so obstructed by dams that the fish could no longer enter, and except in Maine the salmon is almost a historic fish in United States waters.

Its natural range reached to both sides of the North Atlantic, extending on the American coast from Greenland to Cape Cod and probably to the Hudson River. In Canada, where industrial developments have progressed less rapidly, maintaining the salmon population has been helped greatly by providing fishways at dams and by limiting netting at river mouths.

The last recorded annual catch for Maine was only 1,000 pounds, whereas the catch reported for that State in 1889 was 152,740 pounds.

The highly carnivorous Atlantic salmon, like the shad and the alewives, is anadromous, running far up the rivers to spawn. However, it spends more time in fresh water than the other species, sometimes remaining in fresh water until from three to six years old. Its habits in this respect differ greatly according to locality, but also vary greatly even within a restricted area.

Most Atlantic salmon are about six inches long when they enter salt water. When they enter tidewater, they put off their youthful barred and spotted pattern and take on the silvery coat worn during their sojourn in the sea. They remain about the shores for some time and then disappear. There is no good reason to believe that they go far off shore, though little is known of their movements in the sea.

It has been determined that those salmon that return to the rivers to spawn after passing only two years in the sea will always remain small, whereas those that begin spawning after spending more years in salt water reach a larger size.

The largest one was reported from Scotland and weighed 103 pounds. In America, where 50-pound fish are unusual, 10-pounders are near the average weight.

Adult Atlantic salmon, like the Pacific salmon, lose their bright colors and their trim shape, and the males develop hooked jaws, upon entering fresh water. Unlike the Pacific salmon, they do not die after spawning.

The salmon is highly carnivorous, feeding altogether on live animals. It includes in its diet many different sorts of fish, but its favorites are said to be sand launce, herring, and capelin. While in fresh water, adult salmon feed little and near spawning time, not at all.

The Cosmopolitan Striped Mullet (Top) Is the Wariest and Richest of Our Fishes

FEW species of fish have as wide a distribution as the **striped mullet** (top—*Mugil cephalus*). It is found in Japan and Hawaii, and on the Pacific coast of America from Monterey to Chile. It occurs also on the coast of southern Europe and northern Africa, and on the Atlantic coast of the Americas from Cape Cod to Brazil. In some localities it ascends fresh water streams, fish having been taken over a hundred miles from the sea.

Mullets have the habit of jumping out of the water, sometimes clearing the surface by several feet. Whether this is a form of play or has some utility in the life of the fish is not known. Two of its common names, jumping mullet and jumper, were acquired because of its leaping habit. Another name, fatback, refers to its broad round back.

It makes good use of its jumping propensities in escaping from nets. Considerable skill is required to catch this, our most wary fish.

The mullet is a fine food fish, especially if eaten very fresh. The Gulf States, in the latest year for which statistics are available, reported total landings of 31,892,900 pounds.

Fish only eight inches long often enter into the commercial catches and are especially good eating. A maximum length of 30 inches is attained in the South, where it grows largest.

It is said that the mullet is the only fish rich enough to be fried in its own fat.

The **sheepshead** (bottom—*Archosargus probatocephalus*) is among the gamest of salt-water fish. It ranges from Cape Cod to Tampico, Mexico, and rarely to the Bay of Fundy. A member of the porgy family, it reaches a maximum weight of 30 pounds, but 5 to 15 pounds is usual.

Spawning of sheepshead takes place in the spring on sandy shores. The young acquire the characteristics of the adult fish remarkably early. Fish scarcely three-fourths of an inch long look so much like the adults that they are easily identified with them.

The sheepshead has diminished rapidly under heavy fishing and is now comparatively rare north of the Virginia capes. Virtually all the catch comes from North Carolina southwards.

Painting by Hashime Murayama

35

36

For Three Centuries the Lobster Has Been an American Table Delicacy

THE American lobster (*Homarus americanus*), so called to distinguish it from its near European relative (*Homarus vulgaris*), is found from Labrador to North Carolina in a shore strip 1,450 miles long, if measured in a straight line, and 30 to 50 miles wide. It is not taken in any considerable quantities south of Delaware.

It inhabits waters from the shore out to the 100-fathom line and is most numerous off Maine and Nova Scotia. It prefers rocky bottoms, and usually leaves the shallower waters during the winter months to find more agreeable temperatures beyond the 100-fathom line.

All kinds of animals, both living and dead, and some vegetable matter are pleasing to its appetite. Although dangerous prey to attack, the lobsters, in spite of their hard shells, powerful claws, and burrowing habits, fall victim to the cod, the tautog, the skate, and the dogfish. These fish annually destroy millions of lobsters, particularly the young ones and the egg-bearing females.

The early settlers of New England used lobster commonly as food, and the expansion of the lobster fishery continued with the years as the demand increased, with little thought of the future. The fishery as a separate industry was first developed in Massachusetts around the close of the 18th century. It did not spread to Maine, where it later flourished, until 1840.

In 1892 the fishery in the United States yielded 24,000,000 pounds, valued at $1,062,392. Thirteen years later, in 1905, the yield had fallen to 11,-898,000 pounds, valued at $1,364,921. In this short time, the supply had been cut approximately in half, but the value had increased greatly.

Conservation measures have restored the supply, and recently the total yield for the United States was 24,690,000 pounds, valued at $8,902,698.

Lobsters are usually caught in traps known as lobster pots, made of ordinary plastering lath and having a funnel-shaped opening made of tarred netting, permitting easy ingress but closed against exit. The traps are sunk on lobster-frequented grounds and baited usually with pieces of stale fish.

The European variety of lobster seldom reaches a weight of 10 pounds, but those of our shores occasionally weigh as much as 25 pounds.

The average length of the lobster is 8 to 12 inches, but long survival sometimes leads to greater length. It has been estimated that a lobster $19\frac{1}{4}$ inches long is 20 years old, and one $22\frac{3}{4}$ inches long has attained the age of 33 years.

The lobster is enclosed in a hard chitinous shell, which does not increase in size as the animal grows. Hence, it has to molt—that is, cast off its old shell and acquire a new one periodically —in order to grow. Its size, or rather its rate of growth, therefore, is measured by the number of times it has molted.

sea literally would be crowded out of existence.

Indeed, it has been proved that if only three eggs from each female of each species should develop into adult fish similarly productive, fish life would multiply so rapidly that the seas would soon become vastly overcrowded. What does happen is that, in a general average, a pair of cod (or herring, or any other fish) produce only two offspring which live to maturity. The balance of Nature is so adjusted that each species maintains itself at a fairly constant level.

In this connection, it is interesting to note that Nature's need for females in many species exceeds the requirement for males. In the case of the conger eel, the ratio is nineteen females to every male; and in that of the herring, three females to every male.

Sea Alive with Enemies

The perils fish have to face are innumerable. Huxley estimates that only five percent of the herring destroyed annually by all their enemies find their fate at the hands of man.

The other 95 percent are the victims of whales, the porpoise family, seals, and other mammals; cod, haddock, mackerel, sharks, and other fishes; gulls, gannets, and other birds; and the thousand and one other enemies that constantly lurk in their wake.

How tremendous this toll of the other-than-man enemies of the herring actually is may be gathered from the fact that man catches nearly eleven billion herring annually. On that basis, more than two hundred billion herring fall victims every year to their enemies in the sea— enough to load a solid fish train reaching around the earth at the Equator, a distance of 24,902.39 miles.

Huxley has called mankind an association of herring catchers; and if we count those fish that are caught by other fish which feed on them and in turn feed us, he probably has not missed the mark much.

Raiders of the Great Lakes

The history of fishing holds few darker chapters than that recorded in the Great Lakes during recent years. The villain is the sea lamprey (*Petromyzon marinus*), a snakelike pirate that invaded the Lakes from the sea. About 20 years ago the lamprey spread from Lake Ontario to Lake Erie through the Welland Canal and found the whole vast fresh-water chain open to its buccaneering.

Equipped with a suction-cup mouth, this nightmarish parasite literally boards its quarry, attaching itself to the side of a fish. Then its teeth rasp through scales and skin. Like a monstrous leech, the lamprey clings for hours, sucking out the life of its prey. Some fish have been found festooned with half a dozen or more lampreys, writhing like Medusa's locks (page 46).

In the streams feeding the Great Lakes the creatures have multiplied enormously. Today they are killing fish by the millions. Each year the commercial catch of whitefish, lake trout, walleyes, pike, and other valuable Great Lakes species shows a discouraging decline.

In its determined battle to eradicate the sea lamprey, the Fish and Wildlife Service may make a hero of the humble American eel, which closely resembles the lamprey but lacks its revolting habits. Tests conducted in aquaria have demonstrated that eels will attack and destroy lamprey larvae; therefore, why not introduce eels to the waters where lampreys spawn? Whether eels will perform this service under natural conditions is a question yet to be answered.

The conservation agency has also experimented with an electric "death fence" across spawning streams to electrocute lampreys swimming down from shallow waters where they hatch in a life cycle similar to that of the salmon. But the pests survive unbelievable charges.

Chemical warfare is another possibility, for young lampreys seem to be sensitive to chemicals in the waters. In any case, the battle goes on, with the best of brains and ingenuity pitted against a hideous creature that looks like one of Nature's mistakes. Our government scientific agencies hold out little hope of an early victory.

The migration of fishes forms one of the most fascinating romances of the sea. We know how the shad, the salmon, and other species spend their adult lives in the sea and seek fresh water in which to spawn; how the eels, on the other hand, pass their lives in rivers and lakes and seek salt water at spawning time. The mackerel (page 21) and the flying fish (page 224) families wander wide from their usual haunts at spawning time. Other species follow the great schools of menhaden about the seas, "a full dinner pail" being the first consideration in their lives as in ours.

Migration Mysteries Still Unsolved

However, for the most part, keeping a complete check on the movement of the fishes of the seas is a problem still awaiting solution. The exact winter home of the common mackerel is unknown, though a few have been caught with cod lines in deep water off Grand Manan Island, Bay of Fundy, and others have been taken from the stomachs of cod on Georges and La Have Banks, as well as off the coast of New Jersey.

For a long time it was supposed that the hickory shad spawned in fresh-water streams, as is the habit of its near relatives, the ale-

National Geographic Photographer B. Anthony Stewart

A Seagoing "Giant" Deadheads the Rails Back to the Big City

Proud angler, returning home on the Long Island Railroad's special fishing train, displays his mammoth flounder, hooked off Montauk on Long Island's eastern end. Few flatfish this large are caught on sport tackle.

wife and glut herring. But investigations in the Chesapeake Bay region failed to reveal any young which may have been produced in the tributaries of the Bay. The hickory shad's spawning grounds have not yet been located.

The spawning grounds of the tuna (page 212) have never been discovered. This fish has successfully eluded every effort to trace its tracks through the deep seas.

Extensive tagging and scale studies have revealed the general pattern of the strange comings and goings of the sea trout, or weakfish (page 33).

How Fish Are Tagged

The migratory movements of herring are so complex that, although ichthyologists have been trying for many years, a complete solution has not yet been found.

In past years, the Fish and Wildlife Service, by marking cod, pollock, and haddock, made careful studies of their migration habits. Recently this agency has been attaching inscribed tags of metal or plastic to thousands of flounders, weakfishes, shrimps, and other species. After marking, the fish are returned to the sea, in the hope that fishermen of the waters they inhabit will return the tags of those caught, with information about the locality in which they were taken and a record of the date and of their size. For each tag returned, the fisherman received a small reward and the thanks of the Fish and Wildlife Service for his assistance to science.

In the tagging operations the fish are caught in nets or with hook and line. The uninjured fish is measured and its exact length recorded. A tag stamped U.S.F.W.S. is then securely attached to the body, to a fin or to the tail (the placement of the tag depends on the species). Sometimes the tag may be inserted in the abdomen. The fish is released at once, and a record is made of its number, its size, where it is released, and other data. In many thousands of cases the fishermen who take the tagged fish assist the Government by reporting them.

A study of the anatomy of fishes and the

 National Geographic Photographer Robert F. Sisson

⋏ The "Sacred Cod" Has Hung for Generations in Massachusetts' State House

Symbolic of fishing's early value to the Commonwealth, this pinewood effigy was authorized by the House of Representatives in 1784 after Mr. John Rowe "moved the House that leave might be given to hang up the representation of a Cod Fish." It now hangs opposite the Speaker's chair.

Codfishing is a major industry along the northern Atlantic coast, and the quantity and quality of the catch spells feast or famine to thousands of families in New England, Newfoundland and Nova Scotia.

Often repainted and kept carefully dusted, the State House effigy reminds the commonwealth of its obligation to the fish as a factor in its growth and prosperity.

⋎ Greedy Perch Choked on a Small Fry— Sixty Million Years Ago

In waters that then covered southwest Wyoming, *Mioplosus,* possible ancestor of today's white perch of the Atlantic seaboard, opened wide for *Knightia,* a herring forebear. Preserved in lake-bottom ooze that became rock of the Rockies, the fossilized tragedy was quarried with hammer and chisel to become part of Princeton University's collection.

The chances that a fish had to attain immortality as a fossil were only one in millions. Even if their bodies somehow survived predators, fish that became fossilized were obliterated by sun and winds, snows and frosts, if the fossil strata were cracked open by movements of rocks.

National Geographic Photographer Robert F. Sisson

By the Carload, Boston Fish Go to the Highest Bidder

The catch of each boat bringing a scaly cargo to the Boston fish pier is listed early in the morning on the "hail board," showing quantity and species taken. Once posted, the loads are sold by auctioneers standing on a raised platform in the center of the big exchange. Successful bidders notify wharfmen of their purchases and issue instructions for shipping by train, plane or truck.

New England was long the leader among coastal regions of the United States in the importance and value of its fisheries. Now the Pacific coast states have moved into first place, but New England still has close to a billion-pound catch annually, valued at 70 million dollars and employing some 25,000 fishermen. Most of the fish sold on the Boston market is haddock (page 24).

40

Near the Mouth of Chesapeake Bay Shad Start Their Journey from the Waters to the Table

Shad swim up the great rivers and bays of the eastern United States each spring to spawn. Although river pollution has cut their number, great quantities of the migrating fish still are taken in pound nets (below) and by other devices in waters of the eastern United States.

A. Aubrey Bodine

41

evolution of some of their organs throws an interesting light on life in the ocean.

In order to see under the water, the eyes of the fish had to be constructed on lines differing somewhat from those of man and land animals. Dissecting a fish's eye, one discovers that the crystalline lens is almost a perfect sphere instead of the somewhat flattened lens of land animals. This arrangement is necessary to sight in the water, since the difference in density between the lens and the water is so slight. The result is that fish are extremely nearsighted.

Fish Eat Without Tasting

While it is probably true that fish do not "hear" sound waves in the air, they seem to react promptly to disturbances in the water. Whether or not this sensitivity to underwater "waves" should be called "hearing," it is practically utilized in driving fish into nets. To produce "noise" in the water, fishermen beat the surface with a flat object or stamp on the bottom.

What we know as the fish's ears are largely organs of equilibration, as they are to some extent in man.

The sense of taste appears to be largely wanting in fish. Their tongues are without power of motion and lack delicate membranes. They swallow their food very rapidly and largely without mastication.

Out of water, a fish dies of suffocation because it cannot extract oxygen from the atmosphere. Only oxygen dissolved in water can be utilized through the vessels of the gill filaments. Some species, like the catfishes, can live for a considerable time out of their native element. A man requires 50 times as much oxygen as a fish of equal bulk.

The air bladders, or swim bladders, of most fishes help them to solve admirably their respective problems of hydrostatics. In other words, the floating and balancing powers of the fish in the water are controlled by its air bladder, just as a submarine's are by its ballast tanks. Bottom fishes have small ones, and species that range between the surface and the bottom have relatively large ones. The gas with which air bladders are filled is secreted from the blood in most species.

Fins Are Fishes' Limbs

The evolution of the air bladder from a respiratory organ and the perfection of the gills to a point where they furnish oxygen enough, and therefore render the air bladder useless for breathing, may be traced in species still existing. In the more primitive fishes, gills were the principal organs of respiration, but the air bladder served as accessory "breathing" equipment, a function which it has lost in the more specialized fishes. The primitive connection between the air bladder and the gullet is retained in the soft-rayed fishes, such as the herrings, eels, trouts, and salmons. Although these species may renew the supply of oxygen in the air bladder by coming to the surface and "gulping" air, respiration is carried on chiefly through the gills.

Some fishes have no air bladders: for example, the sharks, skates, flatfishes, pipefishes, adult mackerel, some species of tunny, and some rockfishes.

The major fins of fishes correspond strikingly to the limbs of land mammals. Those back of the gills are known as the pectoral fins and correspond to the arms of humans. If the bones to which they are attached are examined critically, they will be found somewhat similar to the shoulder girdle of land mammals.

Below the pectoral fins are the ventral fins, which correspond to the hind legs of quadrupeds. The dorsal fin on the back, the caudal fin at the root of the tail, and the anal fin beneath the body are used to maintain equilibrium or direction.

Nowhere is the art of camouflage more strikingly employed than in marine life. The master breeder of the ages, Nature, has provided certain, if very slow, methods of eliminating the unfit from reproduction.

One method is by tests of brute strength, as in the battles of bull fur seals; another is by the elimination of the sluggards, as in the pursuit of the herring by the mackerel. A thousand and one methods are available.

Use of Camouflage Important

In the fish's struggle for survival, nothing is more important than its proper use of the art of camouflage. The color of a herring's back (page 28) corresponds to the shades of the water in which it thrives; viewed from the air, it has low visibility. Its belly corresponds to the appearance of water when viewed from beneath the surface. The fishes best protected by their camouflage escape their enemies most frequently and therefore have a better chance to reproduce. The ones that are least protected fall victims more easily and therefore are less likely to reproduce.

The flounder, the halibut, and the sand dab, lying on the sand, have harmonizing blotches imprinted all over the upper part of the body, matching the various kinds of sand on which they lie, whether it is common brown crushed coral, or rotting lava.

New England's Lobster Industry

Not a fish but the lobster, belonging to the crustacean group of animals, supports one of

Luis Marden, National Geographic Staff

Cover the Top Two Inches and This Could Be a Rustic Scene Far from Skyscrapers

Shad fishermen are clearing their nets on the New Jersey side of the Hudson River, with George Washington Bridge and New York's Washington Heights as a backdrop. This quarter-million-dollar-a-year industry flourishes only for two months—April and May, when shad seek fresh water to spawn.

the most interesting and important fisheries of the American shores of the North Atlantic.

The lobster, biologically, is a closer relative of the spider than of the fish. It is found only on the eastern coast of North America, although the name spiny lobster is sometimes given to the southern crayfish (page 226). Its known range covers a strip of the North Atlantic reaching from Labrador to North Carolina, with the Maine and lower Canadian shores as the region of its greatest commercial abundance. This strip of water is from 30 to 50 miles wide and from 6 to 600 feet deep.

From the close of its early free pelagic life to its old age, which often stretches into decades, the lobster never leaves the sea bottom of its own accord. Its external world is the ocean floor, and it is content to stay there.

Having considerable power of locomotion, it wanders around as winter approaches, from shallow inshore waters to deeper ones of the 100-fathom line, searching for a comfortable temperature and for suitable food, and attending to the duties of reproduction.

Its instincts constantly lead it to conceal itself, sometimes to take its prey unawares, and at others to hide from its natural enemies.

Feelers Detect Danger

It walks over the sea floor on its slender legs, which are provided with brushes of sensitive hairs. With its large claws put forward to offer little resistance to the water, it waves its "feelers" back and forth continually to detect danger as well as to discover game its eyes may have overlooked.

The buoyancy of the water makes the lobster light on its feet in its native environment, but its body weight is too great for its legs when out of water.

Though a great scavenger and tending to be nocturnal in its search for food, the lobster prefers fresh food whenever that is available. Fresh codfish heads, flatfish, sculpins, sea robins, menhadens, and haddocks make excellent bait; but balls of putrid slack-salted herring also seem attractive.

When hungry, the big crustacean will bur-

Tagging Salmon Keeps Tab on a Canadian Money Crop

Migrating salmon of the great midsummer British Columbia run give employment to some 23,000 in the fishing fleet and 20 canneries. Movement of the fish is checked closely by the Canadian government. Here inspectors attach a distinctive tag to a salmon, to be reported when the fish is caught.

row in the sand like a ravenous pig rooting for grubs. It has been known to attack with its plierlike claws even a full-sized conch, breaking its shell away, piece by piece, and gluttonously devouring the soft parts.

The lobster is a cannibal by nature, preying on its weaker brethren, and if the conditions under which it is hatched did not favor its immediate and wide dispersion, it would largely exterminate itself.

Giants of the Lobster World

Like dogs, lobsters have frequently been observed to drag dead prey to some secret spot, bury it, and then mount guard over the cache, ready to defend it against all comers. Often grim battles are fought over such caches. Indeed, most of the giant lobsters that have been taken bear numerous scars that tell of pitiless struggles where quarter was neither asked nor given.

In the American Museum of Natural His-

tory in New York there is preserved a giant lobster, the living weight of which was 34 pounds. It was captured at Atlantic Highlands, New Jersey, in 1897. The Smithsonian Institution has one of which the living weight was estimated at 25 pounds. But both of these were dwarfed by a monstrous 47-pound lobster taken in 1931.

Dr. Herrick thinks that all of the thirteen titans he lists as weighing more than 20 pounds were not giants by nature but rather simple favorites of fate, which allowed them to live to a riper age than their smaller fellow-creatures. Good luck never deserted them until they became stranded on some inhospitable beach or entangled in some fisherman's gear. Such lobsters as these, he believes, have weathered the perils of at least half a century.

Few living creatures have such striking habits of changing their clothes as the lobster. It begins to molt, or discard its outgrown clothes, the second day after hatching, and continues to do so with decreasing frequency until it has ceased to grow at all.

Nowhere else in Nature is the molting process so striking, so critical, or so abrupt.

When the old shell becomes too small, a new skin begins to grow underneath it. When this growth nears completion, the lobster becomes a "shedder," ready to cast off not only its old shell but even the lining of its esophagus, stomach, and intestine.

Specimens under careful observation have been found to be restless and uneasy as the time of the molt approaches. Suddenly there comes a break where the tail joins the shell. The lobster then turns over on its side and bends itself in the shape of a V, with the break at the apex. Pressure is applied, and gradually the rear end of the shell breaks loose from the new one beneath.

A Crucial Period for the Lobster

Step by step, the process of liberating the imprisoned body from its outgrown armor continues until finally the claws are withdrawn through the narrow openings. The area of a cross section of the flesh in the largest part of one of its big claws is four times greater than that of a cross section of the second joint, through which it must be drawn. The process, therefore, reminds one of pulling wire through the holes of a drawplate.

Enemies by the Million

Presently, with a mighty effort, the lobster emerges from its old coat of mail, casts off the linings of its digestive tract, and steps out, full-panoplied in a soft new shell.

45

Proof That Salmon Come Home to Spawn—and Die

Scientists at the University of Washington School of Fisheries in Seattle prove in a dramatic experiment that Pacific salmon, which spend their adult lives in the ocean, return with unerring precision to their native fresh water to spawn and die.

In November, 1948, newly spawned silver salmon eggs from the state fish hatchery at Auburn, Washington, were hatched in University pools. A year later the fish were marked, 13,368 of them by clipping off the left ventral fin, and 12,434 by clipping the right ventral fin.

In March, 1950, those with the clipped right fin were released in the Lake Washington ship canal. The others were kept in artificial ponds near the canal for almost a month before being released through the outfalls, or fish ladders, leading from the ponds to the canal.

Between October 20, 1951, and January 21, 1952, 31 salmon with the right ventral clipped returned from the Pacific Ocean through Puget Sound, Salmon Bay, and Lake Union to the canal.

Forty-four fish with left fins clipped followed the same route and then climbed the fish ladders to reenter the identical artificial ponds from which they were released.

Professor Lauren R. Donaldson of the School of Fisheries proudly displays one of the fish that returned to the canal.

From six weeks to three months are required for the soft-shelled lobster to become a hard-shelled one again.

The lobster has many enemies; but, next to man and his alluring traps, the codfish ranks as its worst foe. With an appetite that doesn't stop at a hard shell up to eight inches, and with a particular taste for young lobsters from two to four inches in size, the codfish

Andrew H. Brown,
National Geographic Staff

Blood-sucking Sea Lamprey Kills Great Lakes Fishes

The sea lamprey, an eel-like villain that invaded the Great Lakes through the Welland Canal about 20 years ago, kills fish by the million and threatens the lake fishing industry (page 37). This nightmarish parasite attaches itself by a suction-cup mouth, equipped with rasping teeth (left) to rainbow trout (above), whitefish, lake trout, and other fish and literally sucks the life from its prey.

Between 1935 and 1949, the most recent year having complete statistics, the lake trout catch in United States waters of Lake Huron fell from 1,743,000 pounds to a scant 1,000 pounds! In Lake Michigan the drop during the same years was from nearly 5,000,000 pounds to 343,000 pounds. Both these appalling declines were attributed to the sea lamprey.

E. P. Haddon,
U. S. Fish and Wildlife Service

Chubb Crater's Fish Seem Out of Shape: Heads Are Big, Bodies Are Slender

In the summer of 1951, the National Geographic Society and the Royal Ontario Museum sent an expedition to northern Quebec to explore newly discovered Chubb Crater, the world's largest crater of meteoritic origin. Staff Photographer Richard H. Stewart caught these two deformed arctic char in the cold, near sterile waters of the crater lake. They resemble trout but are soft and flabby. Large heads and thin bodies indicate malnutrition. One fish was so hungry it snapped at a paddle. How the first char entered the high-walled lake and how they survived on short rations remains a riddle.

For laboratory examination the expedition's scientists took specimens of the crater lake's plankton, the minute organisms which furnish fish with basic food (pages 317-324). They found it inadequate to support healthy fish life.

Fish caught in near-by Museum Lake were healthy and normal, like the one below being measured and preserved for further study. They weighed up to $13\frac{1}{2}$ pounds, four to six times as much as Chubb's, and made fine eating.

National Geographic Photographer
Richard H. Stewart

47

National Geographic Photographer John E. Fletcher

Hen Lobsters Glue Their Eggs to Their Bodies

This lobster was caught in Maine waters and sent to the State rearing station at Boothbay Harbor, since sale of egg-bearing females is forbidden (page 37). The average female may carry from 8,000 to 10,000 eggs, but 97,000, or nearly a pound, have been counted on some large lobsters. After 10 to 11 months, the eggs hatch, in May, June, and July, and float to the surface where they remain until the third or fourth shell is grown and shed. Then the lobsters sink to the bottom, their natural habitat. The effect of overfishing for lobsters shows more in the steady decline in the size of those taken than in the diminution of numbers. The closed season has never been a very effective conservation method, since the female carries the eggs for such an overwhelmingly long proportion of the year. However, other conservation practices have succeeded in a partial restoration of the lobster fishery.

Come Wind or Rain, Fog or Spray, Pots Must Be Tended

Finding scattered lobster pots two miles or so offshore in a pea-soup fog or heavy weather is rugged work, but lobstermen do it every day. The Nantucket fisherman (right) displays two five-pound beauties, and (below) a lobsterman heads out to the treacherous fishing grounds off the coast of Maine. Lobsters are caught in "pots" or traps made of lath and knitted netting (in the stern of boat, below). Gulled by the bait, lobsters enter through a hole in the netting and cannot escape.

Top: National Geographic Photographer B. Anthony Stewart

Bottom: National Geographic Photographer John E. Fletcher

49

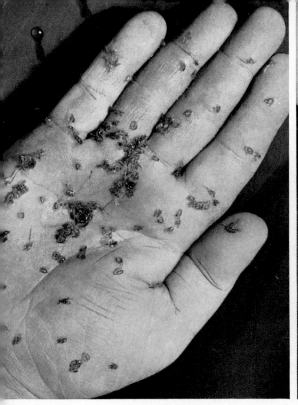

National Geographic Photographer John E. Fletcher

Lobster Babies Wear Their First Shell (Left); Their Fifth (Right)

Day-old lobsters (left) hatched at the Fish and Wildlife Service's station, Boothbay Harbor, Maine, live in tanks of sea water kept constantly flowing to prevent their clinging together and eating one another. Later they will be transferred to the State's rearing station. After the initial shedding within two or three days after birth, they keep their second shell for about five days. Then they discard it and go into the third stage for about seven days. Within three days after reaching the fourth stage, they are carried out to sea in State boats and planted. At this age most of them sink quickly to the bottom and take refuge in crevices among the rocks. Within the first year of life lobsters discard their shells 12 times.

Deep sea creatures below are, left, an eyeless fish from a three-mile depth and, right, a sea anemone from one of the deepest parts of the ocean, 34,000 feet in the Philippine Deep.

Elmer Moss, courtesy California Academy of Sciences

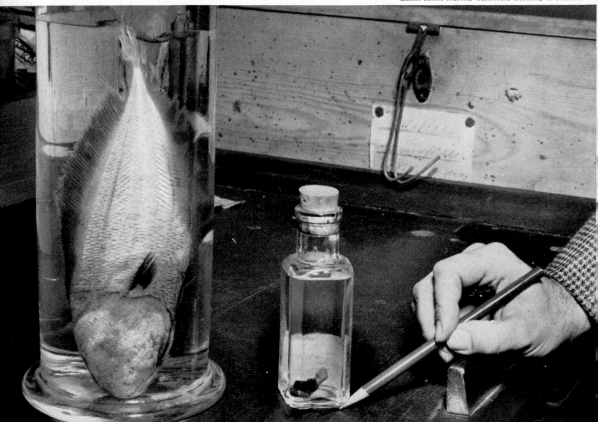

E. Fred Miller

From Open Boat to Cleaning Shed, Cod Climb Pouch Cove Cliffs, Platform by Platform

When the season is on, Newfoundland fishermen stand one above another, like farmers in a hayloft, and toss the heavy cod from step to step with pitchforks called "pews." Though the structure looks flimsy, its stout poles resist sea and gale year after year. Rocks gleam through the clear water. Boatmen stand on the foot of their ramp. Small icebergs drift past the harbor, just a shallow dent in the cliffs. Next stop for the fish may be the Mediterranean, West Indies or South America. Portugal could scarcely exist without its *bacalhau* (cod).

is a tremendous competitor of the lobster palace in the race for survival of the fittest.

During their younger lives, lobsters play into the hands of millions of foes in the sea, for it is not until the fourth or fifth stage that they leave the surface for the bottom. Not until this period does caution seem to dawn in them and guide them to hiding places on the sea floor. During the lobsters' earliest periods, vast schools of surface-feeding fish strain the water through which they chance to pass as effectively as might a towed net.

Lobsters Carry Barnacles

Though only a few parasites of the lobster are known, it has many messmates. Barnacles affix themselves to its shell and cement their tentlike coverings thereon; different kinds of mussels insinuate themselves into attractive depressions in the carapace and joints. Tunicates sometimes fasten themselves on the undersurface of the body, between the legs. Tubeforming annelids, lacelike bryozoans, and several forms of algae make themselves unbidden guests, which the uneasy host can cast off only when it molts.

Grain-eating birds swallow their food whole and, with the aid of gravel or other hard material, pulverize it in their gizzards. The lobster handles the situation differently. It chews its food before passing it into its mouth. The cutting teeth of its outer mouth parts chop the material into mincemeat, which is passed into the mouth proper in a slow stream of fine particles.

From there the food reaches the stomach, which is divided into two parts—the forward section for storage and the rear compartment for sorting, straining, and digesting. Between the two are three teeth, one upper and two lower, which, like upper and nether millstones, grind the food to its appropriate degree of fineness.

Two Types of Pincers

When one examines a lobster carefully, it is seen that the two great claws do not terminate alike. The one ends with a large crushing type of pincers and the other with a seizing type.

One of the strange things in connection with these great claws is that Nature has given the lobster power not only to amputate them in case of danger but to grow others in their place after amputation occurs.

Imagine a man with his hand caught in a machine suddenly giving a severe jerk and severing his arm at the elbow! And then imagine him going off by himself and growing another arm to take the place of the lost one! That is comparable to what the lobster does.

In a census of more than 700 lobsters, 7 percent were found to have thrown one or both great claws, and these showed every stage of the regenerative process. Nature has arranged matters so that no tendons or large blood vessels cross the breaking point; hence there is little bleeding at the operation.

Self-Amputation Is Voluntary

That the self-amputation of the claw is a matter of will is shown by the fact that, when put under an anesthetic, the lobster "forgets" to amputate the captive member.

When the female lobster lays her eggs, she turns over on her back, using her large claws and her tail fan as a tripod to support herself. She flexes her abdomen to make a sort of pocket, to which she glues the eggs fast. An 8-inch female will lay about 5,000 eggs, a 10-inch individual about 10,000, and an 18-inch one some 80,000, there being about 6,000 eggs to the ounce.

The eggs are carried about for ten months. After hatching, the larvae pass from three to five weeks irresponsibly floating around near the surface, somewhat lacking in the powers of coordination and orientation. During this time they undergo four molts. At the third molt after hatching, the lobsters begin to take on the characteristics of the adult. At this stage the instinct to desert the surface and seek the bottom suddenly asserts itself, and the lobsterling settles down to its new environment to eat and grow. It reaches maturity in five or six years.

The Kingdom of the Sea

No creature of the waters dramatizes more forcefully the ever-changing and yet perpetual rhythm and conflict of life in the sea than the lobster. But all other species, over millions of years and long antedating animal life on the land, have also evolved their own rules, their own habits, and their own physical characteristics.

In their primitive struggle for survival, as we have seen, they adapted the very color of their bodies to their environment. In the drama of meeting their needs and surmounting their conflicts, they have developed skills and practices fascinating alike to the scientist and the casual observer.

As the years pass and man's knowledge of aquatic life expands, its intricacy and variety become more rather than less impressive.

Perhaps it is this varied, constant, and colorful life beneath and in the earth's lakes and rivers and oceans that accounts, as much almost as the great fishing industry and the universal sport of fishing, for man's deep and lasting interest in the sea—the source and beginning of all life on the planet.

53

Yellowtail (Middle) and Pacific Mackerel (Lower) Are Spirited West Coast Fighters

THE Pacific, or northern, anchovy (upper —*Engraulis mordax*) is found only from British Columbia to Baja California. Related to the herrings, it differs from them in the size and shape of its mouth, which because of an exceedingly long lower jaw opens to the very rear of the head. With such a mouth and weak teeth, it cannot feed on other fish and subsists on tiny animals and plants that float in the sea.

These delicate fish, averaging 4 to 7 inches, are more important as food for other fishes than they are commercially. The 3,322,300 pounds netted in a recent year were used mainly for bait.

The **yellowtail** (middle—*Seriola dorsalis*), also known as amberjack and white salmon, is a graceful swimmer, and occurs from Monterey Bay,

California, southward to the Gulf of California.

Averaging 10 to 12 pounds, it is classed as both a food and a game fish. Annually commercial fishermen take over 7 million pounds. Many also are caught by anglers, since it is one of the finest of the Pacific game fishes, striking viciously.

The **Pacific mackerel** (lower—*Pneumatophorus diego*) is also called greenback, stripe, zebra, or night mackerel. It occurs from Alaska, southward to South America and Japan.

The fish averages about two pounds, and a recent year's catch was 49,771,300 pounds.

It is known by anglers for its splendid fighting qualities, but because of its abundance and relatively small size, it is not sought by big-game fishermen when larger species are available.

Painting by Hashime Murayama

The Graceless Starry Flounder (Bottom) Is Sometimes Found Partly Buried in the Sand at Low Tide

MEASURING eight inches across the back and weighing as much as three pounds, the **market crab** (top, left—*Cancer magister*) is common only at Monterey Bay and northward, where it lives on sandy bottoms to a depth of 60 feet.

Along the Pacific coast of the United States, the commercial catch averages about 5,000,000 pounds annually. When heaped in the boats the crabs fight furiously, but lose only legs, which would soon regenerate if the creatures were freed.

The **Pacific, or mottled, sand dab** (top, right—*Citharichthys sordidus*) occurs from Kiska Island to Cedros Island, Baja California, inhabiting sandy and muddy bottoms, where they feed on small organisms. The females, larger than the males, reach a length of a little over 15 inches.

A characteristic flatfish of the Pacific coast, the **starry flounder** (lower pair—*Platichthys stellatus*) occurs from Japan to Alaska and southward to Santa Barbara County, California.

Along our coast as far north as southeastern Alaska, about half have the eyes and color on the right side and the other half on the left side.

The starry flounder, averaging 14 inches long, is taken commercially throughout most of its range, but makes up less than a tenth of the 9 to 12 million pounds of "sole" and flounder caught annually in the Pacific States. The food of the starry flounder consists mainly of worms, small fish and crustaceans.

Surf Fishes Give Birth to Their Young Like Mammals

STRIPED, or blue, sea perch (upper left—*Taeniotoca lateralis*) is also called rainbow perch. It is one of the surf fishes, whose name is derived from the habit some have of living in the ocean surf, where they are taken by sportsmen with hook and line.

The blue sea perch ranges from Vancouver Island to the San Benito Islands, Baja California. Abundant in bays and along open shores, it feeds on small shrimps, worms, and other tiny animals.

It lurks around wharves where it can pick its food off the piles. It occasionally reaches a length of a little over a foot in Puget Sound, but the average size is only about eight inches.

The priestfish (right pair—*Sebastodes mystinus*) is one of the rockfishes, so named because they frequent rocky shores. It ranges from Alaska southward to San Diego and is most abundant in the Juan de Fuca Strait.

The large mouth of the priestfish adapts it to voracious habits of feeding, and the patches of sharp teeth on the jaws render its victims helpless at once.

Like the sea perch and other surf fishes, rockfishes are viviparous—that is, they give birth to their young. During the winter or early spring, the 30,000 eggs or more formed in each large female are fertilized and begin their development.

By March, April, or as late as June the tiny young escape into the sea and eventually grow to be about a foot and a half long. The priestfish feeds on shrimp and small fishes.

55

Painting by Hashime Murayama

56

Silvery Midgets of the West Coast Outnumber Their Giant Destroyers

PILCHARD (upper), sometimes called **California sardine** *(Sardinops caerulea)*, belongs to the herring and shad family.

The pilchard ranges in large schools from the Queen Charlotte Islands to the Gulf of California. A recent annual commercial catch for California, Oregon, and Washington was 633,540,400 pounds—the greatest weight taken of a single species among all commercial fishes in North America.

Almost the entire catch is reduced to oil or fish meal. The pilchards, averaging 10 inches, are unloaded at reduction plants and passed through steam cookers to a continuous press where the oil and water are separated from the flesh and bone residue.

The solid portion is dried and sacked as fish meal, of great value for chicken feed and fertilizer.

The **white sea bass** (lower—*Cynoscion nobilis*) is really not a bass but belongs to the carnivorous croaker family, feeding largely on smelt, herring, anchovies, sardines (above), squids, and crustaceans. Abundant in warm seas, there are more than 45 species off Central America. All croakers are food fishes, and some species are game fighters.

The white sea bass ranges farther north than any other member of the family, being common off Vancouver Island, and southward to the Gulf of California.

Off California it is one of the valuable food fishes, reaching a weight of 90 pounds or more. Its flesh is firm, white, and delicious. The latest annual catch was 1,409,600 pounds.

57

Thick, Drooping Lips Give Rubberlip Perch Its Common Name

EXCEEDINGLY thick, whitish or pink lips, silvery sides, and bluish or blackish back of the **rubberlip sea perch** (top—*Rhacochilus toxotes*), common from San Francisco to San Diego, help distinguish it from other surf fishes of the region, all of which are viviparous, giving birth to their young as mammals do.

The fish is taken on hook and line, but the hook must be very small, since the mouth of the rubberlip sea perch is not large.

Though reaching a length of a foot and a half, the species forms only a small part of the commercial catch of surf fishes, the flesh of which is rather watery and lacking in flavor.

The **cabezone,** or **marbled sculpin** (below— *Scorpaenichthys marmoratus*), also known as the blue cod and bullhead, is one of the commonest

and largest of the shallow-water sculpins, family Cottidae, found along the western coast of the United States.

Most of its hundred or more relatives are usually less than eight inches long and of slight commercial importance save for bait.

But the cabezone reaches about two and one-half feet in length, and many weigh 20 to 25 pounds. The flesh, of a slightly bluish tinge, is highly esteemed by anglers, who catch the fish readily on hooks baited with parts of clams or fish. It is found from Puget Sound to San Diego.

The marbled sculpin's colors vary with those of its immediate surroundings. Fish living in the kelp and fucus beds are usually predominantly brownish, while those inhabiting green algae or eelgrass are mostly greenish.

58 Paintings by Hashime Murayama

Pipefish (Top) Have Odd Customs but No Economic Importance

PIPEFISH (upper—*Syngnathus griseo-lineatus*) is the chameleon of the sea, changing its color to correspond with the area where it feeds.

Although there are several other pipefishes, this species is the largest, reaching a foot in length. It occurs abundantly in bays from southeastern Alaska to Monterey Bay, California.

The reproduction methods of the pipefish inverts nature, for the eggs are deposited by the female into an external pouch of the male. There they soon develop into tiny embryos and, like the sea horse, are nurtured by the father.

The **black-tailed, or deepwater, shrimp** (middle—*Crago nigricauda*) is commercially one of the most important species.

The chief method of capture is trawling with 60-foot funnel-shaped nets dragged over the bottom for an hour or longer.

The latest year's catch of shrimp along the Pacific coast of the United States was 871,500 pounds. Known from Alaska to Baja California, the black-tailed shrimp reaches a length of three or four inches.

Not a true perch, the **black sea perch** (lower —*Embiotoca jacksoni*) belongs to that peculiar group of shore fishes that give birth to fully developed young. It inhabits the North Pacific.

Reaching a length of 14 inches, it has considerable commercial value. Anglers catch it on hook and line baited with clams or worms.

59

Mysterious Migrator Baffled Scientists for Centuries

THE mystery of the breeding places of the common, or fresh-water, eel (*Anguilla rostrata*) is one of great antiquity, and only during the present century was any reliable information attained. It was known for a long time that eels moved down the streams of the Atlantic drainage of the United States and southern Canada, as well as the Mississippi River and other Gulf coast streams. But if they were not caught by commercial fishermen, they soon disappeared in the sea, never to be seen again.

Unlike salmon, shad, and other fishes which enter fresh water to spawn, the eel, it is now known, descends streams at maturity to spawn far out at sea.

In Europe the fresh-water eel (*Anguilla vulgaris*) has the same habits and is the objective of a great fisheries industry.

In the United States the catch of eels for market during the last year recorded was around 2,000,000 pounds and worth more than $250,000. The catch is heaviest during the dark of the moon, from July to October, inclusive. Large as is the American catch, that in Europe is vastly greater.

The young eels, three inches or so in length, called elvers, enter fresh waters in the spring in large numbers. The baby eels, before they become elvers, only a few inches long, are thin, flattened, and transparent creatures.

Among First Fishes Known to Pacific Scientists →

THE kelp greenling, sea trout, or rock trout (right—*Hexagrammos decagrammus*) of Pacific North American shores is related to the ling cod, sculpins, and rockfishes. It differs from them and most other fishes by having five lateral lines on each side instead of the usual single one along the mid side. The color of the sexes differs. The top specimen is male and the lower pair are females.

Living around rocks among kelp and other seaweeds (algae) in bays, around islands, and off the coast from Kodiak Island, Alaska, to Point Conception, California, it is known to most anglers, who catch it on hook and line.

Although it reaches a length of 18 inches and a weight of two to four pounds, it is unimportant commercially. Most of the fish are landed at San Francisco and sold on the fresh fish market.

To the north, in Oregon and Washington, a small catch is made by anglers in Puget Sound. Often the flesh has a pale blue-green tinge that disappears upon cooking. The flavor of greenlings when properly prepared is excellent and enjoyed by many.

One of the first group of fishes of the North Pacific to be made known to science was in the family Hexagrammidae, kelp greenlings. Five of the known species were first described in 1810, although the exploration of the fish fauna of the west coast did not begin in earnest until after the Gold Rush in 1849.

Today much of our knowledge of fishes is due to the studies made by west coast icthyologists during the last half century.

At the lower left are **ghost shrimp** (*Callianassa californiensis*). Erroneously called "crawfish" by dealers who sell them as bait, it is so transparent that the beating of its heart can be seen through its shell.

Ghost shrimps live in burrows in the sand from Vancouver Island to San Diego. They do great damage to young oysters, which are often smothered when waves bury them under the shrimps' burrows. The ghost shrimp lives chiefly on worms, which it seizes with its crablike legs. The young shrimp is delicate orange to deep rose pink in color, but as it grows older, its color becomes paler.

← The Ling Cod Is Badly Misnamed

LING COD (left—*Ophiodon elongatus*) is confined to the northeastern Pacific Ocean from the Gulf of Alaska to San Diego, California. A large-mouthed, elongated fish, with strongly protruding lower jaw, it has caninelike teeth in both jaws and a body covered with small scales.

Its closest relatives are the greenlings (below) and sculpins, which are of similar habits and habitat, but it is not related to true cod at all. Probably the name "ling cod" was bestowed by European fishermen, who knew the ling of the North Sea. The Chinook name "cultus," meaning worthless, is also a misnomer, because the fish is valuable food.

This species is extremely variable in color, the coloration appearing not to be associated with the sex. When a fish three and a half feet long was brought up alive by a trawler in Puget Sound, it appeared a marbled dark brown with orange spots. The captain struck it on the head with a gaff hook, and like a flash it completely changed its hue, the dark areas becoming light creamy yellow and the light areas brownish.

Female ling cod grow much larger than the males. The largest male on record was 36¼ inches long and weighed 22 pounds. Females weighing 70 pounds and measuring five feet in length have been taken.

Profitable prey for commercial fishermen, ling cod are caught commercially by the otter trawl, a long baglike net with 5-inch stretched mesh at the mouth and 4-inch stretched mesh at the small end. The float line is supported by corks, and the bottom line is heavily leaded. Attached at each side of the net's mouth are 3 x 5-foot otter boards. When these are set at the proper angle and hauled through the water, they spread the net. A recent year's landings totaled 8,009,500 pounds.

The smaller fish are dressed and sold to restaurants and hotels, or they are cut into steaks for sale in markets for home consumption. Fish that are exceptionally large are filleted. When properly fried in deep fat, they are a delicious food fish.

61

Paintings by Hashime Murayama

62

Fresh-water Drum Sometimes Called Thunder Pumper Because of Its Noise

THE fresh-water drum *(Aplodinotus grunniens)* belongs to the croaker family, which usually lives along the shores of warm seas. None occur in deep water, and a few species are confined to fresh water. Many of the croakers reach a large size and are rated high in commercial importance as food.

Generally distributed throughout the Great Lakes region and Mississippi Valley, the fresh-water drum prefers large rivers and avoids small streams. It is a remarkable species, interesting because of its food and feeding structures and its ability to produce a peculiar grunting sound, which gives it its name.

The fresh-water drum reaches a length of three or four feet and a weight of 40 to 60 pounds. It is a food fish wherever taken and is more popular in the South than in the North. It becomes tough with age, but is considered best when weighing under three pounds.

The drum is a bottom fish, living mostly in muddy waters, feeding on snails, mussels, and crayfish, which it is well equipped to crush. In its throat are located the pharyngeal jaws, bones which have heavy millstonelike teeth controlled by powerful muscles.

Its relation to the pearl mussel that it devours is not altogether one-sided, for it thus exposes itself to infection with glochidia, or mussels in the larval stage, so that of all fishes it commonly carries the heaviest load of young mussels to be fostered, transported, and planted on the river bed. (These grow up to become the food of other drumfish.) According to Dr. R. E. Coker, it is the only known fish that systematically, if unintentionally, aids in the growth of its own food.

The drum, then, is to be accounted a resource of double value—first, as an abundant food fish and, second, as an agent in the natural propagation of fresh-water mussels.

It is not a popular angler's fish, but is sometimes caught with hook and line baited with crayfish. The young are fair pan fish. The net fisheries take the bulk of those marketed. In the North it is often called sheepshead, while in Louisiana it is best known as gasper-gou.

The fresh-water drum makes drumming or grunting sounds not unlike those made by the sea drum, and this is the meaning of its specific name, *grunniens*.

The noises made by drums, croakers, and the other relatively few sound-producing fishes are accomplished in several different ways, but the drumming produced by drums is the result of muscles attached or drawn over the air bladder. The rapid contraction and expansion of the muscles, about 24 times a second, causes the walls of the air bladder to vibrate and to act as a resonator, intensifying the sound. Since fishes lack real vocal organs, noises cannot be produced in the same manner as in birds and mammals.

The ivorylike ear bones, or otoliths, of this fish are popularly known as "lucky stones," a fancy originating in a marking resembling the letter L. Since their growth parallels that of the fish, scientists study them to chart the age of the fish.

63

Night Prowlers Developed Goggle Eyes That Gave Them Nicknames

ONE of our commonest game fishes in streams and lakes throughout the Mississippi Valley, Great Lakes, and eastern and southern United States, the **rock bass** (*Ambloplites rupestris*), is also called redeye and goggle-eye. It was introduced into the States east of the Alleghenies, but in the Roanoke River of Virginia there is a native species, *Ambloplites cavifrons*. *Ambloplites rupestris*, averaging 10 inches, has been introduced into Pacific Coast States.

The rock bass, like other centrarchids (sunfish), excavates a nest on the bottom of a lake or stream, usually on gravel or stones, and protected by the male fish. The male works energetically, fanning out the sediment with his fins, thus making a basinlike depression, 8 or 10 inches in diameter, and cleaned of all debris. The female is driven into the nest and is carefully guarded until the eggs are laid.

During the process of spawning, the two fish lie side by side in the nest. The female reclines on her side, and a few eggs at a time are extruded through her red, bluntish ovipositor. They are fertilized the same instant by the male. After all her eggs are deposited, the female leaves the nest and does not return.

The tiny young rock bass, shifting for themselves, seek weedy places where they can find shelter and ample food for their growth. If weeds are not available, young rock bass occur around rocks and stones, darting in among them at the slightest disturbance. Among the weeds and stones they feed on small aquatic insects,

water fleas, and other tiny organisms that are available. As they get older, they take larger animals, including small crayfish.

Percy Viosca, Jr., in 1936 described as new a rock bass, *Ambloplites ariommus*, from Louisiana and Mississippi. In life the general ground color of this rock bass is olivaceous above, blending into straw or oyster white below; these lighter markings are overlaid with, and often obscured by, black shadowy cloudings, spots, and dots.

Above the lateral line all scales show metallic green reflections. On the sides the color is olive green, and here the reflections vary between greenish gold and old gold, with a pearly iridescence of a bluish or pinkish cast.

Below the dorsal fin is a wide vertical bar of dark blotches. A black spot is discernible on each of the body scales, and this marking often gives the appearance of continuous longitudinal stripes rather than rows of squarish spots as in the common northern rock bass.

This new rock bass is secretive, hiding deep in the shadows, and the large eye might indicate nocturnal feeding habits, Mr. Viosca believes. That it is seldom taken and practically unknown to anglers can be attributed only in part to the fact that Louisiana anglers fish in large streams or in bodies of water where the species is not found.

Its game-fish associates are well known and take the artificial fly readily. It is more than six inches in length and can be classed as a first-quality food fish, since its flesh is firm, flaky, and of delicate texture and fine flavor.

Prized Sturgeon Overfished for Caviar

EXCEEDED in length only by the largest sharks and probably by a Eurasian relative, the **Atlantic sturgeon** (top—*Acipenser oxyrhynchus*) is occasionally 12 feet in length, with females 7 to 9 feet long not uncommon. A 10-foot fish in good condition weighs about 500 pounds.

If the Atlantic sturgeons of America and of Europe are considered identical (of which there is doubt), the range extends from Scandinavia to the Mediterranean Sea and from the St. Lawrence to the Gulf of Mexico.

Because of its small, toothless mouth, this large fish must feed on small organisms. It has the same feeding practices as the **lake sturgeon** (below—*Acipenser fulvescens*), the largest fish of the Great Lakes. Its sensitive snout and the four barbels in front of the mouth are used for locating food on the bottom.

While feeding it cruises slowly along, with the barbels dragging or touching the bottom. As soon as these sensory appendages touch some food object, the tubular mouth is shot downward and sucks in the food discovered.

Long neglected, the sturgeon was recognized as commercially valuable at the end of the 19th century, and the stock has since been badly depleted for its roe.

The Fork-tailed Giant of the Trout World Likes Deep, Cool Fresh Water

VARIOUSLY called the mackinaw trout, the salmon trout, and the fork-tail trout, the **lake trout** (*Cristivomer namaycush*) is chiefly a commercial fish, but throughout its range in most of the large lakes of British Columbia, Alaska, northern United States, and northward beyond the Arctic Circle it is also a game fish of importance. In the Great Lakes the angler's share is small in comparison with the commercial catch.

Largest of all trouts, the lake trout is known to have reached a weight of 100 pounds. The average of those taken commercially at the present time is less than 10 pounds, but those caught by anglers along the shore average only half that weight. Although the usual length is 24 inches, many years ago in northern Alaska specimens exceeding three and a half feet in length were taken.

The lake trout is easily distinguished from other trouts by the numerous small pale-yellowish spots which cover its body.

Lake trout occur only in the larger deep lakes. They are essentially fish eaters and seldom grow to a large size on other than a fish diet. One 20-pound lake trout was reported that had 13 good-sized lake herring in its stomach. Thus an abundant population of forage fishes, such as smelt, ciscoes, or alewives, is needed. The presence of weed beds is not essential for the production of lake trout. They are voracious fish.

There are many vessels in the Great Lakes engaged in wholesale fishing, as long as the Lakes are free from ice. The most recent annual American catch of lake trout in the Great Lakes was more than 3,000,-000 pounds. In former years the catch has been as high as 10,000,000 pounds; the decline is largely due to the lamprey-eel infestation, perhaps the gravest problem besetting Great Lakes fisheries.

Lake trout are taken in Georgian Bay at depths of about 50 feet with hand line and trolling spoon, but the sport would be better if rod and reel were used. Anglers who have used the rod with 300 feet of line and minnows for bait find that the fish can be played in a satisfactory manner.

Surface trolling, when the trout are found in shallower waters, affords wonderful sport. In smaller and shallower lakes, like those in Maine, where summer temperatures are higher than in the Great Lakes, the lake trout is often taken with the fly. In Seneca Lake, in New York State, it is taken with a special trolling rig, designed to play the spoon 10 or 20 feet under the surface.

Painting by Hashime Murayama

65

The Feelers of the Catfish Help It to Find Food at Night

DISTINGUISHED by scaleless skin, small eyes, and long feelers that resemble cat whiskers, the many kinds of catfishes in America are among its most numerous and popular fishes.

One of the best known is the **brown bullhead**, or **horned pout** (left, top and center—*Ameiurus nebulosus*), of ponds, lakes, and streams of the eastern middle States. It is distributed north to the Dakotas and south to Texas. It has been introduced on the west coast, too, where it is well known.

Preferring shallow, warm, weedy, and muddy waters, bullheads are caught on worms, meat scraps, bits of fish, and crayfish by still fishing. Small traps and nets are used by the commercial fishermen.

The brown bullhead, averaging 10 inches in length, eats mostly at night, prowling along the bottom with barbels (feelers) widely spread. It will suddenly pause, then sink headforemost into the mud for some unseen prey. It is not particular what it eats, bolting almost anything convenient, but it prefers insect larvae, pupae, nymphs, and crustaceans, bivalve mollusks, and snails.

Catfishes make their nests usually in sheltered spots, as under rocks and submerged logs or stumps. Apparently both male and female do considerable excavating and finally make a saucerlike hole. Both fins and mouth are used to clear the bottom so that the gravel is exposed. Both fish remain at the nest and help incubate the eggs, the male doing most of the guarding.

The **channel**, or **spotted, catfish** (top right—*Ictalurus lacustris*) belongs in the Mississippi Valley and the Great Lakes, but is also in the Potomac River, where it was undoubtedly introduced many decades ago. A trim, active fish, it is bigger than the bullhead, usually being 10 inches long.

The **blue catfish** (lower pair—*Ictalurus furcatus*), inhabiting the Mississippi Valley and now in the Atlantic coast streams too, is the largest and best of all catfishes as a food fish. It occasionally attains a weight of 125 pounds, and 80-pound specimens are not uncommon. But the average weight is up to 20 pounds.

The blue catfish is less fond of muddy waters than other catfish and prefers the clearer and swifter streams. It is a clean feeder, living much on fishes and crayfish. A strong fighter, it is one of the best game fish in the catfish family.

In general, catfishes are omnivorous, feeding on animal life. They are very hardy and can live out of water longer than most fishes. Several kinds of catfish are preferred to trout as food by many people.

© National Geographic Society

Painting by Hashime Murayama

66

The Most Important of Lake Fishes Has Been in Heavy Demand as a Food Resource

N OT far removed from the salmon family, members of the whitefish family, Coregonidae, are found throughout the Northern Hemisphere, in Eurasia and North America. Whitefishes, with few exceptions, are lake fishes, though some species live most of their lives in streams.

One of the most abundant and important food fishes of the North is the lake whitefish (*Coregonus clupeaformis*), which inhabits the Great Lakes and some other large lakes of the United States and Canada. A recent annual American catch of lake whitefish in all lakes was 8,837,100 pounds. It is doubtless the favorite food fish derived from inland waters.

Planked whitefish is considered as great a delicacy in the Lake region as planked shad is around the shores of the Chesapeake.

The largest part of the catch is made in Lake Michigan and the least part in Lake Ontario. The gill net is the principal apparatus used, but many fish are taken with pound nets and seines. It is seldom taken with hook and line.

It inhabits chiefly the deeper parts of the lakes, moving into shallower waters early in summer, in midsummer seeking again the cooler depths. In the fall months, whitefish again come inshore to spawn, some of them entering streams for that purpose, but the migratory movements vary somewhat in the different lakes.

The average-sized lake whitefish lays between eight and fifteen thousand eggs. Spawning takes place during late October, November and December, and the eggs are found between the stones and in the crevices. They hatch by the next April.

The whitefish larvae, after hatching, come to the surface over the spawning grounds, where they remain for a few days. Then they make their way to the shore where they concentrate in water of about one-foot depth. When they reach a length of more than an inch, they seek the bottom in deeper water.

The young and the eggs of whitefish are devoured in great numbers by predatory fishes. Fortunately, the lake whitefish responds readily to artificial methods of propagation, and there are several hatcheries along the Great Lakes devoted to increasing the depleted stock.

In rare cases, the lake whitefish has reached a weight of 20 pounds, but the average brought to market is only 3 or 4 pounds. The usual length is 18 inches.

Painting by Hashime Murayama

© National Geographic Society

67

68

Their Flavor and Abundance Have Dubbed Crappies "The Fish for the Millions"

THE white crappie (upper—*Pomoxis annularis*) and the black crappie (lower—*Pomoxis nigro-maculatus*) occupy the same area, namely the region east of the Rocky Mountains and from southern Canada to the Gulf States. Fond of warm, muddy bottoms, the white crappie is abundant in lakes, ponds, bayous, and small rivers and creeks where the waters are sluggish. Both crappies abound in the Mississippi Valley, where the young literally swarm when the river overflows into ponds and bayous. Vast numbers perish each year when these waters dry up.

A fish of so wide a range naturally has many local names. Around the Great Lakes the white crappie is called ringed crappie, pale crappie, and strawberry bass. In Louisiana the name sac-a-lait is most commonly used, but it is well known elsewhere under no fewer than 22 other local names, ranging from strawberry perch to lamplighter. The black crappie is very commonly called calico bass, but is also called papermouth and tinmouth.

The white crappie spawns during May and July in water three to six feet or deeper, commonly under submerged brush or against a stump, and has practically the same habits as the black crappie. The male jealously guards the eggs and nest and keeps the water about them in constant motion with his pectoral fins. Other fish are kept away and, if they come too close, are savagely bitten.

Both white and black crappie are fine, delicious pan fish. Since they are also easily adaptable to fish culture, they have been planted widely, including on the Pacific coast.

The black crappie can be distinguished from the white by its relatively deeper and darker body and by the usual absence of the vertical bars or rings of the white crappie.

The black crappie, usually eight inches in length, is chiefly a feeder among aquatic vegetation on insects and their larvae and small forage fishes like minnows. It is most active during the early morning and evening and at night. When kept in ponds, it lives peaceably with other fishes.

The most successful bait used in fishing for crappies seems to be live minnows, although they will also take artificial flies, spinners, and insects. Of negligible commercial consequence, crappies are caught in huge numbers by millions of anglers, many of whom regard them as a favorite food.

Although the male black crappie guards the nest and eggs, the fry become active early and seem to seek their own cover. But the species is not notably a shelter-loving type. Nevertheless, it likes quiet waters and when it comes to the surface is apt to be found in weed beds or brush piles.

Our Heritage of the Fresh Waters

By Charles Haskins Townsend

Revised by Dr. Charles M. Breder, Jr., Curator, Department of Fishes and Aquatic Biology. American Museum of Natural History

SINCE the beginning of time, mankind has been able to get some part of his food from the waters; among the relics of the Stone Age are shell hooks and stone sinkers. Ancient sculptures—Assyrian, Egyptian, and Aztec—portray the taking of fishes with spear, hook, and net.

The prophet Habakkuk—who knows how many centuries B. C.?—placed some details on fishing in the earliest literature: "They take up all of them with the angle, they catch them in their net, and gather them in their drag."

In some of the far corners of the world, amazingly primitive ways of getting fishes are still in use.

In the mountain streams of New Guinea, the still-savage native has been found using a dip net made of hoop fitted with a piece of unbelievably tough spider web.

We have seen the Aleut drag up a heavy halibut with a huge hook of bent wood, the Fuegian make a successful throw with his bone-pointed spear, and the Tonga islander stupefy hundreds of fishes with the juices of a poisonous plant.

The modern Japanese fisher has not yet lost the ancient art of making the cormorant fish for him without the trouble of providing either hook or bait.

Fresh-water Resources Are Diminishing

In considering the resources of our fresh waters, we find everywhere exhaustive methods of fishing and a diminishing supply, in spite of restrictive measures and extensive fish propagation.

The means by which diminution is measured are to be found in the fishery statistics of the last half century. The annual yield of products, still very large, can be safely viewed only in comparison with the continual increase and improvement in the apparatus of capture.

It takes more and more gear to make the same catch. In the Great Lakes, our largest reservoirs of fresh-water fish food, the investment in the fishery industry runs into many millions of dollars. The principal fish-catching devices, such as pound nets, fyke nets, and gill nets, practically automatic in operation,

are filling day and night as long as the Lakes are free from ice.

The rivers and lakes of the United States have fishery resources unequaled elsewhere. The Great Lakes are virtually inland seas, and the navigable rivers are among the largest in the world. The mighty Mississippi, with its tributaries reaching in all directions, fairly dominates the map of the country.

These waters, together with the rivers of the Atlantic and Pacific coasts and many lakes of the northern States have been enormously productive in food for our ever increasing population.

Tons of Food from Great Lakes

The latest year for which complete figures are available, commercial fishermen alone took from the Mississippi River and its tributaries more than 80,000,000 pounds of fish. The 1949 catch by United States fishermen in the Great Lakes was more than 85,000,000 pounds.

Large as are the food supplies of these two regions at present, they must have been vastly greater before the exploitation of their resources began. Unfortunately, there are no official records by which the extent of the earlier fishery operations may be measured.

While the fish food derived from our fresh waters is vast in quantity, it is also notable in variety. There are many kinds of trouts, salmons, whitefishes, sturgeons, pikes, black basses, sunfishes, perches, catfishes, the shad, and the eel, as well as the less important, but abundant and widely distributed, chubs and suckers.

In addition to the familiar food and game fishes, our waters are rich in minnows, darters, shiners, and other small fry of no direct economic value but of vast importance as the food supply of larger fishes. Every great watershed has its peculiar forms of these, all well known to ichthyologists, who have described and named them by the score.

United States Has Hundreds of Species

The richness of fish life in our fresh waters continues to be amazing. The United States has a smaller area than Europe, yet it has

National Geographic Photographer Justin Locke

Trout for Southwestern Streams and Lakes Grow in These Round Hatchery Pools

Largest of five trout hatcheries in New Mexico is this one at Red River, close to the State's northern border. Fresh water streams through the circular ponds cradled in the Sangre de Cristo Mountains. The seven-month-old trout visible in the foreground pool are ready for shipment to waters where they will test anglers' skill.

"Sound Off!" Trout Files on Parade

A fish's life is not always completely aimless swimming. Witness rank and file in this military school of rainbow trout in clear, shallow water of Brule River in northeasternmost Minnesota. The social basis for their soldierly formation is unexplained by authorities.

nearly five times as many kinds of fresh-water fishes. We have upward of 500 species of these, while Europe has some 126 species.

We find that a single State may have considerably more than 100. The number known to Illinois is 150, and New York is credited with 141. It could doubtless be shown that our fresh-water fishery resources are greater than those of any other country.

Many of the fishes commonly taken for food or in sport fishing, and naturally of wide distribution, have been established, as a result of fish-cultural operations, in sections of the country far removed from their original habitat. A fish belonging to the Mississippi system or to the Atlantic slope often takes full possession of a new watershed, as a result of mere transplantation of limited numbers.

Although the numbers of fishes caught by anglers do not figure in statistics of the catch made for market, they are not without high economic and other values. Most of the northern States are visited in summer by thousands of tourists interested primarily in good angling waters.

Lakes far and wide have become summer resorts for people who find much of their recreation in fishing. Railways and summer resorts widely advertise the resources of their waters. Seasonal visitors, moving actually by hundreds of thousands, carry into these States

and pay out for expenses millions of dollars. The trade in angling equipment alone annually amounts to millions.

Who can measure the health and esthetic values attendant upon the angling idea? The angling habit seems to be conducive to long life, and, beginning with Izaak Walton, who lived to be ninety, presents a long list of celebrated fishermen who lived well into the eighties and nineties, many of them prominent in the literature of American angling.

Fresh-water fish culture in the United States has been carried on for more than fifty years in steadily increasing volume, in the effort to keep pace with a depletion by fishery industries which constantly threatens exhaustion of the fish supply.

Pollution a Dangerous Menace

The great fishery problem of the time in our country is the pollution of the fresh waters by innumerable agencies, rapidly affecting their productiveness. Unless stern measures are introduced by law to correct this, soon one of our great natural economic gifts will be seriously stricken.

When we consider that the market catch in the Great Lakes alone has sometimes exceeded 100,000,000 pounds in a year, that legions of anglers are overfishing the trout and bass streams everywhere, and that pollution of the

W. T. Davidson

Speckled Beauties Dance to the Lure; Two Fish Leap for the Same Fly

Any angler would part with a dozen of his prize flies to have two big, hungry brook trout form this circle as they strike at his single fly. This extraordinary stroboscopic photograph was made at the Corry, Pennsylvania, State fish hatchery.

The brook trout (page 100) feeds on insects and smaller fishes but responds readily to artificial baits. One of the top favorites among American game fishes, it is also an excellent food fish—a combination that has made trout fishing a great American pastime.

Some species of trout are highly localized, such as the golden trout of Lake Sunapee (page 122).

rivers by manufacturing industries, pumping out acids and residue of their mills which poison and destroy fish life, has reached appalling proportions, it is apparent that our heritage of the waters is endangered to a serious degree.

Fish culture alone cannot save it, even if greatly increased. We are already wasting expensive propagation work in stocking waters no longer suitable for fish life, and many streams have been abandoned to their fate. One could name a score of rivers in mining and manufacturing States, once contributing to the food supply, that now contain no living thing—no fish or mussel or crayfish, not even the air-breathing frog. These rivers represent damaged resources, and there are others that may soon be like them.

Reforms come so slowly that the great cleaning-up task ahead of the American people is not likely to be undertaken seriously until conditions become intolerable. In many countries all wastes available for fertilization are restored to the land and not sent insensately through sewers into the streams, and manufacturing wastes are converted into valuable by-products. The exhaustion of our fresh-water resources through overfishing and water pollution is not inevitable. A saving fund of knowledge, relative both to propagation and to protective measures, now awaits application through the force of public demand.

Many as are the sportsmen taking toll of our wildlife with the gun, those who use the rod are vastly more numerous. It is as easy to exhaust a small stream by overfishing as it is to exhaust the quail supply of a neighborhood. Fortunately, the preservation of the fishes is always possible through the employment of safeguards and restorative measures. Our fishing will doubtless last longer than our shooting.

Private fish culture would be of great service in maintaining and increasing our supply of fish food. Although it has been practiced for centuries in some European countries, it has but little more than commenced in America.

National Geographic Photographer Edwin L. Wisherd

Alligator Gar Is as Formidable as He Looks

This savage-looking seven-footer is an alligator garfish, a predaceous species abounding in Louisiana bayous. It destroys much valuable food fish. Its own flesh is tough and unpalatable.

The possessors of strongly flowing springs, brooks, and small lakes should be awakened to the value of their home resources for water farming. Approved methods for the construction and management of fish ponds have been worked out at public fish-cultural stations, and instructive public documents on the subject can be had for the asking.

Fish culturists assert that an acre of water can be made to yield more food than an acre of land, and the truth of the assertion has been demonstrated.

Mussels Dependent upon Fish Hosts

An interesting work in agriculture was once carried on in the Mississippi Valley originally under the direction of the old Bureau of Fisheries, now incorporated into the Fish and Wildlife Service. It was based upon the fact that the propagation of the mussel is dependent upon the presence of fishes to which the young,

free-swimming mussels may attach themselves as parasites until they are old enough to form shells and begin an independent existence.

The large, heavy-shelled mussels of this region had been gathered in such numbers for the manufacture of pearl buttons, and also for the valuable freshwater pearls they sometimes contain, that the supply was being exhausted, and the important industry dependent upon the mussel was in danger.

The mussel industry sometimes yielded as much as 20,000 tons of shells worth upward of half a million dollars. This supply of raw material for the button industry was threatened by the possibility of the river becoming too foul for the growth of mussels.

Young mussels attach chiefly to the gills of fishes, and in some species to the fins, early in their lives. It is now certain that all mussel spawn which fail to find a suitable fish host sink to the bottom and die.

The young mussels are temporarily provided with minute hooks for attachment and are soon enveloped in the epithelium of the fish, where they remain encysted until the shell begins to form and they can safely drop off.

Not all fishes are equally susceptible to these temporary mollusk parasites. Some receive very few, others shed them too soon, still others die as a result of carrying too many. As part of the agriculture program, large numbers of fishes were "infected," as it is called, with young mussels and then liberated to stock the public waters, as their "parasites" develop and fall off.

Turtles, Frogs, and Crayfish

There are several species of large turtles of the kinds known as "sliders" in our freshwater streams and lakes, especially in the middle and southern States, that contribute to the food supply. They have long been used in filling the ever-widening vacancy in the markets formerly occupied by that favorite of the epicure, the diamond-backed terrapin of the salt-water marshes.

They have so high an edible value that it is whispered we often pay terrapin prices for turtles that never saw brackish water. Fishery officials are aware of their importance and have studied their distribution, methods of capture, and conservation.

Frogs of several kinds are valued food delicacies, and their habits have received considerable attention with the view to developing a practical system of frog culture. It is to be hoped that some practicable and efficient method of conservation will be found before the natural supply approaches exhaustion.

The annual market supply of fresh-water turtles and frogs has been known to exceed half a million pounds of each, the great bulk of the catch being derived from the Mississippi and its tributaries.

Fenno Jacobs, Three Lions
Catfish Grandpappy
Channel cats can come in all sizes, but this 50-pounder is a real prize.

 Wide World

Most Likely Catch: Another Eager Angler

Addicts call trout fishing sublime, but it can easily become humorous. Opening day of the New Jersey trout season found this crowd of hopefuls tangling lines at the foot of Saxton's Falls on the Musconetcong River!

A subject of perpetual interest to all who fish with the rod is the food of fishes. There are moments in the lives of all of us when the most important thing in the world seems to be how to get the fish to bite. The problem is taken as seriously by the captain of some great industry, off on a fishing trip, supplied with the most expensive tackle, as by the barefooted urchin with a homemade pole, and doubtless the man of business is the more serious of the two.

Thanks to the patient laboratory investigations of Prof. S. A. Forbes, this dark question has been made luminous. He learned that while the food of fishes consists chiefly of other fishes, it includes virtually the whole aquatic fauna—a comfort when we would seek for baits.

Carnivorous Fishes

Fishes not only feed on other fishes and on insects but on crustaceans, mollusks, and worms. Plants do not constitute much of their food, although a few kinds feed on them, such as buffalo fishes, carps, and minnows. Some fishes get food by rooting in mud; others are inclined to be scavengers.

Among the chiefly fish-eating fishes may be mentioned pike, pickerel, muskellunge, pike-perch, burbot, gar, black bass, and channel catfishes. Those taking fish food in moderate amounts are represented by bream, blue-cheeked sunfish, bowfin, white bass, rock bass, and crappie.

Fishes which feed on other fishes to a trivial extent are white perch, suckers, spoon-bill, the various darters, top minnows, and silversides, sticklebacks, mud minnows, stone cats, and common minnows. The whole minnow tribe contributes to the food of the smaller fish eaters.

In the Mississippi region the gizzard shad constitutes 40 percent of the food of the wall-eyed pike, 30 percent of that of the black bass, half that of the pike, and a third that of the gars. This is a good illustration of the usefulness of an abundant species of little importance as food for man.

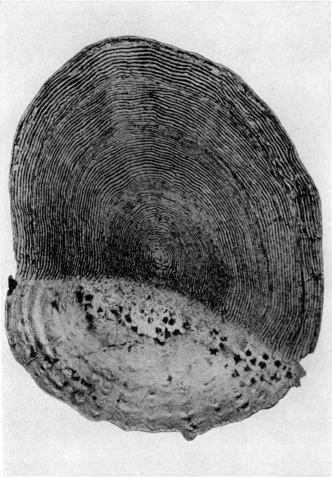

The Magnified Scale of a Salmon Tells Its Age

This specimen was taken from a male in its fourth year. The revealing "rings" resemble those of the cross section of a tree.

from the water not too large to be swallowed. Therefore, if the fish will not take the bait or the fly first offered, it may be tempted with another, and the resourceful angler need not return with an empty creel.

Little can be learned definitely about the ages attained by fishes unless individuals are kept under observation in captivity.

Age, Growth, and Habits of Fishes

The records of public and private aquariums, however, furnish data that we may consider reliable. The European eel has undoubtedly lived for long periods in captivity. According to accepted authorities, a few specimens kept in aquariums have lived for periods varying from 20 to 55 years.

Boulenger, in the Cambridge Natural History, states that an eel kept by the French naturalist Desmarest for "upward of 40 years" reached a length of four and a half feet.

It is recorded that four Russian sterlets had lived in the private aquarium of Captain Vipan in Northamptonshire for 25 years. He also had a golden orfe living after 24 years of captivity. The Brighton Aquarium had a sterlet which died after having been kept there "about 38 years."

Mollusks—the snails and mussels of various species—are also important as fish food. They form large proportions of the food of catfishes, suckers, fresh-water drum, and mudfish. About 16 percent of the food of perches, sunfishes, top minnows, and shiners is molluscan in character.

Fishes feed freely on insects, not only on the aquatic forms in their larval and mature stages but also on terrestrial insects cast into the water in many ways.

Crustaceans appear to be of even more importance as food, especially the minute entomostracans. The crayfishes are also eaten.

The food of adult fishes naturally differs greatly from that of the young. In addition to natural foods, both alive and dead, fishes in captivity will devour many kinds of meats and prepared foods. The question, then, as to what constitutes the food of fishes may be answered: almost any living animal forms

The Australian lung-fish is known to have lived at the London Zoological Gardens more than 19 years.

There are accounts of European trout said to have been kept in captivity for 53 years, and of carp kept still longer, but such are hardly comparable in verity with the records of existing public and private aquariums.

In the old Aquarium certain North American fishes lived for long periods: striped bass, 20 years; whitefish hatched in the building in 1913 lived until 1928; large-mouthed black bass, 11 years; muskellunge, calico bass, rock bass, and yellow perch, 10 years.

A striped bass kept in captivity for 19 years weighed 20 pounds and was three feet long when it died. Its length when received was about six inches. This species sometimes attains a weight of 120 pounds or more. It is likely that some species grew faster in freedom, where they find their natural foods, but other

E. Fred Miller

Cascades Do Not Stop the Salmon's Migratory Urge; He Leaps as if Jet Powered

From July to September, the Atlantic salmon, quitting the ocean, seek their spawning grounds in fresh water's gravelly headwaters. Unlike their Pacific kindred, they do not close their life cycle with this adventure, but descend again to the sea. This pair climbed the falls on Northwest Brook, Newfoundland, by taking one desperate leap, then swimming violently the rest of the way.

kinds may develop faster in suitable ponds where they are well cared for and protected from enemies.

Telling a Fish's Age by Its Scales

Since wild fishes of exceptionally large size are often found, we may assume that fishes continue to grow through life, the period of life depending largely upon enemies. In a world beset with sharp fangs and claws the life of a wild animal, either in the water or on land, is apt to end in a tragedy.

It is now known that the scales of fishes bear marks which indicate the length of life and the rate of growth in different years. Studies of the Atlantic salmon in Scotland and of the several species of Pacific salmon have proved this.

The scale grows in proportion to the rest of the fish, principally by additions around its border. The fish grows at different rates during different seasons of the year. Concentric ridges form around the edge of the scale, its marginal expansion in summer being more rapid than in winter, so that the growth during each year is usually distinguishable.

Studies of the five species of Pacific salmons have shown the ages at which the different species return to the rivers to spawn. Thus the ridges on a fish's scales are comparable to the annual ring growths revealed on a cross section of a tree trunk, which tell its age.

Studies of the scales of whitefishes in the Great Lakes have shown that the scale characters are so well defined that they indicate the age of the individual fish and the rate of growth of the species.

Scales from whitefishes hatched and reared in the old New York Aquarium and therefore of known age have been used by Government biologists in checking the results of studies of the scales of wild fishes.

The sexes of fishes are not so readily distinguishable as the sexes of birds. Males and females are usually so much alike that

The Bass Are Wary and They Grow Big in Florida

Largemouth black bass in the fresh-water lakes and streams of Florida are known to attain a weight of 22 pounds or more. The bow angler on Marion Creek has hooked a big one on light fly tackle and is attempting to bring it alongside the boat for the guide's waiting landing net.

only the expert recognizes the differences, and in many species the dissecting knife must be employed to determine the sex.

The colors of fishes vary somewhat according to the waters which they inhabit. This characteristic applies also to fishes held in captivity, where their colors tend to become more subdued. The specimens of exhibition tanks, however, brighten their colors during the spawning seasons, much as do wild fishes.

The habits of fishes have not been studied so thoroughly as those of birds, mammals, and other vertebrate animals. Books on fishes are largely of two classes: those written by anglers, relating chiefly to methods employed in the capture of the fish, and those written by the systematic naturalist, dealing chiefly with classification and distribution.

A Big Field for Science

In neither class of books is the life of the fish in its own environment very fully considered. There are, of course, satisfactory life histories of certain common species, especially those inhabiting the smaller streams, and fish culturists are contributing new information on the ways of fishes reared in ponds.

Since the keeping of fishes in aquariums became common, many important facts have been recorded, but observations on creatures in captivity can manifestly deal with little of their real life.

Richard Harrington

Spears Poised, Patient Eskimos Await Arctic Char Swimming under the Ice

Early in July the ice begins to break away from the Spence Bay shore of Canada's Boothia Peninsula, well north of the Arctic Circle. Netchilirmiut Eskimos make holes in the thinning ice. Watching motionless for hours, if necessary, they spear char, big cousins of the trout, with lightning-like thrusts of spears.

For many important facts about the senses of fishes, we are indebted to the modern biological laboratory. Results of scientific experiment relative to fishes' powers of hearing and memory, their color changes, sleep, electrical and poisonous properties, the sounds they make, and so on are slowly being revealed.

In recent years, scientists have devoted considerable time to the study of the breeding activities of American fresh-water fishes. Odd as it seems, the breeding behavior of salmon and trout was not correctly analyzed until the present decade, even though the spawning activities had attracted the attention of fishermen and naturalists.

Credit for observations and interpretation of the spawning activities of brook trout must go to Dr. Albert S. Hazzard; for brown and rainbow trout to Dr. John R. Greeley. Dr. C. M. Breder, Jr., summarized the breeding habits of basses and sunfishes. One of the first and most detailed accounts of breeding habits of fishes was written by Dr. Jacob Reighard, University of Michigan, with respect to suckers and minnows.

There are a number of papers about other species, but as yet the ecology and habits of most of our commonest fishes are little known. The naturalist who can devote himself to the study of fishes will find a fascinating field awaiting him.

U. S. Air Force, Official

Salmon Climb Sweeping Stairways Around Bonneville Dam

Huge Bonneville Dam stands between the sea and upstream Columbia River salmon spawning ground. To allow fish to jump and swim around the obstruction, biologists and Army engineers designed a $6,500,000 system of by-passing "ladders." The flumes consist of foot-high "steps," 40 feet wide and 16 feet long. Two curve upward to unite on Bradford Island (center). A third encircles the end of the dam (bottom). Industrialization has endangered fresh-water fish, and conservation methods have occupied an increasing number of scientists. Remedying the depletion of sockeye salmon (page 89) was the subject of a Canada-United States treaty in 1937.

Fishing in Pacific Coast Streams

By Leonard P. Schultz

Curator of Fishes, U. S. National Museum

M Y EARLY fishing experience was confined to sitting on a railroad bridge and coaxing sunfish, rock bass, and catfish to take a hook baited with angleworms, or going with my father to a lake and angling from a boat for bluegills. Now, after summers in Glacier and Yellowstone National Parks, and several years on the Pacific coast, I am converted into an enthusiastic fly fisherman.

Unlike many fishermen, I did not limit my interests to the trout, but sought all the other species of fresh-water fishes that occur in western North America. A few of these are discussed in this article.

No Fur on Fishes

In Glacier National Park I did not find the celebrated fur-clad trout that old-timers describe to gullible tenderfeet. Fish do not grow fur, despite the rumors; they are, however, provided with scales, spines, plates, naked skin, and prickles. Some, such as catfishes and sturgeon, have "whiskers," but these are long fleshy barbels, without the slightest resemblance to a hair.

When trout have not responded to artificial lures, I have searched the submerged rocks, logs, and vegetation for natural fish foods. The tiny clams that live in the mud or sand bottoms of lakes and streams are not readily taken by trout. However, crustaceans, such as the fresh-water shrimp, amphipods, and crayfish, as well as aquatic insect nymphs or larvae of stone flies, May flies, caddis flies, and worms, make excellent bait. Land insects, especially grasshoppers, are attractive, too, causing trout to strike when they refuse artificial bait.

The salmon and trout of western North America are of the greatest interest to sportsmen, fishermen, and scientists, not only for their recreational and economic value, but for their grace, beauty, and absorbing life stories. To maintain the supply of these species, the several States and the United States Fish and Wildlife Service artificially propagate each year many millions and distribute the eggs, fry, and young fish to the streams and lakes, sometimes dropping them from planes.

In addition to this restocking, some streams in western national forests and parks have been improved by the establishment of environments attractive to trout. Covers or shelters have been built, and current deflectors have been made of stones, logs, and brush, causing pools to form. In streams with soft sand bottoms little food grows, but on gravel or rubble much develops, so that devices to remove the sand and expose the gravel greatly improve trout and salmon habitats.

Clearing streams of snags and brush or straightening them to enhance their beauty is a mistake from the fisherman's viewpoint. Such changes remove the natural shelters for fish and for the production of fish foods.

Salmon fisheries extend from Monterey Bay, California, to the Yukon River in Alaska, and westward to Kamchatka and northern Japan. In North America alone the average annual pack of canned salmon for the past several years has exceeded six million cases (48 one-pound cans to the case).

The total value of salmon to the fishermen of the United States and Alaska for the period of 1940 to 1949 was $301,352,000 representing 4,872,476,000 pounds.

Chinook a Better Name for Salmon

The name "salmon" was first used in Europe for the Atlantic salmon (*Salmo salar*), closely related to the steelhead trout of the Pacific coast. Unfortunately the term "salmon" was applied to these fish of the Pacific, when the local Indian name "chinook" would have avoided confusion with the wholly different Atlantic salmon.

The spawning migration of salmon is anadromous, or from the sea to fresh-water streams. This is the reverse of that of fresh-water eels, *Anguilla,* which have a catadromous migration, or from fresh-water streams to the sea. In the Yukon River the late Dr. C. H. Gilbert discovered that some king salmon or chinook go upstream about 3,000 miles. Their migration is probably longer than that of any other species of salmon or trout. The pink salmon migrates least of all Pacific salmon; it spawns only a few miles above salt water. The catch of pink salmon is highly variable in Puget Sound where they are taken in quantity only in the odd-numbered years because of their two-year life cycle. For instance in 1947, about 52,000,000 pounds were taken, whereas in 1948, only 1,600 pounds and about 44,000,000 in 1949, the latest year for which statistics are available.

In trout, *Salmo*, and charrs, *Salvelinus*, the migratory instinct is definitely developed, but these forms pass most or all of their lives in fresh water, and thus there is no necessity for their migrating so far.

The salmon, in their urge to reach the proper place to deposit their eggs, often wear themselves out trying to navigate waterfalls or fish ladders placed in dams. Pacific salmon will jump vertically four times their length or more.

Sometimes they are killed by falling backward and striking sharp rocks. If not seriously injured, they continue to leap until they either go over the obstruction or drift exhausted downstream to fall prey to birds, bears, or other predators. By the time they have spawned, both salmon and trout are weakened and often emaciated.

This worn-out condition is not, however, the chief cause of the death after spawning of the five species of Pacific salmon. They have reached the end of their life cycle, and even fish in good condition die soon after their reproductive period is completed. Trout, steelhead, and charrs may spawn for several successive years.

Live Fish Related to Fossils

One remarkable trait of salmon is their "homing instinct", their mysterious ability to return to the stream in which they developed as fry and fingerlings. When eggs have been taken from females in one river and transferred to another stream for development, the young produced have gone through their life cycle and returned to spawn in the waters where they were hatched rather than in the habitat of their parents. Returning of tagged or marked fish and study of their scales have proved that most salmon return to their "home stream." This has been fully established by the International Pacific Salmon Fisheries Commission with authority to study the sockeye salmon fisheries of the Fraser River system of British Columbia. Back in 1913, the salmon runs were practically destroyed at Hell's Gate by big rock slides that blocked the river. The commission has built new fishways over the obstruction and in recent years, as a result, barren areas have been restocked, runs have been rebuilt. From the cyclic run for 1939, 91,050 cases were packed. However, in 1951, 252,551 cases were packed. Most of this increase is credited to the installation of fishways.

With the great development of waterpower in the western rivers by construction of dams, the sport fishing and the fisheries industries are greatly endangered. The State of Washington by popular vote a few years ago set aside the Cowlitz River as a salmon sanctuary with the idea that no dams would be built. Although fishways do aid in getting salmon over dams to spawn, the downstream migration of the young is a much tougher problem. Many of the young pass through the turbines and are killed, perhaps not so much from hitting something en route as from the sudden release of great pressure and formation of a vacuum.

Different Species May Inhabit Neighboring Waters

The faunas of the Pacific coastal drainage system have much in common, yet the species differ among the river systems and lake basins.

Fish of the isolated lakes of southeastern Oregon and of the Lake Lahontan Basin are distinctive. Some forms found in the Columbia River are represented by similar forms in the Sacramento-San Joaquin system, but in both rivers are species found nowhere else.

The fish fauna of the Great Salt Lake drainage system is characteristically that of the Snake River, a tributary of the Columbia. That of the Fraser River is similar to that of the Columbia, too.

In none of the streams west of the Continental Divide in the United States occur endemically such species as the paddlefish, the bowfin, the pirate perches, pickerel, the gar pike, darters, and yellow perch. But such fish as the cyprinids (minnows and dace), centrarchids (basses and sunfish), the ling, sculpins, trout, and whitefish, are found on both sides of the Divide.

Among the fresh-water fishes of the Pacific coastal streams are to be found the largest minnow in North America, the squawfish, and the largest anadromous fish, the white sturgeon.

In the Sacramento-San Joaquin drainage system occur 40 endemic species, as contrasted with 46 in the Columbia system, 15 of which are common to both streams. In addition to the endemic forms, 18 species have been successfully introduced into the Columbia and 19 into the Sacramento-San Joaquin, 17 of which are reported from both stream systems.

Farm Ponds

During the past two decades and especially since the war, there has been a tremendous development in farm ponds. These are usually constructed by making an earth dam across a small creek or across a natural watershed. The most successful ponds are an acre or more

W. D. Staats

Census Takers Count Fish as They Reach the Top of the "Water Stairs"

A submerged white platform shows up weary salmon as they cross the upper "landing" of a Bonneville Dam fishway. In one six-month period, by actual count, almost half a million salmon and steelhead trout passed the dam on the way up the Columbia River.

in area and 6 feet or more in depth. Natural small ponds may be excavated to a greater depth, but in all cases, the soil must be non-porous such as clay or the water will disappear in the soil. These ponds serve not only for fish production but are valuable in retaining water for domestic animals.

The management of fish ponds is a problem similar to running a farm or growing a garden. The pond needs fertilizer so that plankton will form to start the food chain. Weeds may grow to a damaging extent, but they may be controlled through the increased cloudiness of the water as the result of fertilization. The sunlight is absorbed by the turbid water so much that aquatic plants do not grow except in the most shallow places.

Warm water ponds that completely lack fish may be stocked with a combination of large-mouth blackbass and bluegills. The bass feed on the bluegills which are highly productive all summer. To keep the cycle going, it is necessary to fertilize the pond at intervals and to fish out bass and bluegills of legal size. There may be overfishing of the bass but little danger of catching too many of the bluegills.

Ralph Burress stated that in a heavily-fished 3½ acre pond "even though 115 pounds of bass and 387 pounds of bluegills had been removed by anglers during a 79-day open season, the following fish were left in the lake:

67 adult bass weighing 80 pounds, 728 young bass weighing 75 pounds, 160 adult bluegills weighing 43 pounds, and 46,168 small blue-gills weighing 494 pounds—a total of 692 pounds of fish." Small ponds may be over-stocked so that the fishes present do not have enough food and are runts. Far more ponds are ruined by underfishing than by too much fishing.

The analysis of many such fish ponds points out one fact very clearly that no panfish (in this instance bluegills) of any size, once caught, should be returned to the pond alive. If it is too small for table use, kill and return it to the pond as fertilizer. "Such reduction in numbers allows the remaining fish to grow more rapidly and reach a more desirable size."

Fisheries biologists in a number of states are finding that in streams, rough fish may greatly outnumber game fishes. Anglers are contin-ually catching the game fishes but the rough fishes such as suckers do not take the hook, they remain to compete in the food chain. This selective fishing operates to the advantage of the rough fishes. Recognizing this problem, the Kentucky Division of Game and Fish opened the states streams to gigging in 1950. In 1951, a check was made of the catch taken by 3,432 giggers and 534 snaggers. "They had taken 11,481 fish weighing 12,435 pounds. Of the fish caught, over 95 percent were suckers. About one percent were panfish and illegal game fish. If the giggers take only rough fish, their action will be very helpful to the hook and line angler, but if they also take game fish in appreciable numbers, the activity must be outlawed, to their own disadvantage, and to the disadvantage of the hook and line fisherman."

Thus the newer theories of managing the fishing in our streams and lakes applies as much to non-game fishes as to the game species.

Atomic Energy and Fishes

The atomic age has its effect on our fresh-water fishes and on fishing. Although the Atomic Energy Commission makes proud boasts and apparently proves it with carefully prepared records that its thousands of employees working in the vicinity of atomic piles have as good or a better health level than employees working around the great industrial plants of our large cities, it is greatly concerned about the effect of radiation on our wild life and on stream fishes.

The source of this radiation originates in the radioactive wastes from the atomic piles of the manufacturing plants of the Atomic Energy Commission such as at Oak Ridge, Tennessee and at Hanford, Washington on the great Columbia River. "When uranium metal placed in the reactor to produce plutonium is bombarded by neutrons, energy is added which produces a state of excitation in atomic nuclei. In an inconceivably short time the atoms split into two unequal fragments. This is called fission." As this process goes on more than a hundred isotopes of various elements are formed, most of which are radioactive. Although the majority of these fission products have high activities but very short half lives, some have a half-life of 40 days or more. The products of plutonium manufacture are tremendously complex and at the present time only a few are used whereas the rest are discarded.

The four principal methods of radioactive waste disposal used are air dilution; water and mud dilution; storage and shipping; and burial. From the first two methods some wastes have gotten into streams. In the event of an atomic war large amounts might pollute our streams so it is necessary to know the effect of radiation on aquatic organisms and on fishes. These waste materials settle on the bottom where aquatic organisms burrow and feed. The radioactive particles are ingested, absorbed and accumulated in the organism which later enters the food-chain from bacteria to forage fishes, then is passed on to our game fishes that cannot escape the contaminated environment.

Research work is in progress on the effect of radiation on fishes especially at the Applied Fisheries Laboratory, University of Washington, Seattle. Dr. Welander exposed eggs and larvae of chinook salmon to various doses of radiation. Then the embryos and young salmon were raised, and the effects studied. The damage to the cells was in direct proportion to the amount of radiation.

Exposure of adult rainbow trout to 500 Roentgen units caused considerable cell damage, whereas an exposure to 1,500 Roentgen units caused 56 percent mortality in 13 weeks, and 87 percent in 64 weeks.

These and other experiments have shown that fishes can withstand far greater amounts of radiation than man. The maximum safe daily exposure for man is only 0.1 r.

Elmer Higgens states that "if a group of people were given a single dose of gamma radiation of about 450 r., about half of the group would die. However, most individuals could take 450 r. if it were not given in a single dose but in a series of small doses over a period of several months. A diagnostic chest x-ray is equivalent to about 10 r."

Since people are more easily affected by radiation than fishes, it is important to be able to determine which streams are contaminated, and if edible fishes are present, how much radioactive materials have been absorbed by them, because these can be passed on to man where they may accumulate in the tissue of his body and in later years cause cancer or other damage.

The Need for Scientific Studies

Half a century ago few fish culturists had a scientific background or advice from scientifically trained men. The chief aim was to produce millions of fry in the hatchery, and when they were planted in a stream it was assumed a large percentage would survive. However, that was not the usual result.

I was asked to check the mortality of cutthroat plantings in streams of Yellowstone National Park. In one stream, where natural spawning occurred successfully, several thousand recently hatched fry were planted in a favorable location. By the end of the fifth day, daily samplings revealed, 2- or 3-inch long trout had completely eaten all the fry planted.

Such unbiased observation and analysis make it possible to correct long used but obsolete fish cultural practices. Such universities as Michigan, Washington, California and New York have aided by offering excellent courses leading to the proper management and conservation of our aquatic resources, insuring a maximum yield to benefit both commercial fishermen and sportsmen.

85

Electric Batteries of This Ray (Top) Are Effective Weapons

ELECTRIC RAY, or **crampfish** (top— *Tetranarce californica*), is found in moderately deep to shallow water from Nootka Sound, Vancouver Island, to San Diego Bay, being very rare northward. On the Atlantic Coast there is an electric ray or torpedo fish difficult to distinguish from the Pacific form.

The electric rays have, at the sides of the head and gill chambers, electric glands which generate shocks sufficiently strong to stun other fish and to be disagreeable and painful to the hands or to the bare feet of bathers. This living battery shows all the properties of electricity, the discharge registering voltage on electrical instruments. The electric ray ranges in length from a foot to three feet and in weight to 75 pounds or more.

Sheep, or kelp, crabs (bottom—*Loxorhyn-chus grandis*) belong to the family of spider crabs, Majidae, with numerous members occurring along the shores of Pacific North America. They are noted for their habit of masking themselves by placing, with their long, ungainly legs, bits of seaweed or other objects on their backs. This disguise probably aids the crab to escape from its enemies.

Reaching a length of eight inches across the back, the sheep crab is found from San Francisco to Puerto San Bartolomé, Baja California. Although these big crabs are abundant, their slender legs do not contain as much meat as those of the market crab, and they are not caught commercially. Even those in Alaska that measure 3½ feet between the tips of opposite legs are used only locally.

Painting by Hashime Murayama

86

The Shark's Reputation for Ferocity Is Not Shared by All Kinds

KNOWN from San Francisco Bay to Ballenas Bay, Baja California, the leopard shark (*Triakis semifasciatum*) is distinguished by conspicuous black bars across the back and upper sides. It is one of the commonest species in the markets of southern California and is frequently taken by anglers.

Shark meat is hard, firm, and of a sweetish taste, but is not used so extensively here as in Europe and Asia. Sharks captured in the commercial fishery are skinned, and the hide is used for shoes, pocketbooks, and bags.

While most sharks are voracious, only a few are known to have attacked man. Some of the more vicious species, such as the tiger and hammerheads, attack any animal life, including humans, often fatally mutilating their victims. Other sharks are harmless even to fishes and feed only on plankton. The basking shark and the whale shark are the largest species of living fishes known, reaching a length of 45 feet. The leopard shark of the Pacific averages only about 40 inches long, and is perfectly harmless to man.

The International Game Fish Association angling record for sharks was a 14-foot 8-inch man-eater that weighed 1,919 pounds.

Formidable Mouth of Red Rockfish Swallows Other Fish Whole in One Gulp

ONE of the most attractively colored species among the rockfish family along the Pacific coast, the red rockfish (upper pair—*Sebastodes rosaceus*) is found from Puget Sound to Baja California. The usual length of the red rockfish is ten inches, and it feeds on herring, perch, crabs, and shrimp.

The rock crab (bottom—*Cancer antennarius*) has along the Pacific coast eight close relatives, one of them the common market crab. Although edible, it is seldom seen in the fish stalls, probably because it is unprofitably difficult to catch in sufficient numbers due to the rocky shores which it inhabits. It ranges from Tomales Bay, California, to Baja California. Averaging seven inches across the back, it is, like other crabs, inclined to scavenging.

Painting by Hashime Murayama

88

In Alaska Salmon Is an $85,000,000 Industry

BOTH pink, or humpback, salmon (top pair —*Oncorhynchus gorbuscha*) and chum, or dog, salmon (lower pair—*O. keta*) are found from northern Japan to Alaska and southward to central California, but are taken commercially in large quantities only from Puget Sound northward. Throughout their range they pass part of their life cycle in the sea and part in streams.

In southeastern Alaska salmon begin their migration from the sea in late June, the pink salmon continuing until late September and the chum salmon to November. Usually Pacific salmon die after spawning.

The name "humpback" is derived from the hump found on the back of the male pink salmon (second from top) while on its spawning grounds, where it also develops a hooked snout. The humpback is caused by the sudden formation of cartilaginous tissues between the back of the head and the beginning of the dorsal fin. The hooked snout results from rapid elongation of bones.

Both these salmon are usually 18 inches in length and are caught in far greater commercial abundance in Alaska than in the Pacific States. Salmon constitute 85 percent of Alaska's $100,-000,000 fishing industry.

89

Red Salmon Has Become a Favorite Canned Food in America

RANGING from northern Japan to Alaska and southward to San Francisco Bay, California, the **red, or sockeye, salmon** (*Oncorhynchus nerka*) averages about 5 pounds, with a maximum of 12 pounds.

Also known as blueback salmon, its flesh is deep red and of excellent flavor. The latest recorded annual catch was 77,987,000 pounds, with a market value of $7,110,000.

At one time the greatest red-salmon stream was British Columbia's Fraser River, the surface of which was paved with red salmon as they fought their way from the sea to spawning grounds. But in 1913 and 1914 heavy slides occurred during railroad construction and blocked the migration to the spawning grounds. The species has not yet regained its former abundance in this river, even though the obstructions have long been removed.

Some red salmon are landlocked in lakes and never go to sea. They may be caught in Lake Washington during the spring and early summer before their color changes to dark red. While in the lake they are called "silver trout," but by autumn, when they go to the mouths of adjacent streams, they are called "redfish."

90

Dolly Varden Trout Is Abundant but Unpopular with Anglers

LIKE its nearest relative, the eastern brook trout (page 100), the **Dolly Varden** (*Salvelinus malma*) belongs to the charrs, family Salmonidae. These two species differ from other trout (*Salmo*) in having light spots on a darker background instead of black spots on a lighter background, and a few scarlet spots on the sides of the body.

Dolly Vardens occur from northern Japan to Alaska and southward to northern California. Throughout this vast area they inhabit the coastal streams, often going to sea as "steelhead Dolly Vardens" and growing to large size. Although this species is not cultivated artificially and is the subject of continued fishing, it nevertheless persists in most of the coastal streams and in

Alaska occurs in great abundance. In most Alaskan streams they occur in schools.

The Dolly Varden trout is not a leaping fish like the rainbow trout or black bass when hooked, although it may rise from the water when striking the fly or other lure.

Fish two-and-a-half feet long and from 8 to 10 pounds are common. Voracious feeders, they prey on young trout and salmon, and are consequently out of favor with sportsmen. They will take lures, such as artificial minnows and spinners, and will rise to a fly. Since the flesh, delicious when properly cooked, if often pale pink like that of the Yellowstone black-spotted trout, both these species are known in some localities as "salmon trout."

91

Economic Value of Salmon of the Pacific Coast Is Fabulous

LARGEST of the species of Pacific salmon in the genus *Oncorhynchus*, family Salmonidae, the **chinook,** or **king, salmon** (top pair—*Oncorhynchus tschawytscha*) occurs from northern Japan to Alaska and southward to Monterey Bay, California.

Its average size is about 22 pounds, though it has exceeded 100 pounds. Usually the flesh is a deep salmon-red, but in some localities it is pinkish.

The chinook salmon usually migrates in the spring, April to June; and another run occurs in the autumn, August to November, the time of the migration depending on the river. In the larger rivers of its range, such as the Columbia, an additional migration takes place in summer, with stragglers going upstream most of the time.

The total commercial catch of the Pacific Coast States averages some 33 million pounds annually, with a value of $1,500,000 to $2,500,000.

Of the same range as chinook, **silver,** or **coho, salmon** (lower pair—*Oncorhynchus kisutch*) is much smaller, averaging five to eight pounds. Its flesh, which varies from pinkish to deep salmon-red, is canned extensively. About 20 million pounds are taken annually in the United States, the value of the catch ranging from a half million to nearly a million dollars.

Large quantities of silver salmon are quick-frozen and glazed, then stored in modern refrigerator plants. As the market will absorb them, they are shipped to the East.

92

Stickleback Builds Nests →

FOUND in Asia, Europe, and North America, the **three-spined stickleback** (right—*Gasterosteus aculeatus*) is so named because of the sharp isolated spines on the back.

Sticklebacks are known for their ability to build barrel-shaped nests with front and back entrances leading to a tubular hallway. The male alone builds the nest out of "vegetable bricks" and cements them together with a sticky secretion from his body. The nest is concealed in vegetation or in rock pools where there is a moderate flow of water.

The male continually goes in and out of his house, working the marine glue from his body over the inner sides, where it hardens. Upon completion of the nursery, he searches for a mate, and after a courtship induces her into the nest, often by poking her with his snout or spines.

Sticklebacks are of no value as food for man, but in salt marshes, along shores of lakes, and in streams, they keep down mosquitoes by eating the larvae.

ONLY member of the sunfish and bass family occurring endemically west of the Rocky Mountains, the **Sacramento perch** (left—*Archoplites interruptus*) is confined to the Sacramento-San Joaquin River basins.

Presumably this fish is a representative of the ancient fauna which extended across the North American Continent prior to the elevation of the Rockies. Fossil remains of this fauna are found in the Eocene Green River shales of Wyoming.

The perch do not build nests on the bottom in sand or gravel as do sunfish or bass, but spawn among submerged objects. The eggs are held together by a gelatinous substance and laid in long strings, somewhat like those of the common yellow perch in the East. They are draped over submerged roots, old limbs of trees, and branches sunk in the water.

This species has been reported to reach a length of two feet, although the average size is from 8 to 12 inches. It takes the hook readily and ranks high as a game fish. Its food consists mostly of worms, insects, and small fishes.

The color of the Sacramento perch varies. Some are almost entirely black and some almost entirely silver.

Yellowstone trout (below—*Salmo clarkii lewisi*) is the only game fish in Yellowstone Lake. Common in the mountain streams of much of British Columbia and the northern Rocky Mountain States, it is a close relative of the coastal cutthroat (page 127) but has fewer anterior and more caudal black spots.

In the springtime these gorgeous trout take nearly any kind of bait. Sometimes one can catch a trout in the cold water of Yellowstone Lake and, without moving a step, boil the fish in a hot spring on the shore.

In the Flathead River at Glacier National Park it is caught by hundreds of visitors, some of whom hike to the headwaters of tributary creeks or to mountain lakes where fishing cannot be excelled. There Dr. Leonard P. Schultz once took on a fly 10 one-pound trout in a little more than 15 minutes.

The fish spawn in May or June in the smaller creeks to which the adults have migrated as soon as the ice is gone. The eggs hatch in from four to six weeks, and the baby trout soon begin to feed. After spawning, the large adult trout, reaching 12 inches in length, usually move back into the lake and leave their progeny to the care of Nature.

Paintings by Hashime Murayama

Painting by Hashime Murayama

Fresh-water Giant Was Bigger and More Numerous in Preindustrial America

LARGEST fresh-water fish in North America is the **white**, Columbia River, or **Sacramento sturgeon** (large pair—*Acipenser transmontanus*), found in both fresh and marine waters along the Pacific coast from Alaska to Monterey, California. It belongs to a remarkable group of fishes, the sturgeon family, Acipenseridae (page 64).

A white sturgeon reaching 12½ feet in length and weighing 1,285 pounds was caught once near Vancouver, Washington, but the day of the big sturgeons is probably over in the Columbia River. Modern power and irrigation dams may prohibit adult fish of this size from going upstream to deposit their eggs, or, if the journey is accomplished, the young may find it impossible to reach the sea by way of fish ladders built for salmon and trout migrants. At present the total commercial catch of sturgeon for the Pacific coast of the United States is from 75,000 to 150,000 pounds annually.

The small fish above are **eulachons** (*Thaleichthys pacificus*), members of the smelt family (page 31). They are common from the Bering Sea to the Klamath River in northern California. Their flesh is of a delicate flavor and highly esteemed as food.

Minnows of the Pacific Coastal Streams (Top)
Sometimes Reach Length of 3 Feet

A MEMBER of the family of minnows and carps is the **Sacramento squawfish** (top three—*Ptychocheilus grandis*). It and its close relatives, Columbia squawfish (*Ptychocheilus oregonensis*), from which it is barely distinguishable, are common in Pacific coastal streams from central California to British Columbia.

The squawfishes are the largest minnows of North America; in the Colorado River another species is said to reach a weight of 80 pounds. Frequently those taken in the Columbia River system are nearly 3 feet long and weigh from 6 to 10 pounds.

They are voracious minnows with pikelike habits, the adults feeding mostly, if not exclusively, on other fish, including young trout and salmon. Like all other minnows or cyprinoids, they are without jaw teeth, but they are quick enough to capture fish with their large mouths and to crush them far back in the throat by using their pharyngeal teeth.

Squawfish have a poor reputation among sportsmen. They are greedy for salmon eggs, worms, and insects, and will readily take artificial lures as well as frogs. The young make excellent bait for rainbow trout or bass.

Several species of suckers, so called because of their peculiar mouths, occur in North America and Asia, but the **Sacramento sucker** (lower three—*Catostomus occidentalis*) and its close relative, the large-scaled Columbia River sucker, are confined to the coastal streams of western United States and British Columbia. By protruding their papillate lips, these fish feed on small organisms and plants growing on the rocks of stream bottoms.

Sacramento suckers may reach a length of nearly two feet, but average about 15 inches; the larger ones weigh several pounds. Because of their odd mouths and feeding habits, they are seldom taken on hook and line. They are not at all gamy and are of slight commercial value, except locally.

Savage Pickerel Family

L ARGEST member of the pickerel family, the **muskellunge** (top pair—*Esox masquinongy*) is known to exceed 80 pounds in weight, and 40-pound specimens are fairly common.

It is a northern fish, inhabiting mainly the Great Lakes, Lake Champlain, Lake Chautauqua, lakes of Canada, the St. Lawrence River, and the upper Mississippi and tributaries.

Celebrated as a game fish for size and strength, it is a tough fighter and rivals the salt-water barracuda in fierceness.

Smaller but more widely distributed and abundant than the muskellunge, the **pike** (lower center—*Esox lucius*) is also a notoriously voracious fish, destroying great numbers of other fishes, water birds, and small aquatic mammals, and eating about an estimated fifth of its own weight daily during the summer months. It is the enemy of all fishes inhabiting the shallower waters.

In winter the pike seeks greater depths and is taken through the ice. In summer it is a solitary, still hunter, lurking about the edges of weedy or brushy places. It usually reaches 24 inches in length.

The **chain pickerel** (bottom—*Esox niger*) belongs chiefly to the region east of the Alleghenies, from Maine to Florida. Although it reaches a weight of eight pounds, the average size, which varies with the locality, is two or three pounds.

Like others of the pickerel family, it is solitary and voracious, sometimes seizing a fish half as large as itself and swallowing it by degrees (pages 10, 11).

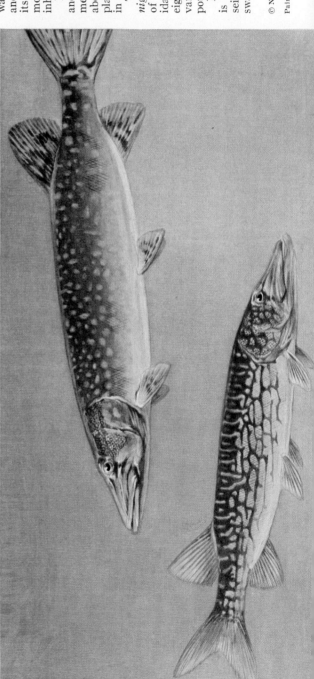

Generations of Fishermen Have Mistakenly Thought the Yellow Pike-Perch (Lower) a Form of Pike, Dubbed It Wall-eyed Pike

YELLOW pike-perch (lower pair—*Stizostedion vitreum*) and sauger or sand pike (top—*Stizostedion canadense*) are close relatives of the yellow perch (page 128), and all of them belong to the family Percidae, the true perches. Another species was discovered by Dr. C. L. Hubbs and made known in 1926 under the name of *Stizostedion glaucum*. This latter fish is called the blue pike and occurs in the Great Lakes in abundance, helping make up part of the commercial catch of pike-perches.

Although the yellow pike-perch prefers clear waters everywhere in its range, it is a fish of the lakes rather than the rivers. It is seldom found in lakes or streams with mud bottoms. During the spring and summer, it frequents the shallow waters near shore in the Great Lakes, but as cold weather comes on, it seeks deeper water.

Yellow pike-perch is found from Lake Champlain westward to Minnesota, in the interior lakes of New York, in the Great Lakes basin and in the Mississippi Valley, but through fish-cultural operations its habitat has been greatly expanded. Its range also extends well into Canada.

The yellow pike-perch ranks close to the whitefishes and the lake trout in quality and commercial importance among the fishes of the Great Lakes, where a recent annual market catch amounted to 7,115,700 pounds, with a value of $1,554,191. It is also a favorite of anglers and strikes willingly at lures.

Though the average weight of this fish in the Great Lakes is less than 10 pounds, a specimen occasionally reaches a weight of 25 pounds and a length of 3 feet. In other northern waters the average is less than 5 pounds. It is a swift and powerful swimmer, capable of overtaking bass and perch.

The yellow pike-perch is essentially a piscivorous fish, but feeds upon crayfishes too. Minnows, shad, and small sunfishes are common in its stomach.

The yellow pike-perch spawns in April. The eggs are small and hatch in two or three weeks after fertilization. Sometimes it runs up rivers to deposit its eggs, but also spawns on gravel shoals in lakes and probably on weed beds too. No definite nests are made, and the eggs are deposited over the bottom.

Resembling the yellow pike-perch in general appearance and having the same range, the sand pike is much smaller, averaging only about a quarter of the former's weight.

Painting by Hashime Murayama

© National Geographic Society

97

98

The White Perch Is Equally at Home in Fresh or Brackish Water

BELONGING to the tidal region of the Atlantic coast from Nova Scotia to South Carolina, the **white perch** (*Morone americana*) is abundant around Long Island and in the Hudson River up as far as Albany. It is taken through the ice in the Hudson, where it is present throughout the year. It is equally abundant in the Delaware and Susquehanna Rivers and Chesapeake Bay, ranging well upstream, and is commonly taken in pound and fyke nets along the coast.

Commonest in brackish tidal water, it is taken in largest numbers in the lower sections of tributary streams. Good catches are also made in the spring during the spawning season, far up rivers where the water is always fresh.

Along the Atlantic coast millions of pounds of white perch are caught annually by commercial fishermen. Anglers catch it in abundance and consider it a good food fish, though its average weight is a little less than a pound. White perch sometimes reach 15 inches, but average half that length.

Whether from fresh or brackish water, the white perch is delicious prepared as a pan fish.

Hook-and-line fishermen find shrimp or bloodworms the best bait, but the fish responds readily to minnows, young eels, small crabs, or any of its natural foods. In fresh waters, worms, grasshoppers, and other insects are effectively used. The white perch rises to the fly, especially in fresh waters, and resists bravely when hooked.

A gregarious species, usually frequenting the shallower waters alongshore, the white perch is better adjusted to living equally well in either fresh or brackish waters than most native fishes, and ranges freely into both.

In rivers it passes up beyond all trace of salinity and often becomes landlocked in strictly fresh ponds, where it breeds for considerable periods. On the other hand, it is taken in abundance about coastal islands where conditions are altogether those of the salt sea.

The white perch normally spawns from April to June, although evidence has been found that it may spawn in December in Chesapeake Bay.

It is taken chiefly in the spring and fall, from March to May and September to November.

99 Painting by Hashime Murayama

Widely Distributed Black Bass Are Most Popular of Fresh-water Game Fishes

DISTINGUISHABLE from the other three black basses by its large mouth, the **large-mouth black bass** (left—*Micropterus salmoides*) has the upper jaw extending beyond the eye instead of just below its rear margin. The color consists chiefly of a more or less regular longitudinal dark stripe and a small but distinct caudal spot. Originally it occurred throughout the Mississippi Valley, Great Lakes region, Gulf coast streams, Florida to North Carolina, but now has been extensively introduced into most sections of the United States.

The large-mouth bass is a fish of warmer waters than the **small-mouth bass** (right and jumping —*Micropterus dolomieu*) and is most abundant in weedy, mud-bottomed lakes and ponds, sluggish streams, backwaters, and swamps. The favorite habitats of the small-mouth bass, on the other hand, are cool flowing streams and large clear lakes.

Among the black basses the large-mouth is the largest, and in Florida specimens weighing 25 pounds are occasionally taken. The usual weight is two or three pounds. The size of the bass

depends largely on the waters it inhabits, and the extremely large sizes occur in waters rich in food organisms. The young eat insects and water fleas, and the adults feed mostly on fish.

The small-mouth black bass reaches a maximum length of a little more than two feet and a weight of about 10 pounds, though one weighing four pounds is a good prize.

The expert angler thinks he can distinguish the species of bass he has hooked before seeing it, since the small-mouth bass is by far the gamier and more active. Its reputation as a game fish is not surpassed by any other of its size. Both large and small-mouth species readily take spinners, plugs, live minnows, and worms, offered by casting, trolling, or still fishing, and both will leap several feet out of the water.

Small-mouth bass build nests from April to June, when the temperature becomes suitable at 59° to 65° F., on beds of gravel rubble, bedrock or coarse sand, usually in 3 to 6 feet of water. The male constructs the nest by cleaning the debris from the bottom with his fins and mouth. He then guards it after the eggs are hatched.

Painting by Walter A. Weber, National Geographic Staff Artist

Of All Fish, Beautiful Eastern Brook Trout Is Most Sought by Fly Casters

ORIGINALLY endemic in cold streams from Labrador to the Saskatchewan and southwesterly along the Alleghenies to Georgia, the **eastern brook trout** (*Salvelinus fontinalis*) has been introduced into nearly all suitable streams and lakes. Through deforestation and pollution, it has disappeared in most lowland streams and been replaced by rainbow and brown trouts. It once reached the rare weight of 10 pounds, but today a one-pound trout is large.

Angling in the United States

By Luis Marden

NEVER in the history of angling has so much fishing been available to so many.

Approximately twenty-two million Americans, one-seventh of the total population, went fishing in 1951. Some, using cane poles, caught catfish on worm-baited hooks; others fished for wary mountain trout, casting tiny dry flies with delicate four-ounce rods of split bamboo. Between these extremes all kinds, grades, and degrees of anglers follow the Nation's favorite pastime.

Familiar to every farm boy and to many city boys of the Mid-West is the ubiquitous and abundant bluegill (page 125). The first catch of thousands of young fishermen was this game little fish of the sunfish family, often generally referred to simply as "panfish."

What makes this recreation so popular? One reason is that no other continent has so great a variety of game fish as North America. Some 220 sport species swim in every imaginable type of water: cold mountain torrents and slow lowland streams; deep blue lakes and brown-water trout bogs; roaring salmon rivers, broad bays and thousands of miles of ocean shore line.

Millions find in fishing refreshment and escape from the pressures and hurry of everyday life. For the true fisherman, there is no competition on the water; he fishes for himself alone, his only opponent the fish.

As "that undervaluer of money," Sir Henry Wotton, said, fishing is to the angler " a rest to his mind, a cheerer of spirits, a diverter of sadness, a calmer of unquiet thoughts, a moderator of passions, and a procurer of contentedness."

Fishing Is Everyman's Sport

And what fisherman does not love the delightful gadgetry of angling? There are so many wonderful things to play with! So many, that today tackle making is really big business. Anglers spend the astounding total of some $90,000,000 a year for a bewildering array of practical equipment and gadgets, from glass fishing rods to big-game reels, and from floating hollow nylon lines to instruments for predicting fish feeding time by barometric pressure. Not all the bright-colored flies and lures seen in the shops catch fish, but all of them seem to catch fishermen.

Another reason for angling's universal appeal is that the diversion may be followed by almost anyone, almost anywhere. The fisherman may outfit himself with a hazel switch, a length of twine, and a few hooks, or he may use a $100 fly rod or a $500 deep-sea reel. And lighter and simpler tackle attracts an increasing number of women to the sport.

Consider two typical American anglers:

The fisherman leans back against the oak tree and stretches his legs contentedly. In the meadow behind him bees drone through the summer heat. From the crook of his arm the long native cane pole slants out over the muddy river, the red and white cork float under its tip motionless as if embedded in opaque glass.

Idly the fisherman wonders if the impaled pink worm, hanging invisible beneath the surface, is still wriggling attractively, when the float disappears and the pole dips sharply. Seizing the pole in both hands, the fisherman holds the straining cane far out over the water as the tip bends and the line cuts through the water. His line, only as long as the pole, is tied to the bamboo's tip, and the pole curves in a deep parabola as he points the butt at the water and walks back up the sloping bank.

Suddenly the red waters part as a struggling yellow fish flops against the bank. Dropping the pole, the angler hand-lines the fish in swiftly and drags up on the grass a glistening 5-pound mud cat.

Holding the catfish carefully to avoid the sharp spines in its fins, he removes the hook from the gaping bewhiskered mouth, then strings a line through the gills. Wiping his hands on his blue jeans, the fisherman gathers up pole and fish and starts back across the meadow. Already he can almost hear the frying pan sizzle and taste the catfish's succulent white flesh.

Five hundred miles away and 2,000 feet higher, another angler fishes a mountain stream. Beneath alders and hemlocks the rushing torrent tumbles over boulders and gravel beds. He stands waist-deep where the green water rushes at a rock wall, shatters in a burst of spray, then rebounds in turning patterns of white-flecked whorls and eddies.

W. T. Davidson

Leaping for a Fly, a Brook Trout Takes Its Own Picture

Fourteen inches of mottled fury is disporting himself in the Corry, Pennsylvania, State fish hatchery, to show what he and his progeny can do when they are released into the State's hundreds of fine trout streams. The photographer, W. T. Davidson, perfected an ingenious system by which interruption of an electric-eye beam sets off stroboscopic light synchronized with the camera shutter. In striking for the barbless lure the trout cut the beam and caught himself on film!

 From John Alden Knight

With a Sweep of the Arm and a Flick of the Wrist the Expert Lures the Gamesters

John Alden Knight—master angler, naturalist, and writer—produces a perfect roll cast. Like many a prideful fisherman, he lands his fly on almost any dime-size spot he chooses, where it will hover and dance in tantalizing May-fly style.

He ties a small gray-brown dry fly to his hair-fine leader as the icy stream presses and tugs at waders that reach nearly to his armpits. From a snap at his back hangs a landing net, and his slender 8-foot split-bamboo rod rests in the bend of his arm as he dips the fly in a vial of waterproofing solution.

Six Countries Equip One Angler

Five countries besides his own had contributed to this angler's equipment: rod bamboo from China; cork for the rod grip from Portugal; the leader's silkworm gut from Spain; the line guide's agate from Madagascar; and favorite hooks from England.

The reel buzzes intermittently as the fisherman makes some false casts methodically, lengthening line in the air without permitting it to touch the water. When about forty feet of the heavy oiled line are out, he puts a bit more wrist power into the forward cast, then stops the rod sharply just above the horizontal. The line rolls out, the 9-foot leader turns over and straightens, and the little fly hesitates, then drops softly into the eddy behind a boulder black and shining with spray.

A dry-fly fisherman sees with his mind and instinct as well as with his eyes. It seems to the angler that he can distinguish each quivering fiber of the small fly's feather ruff as it floats, wings cocked in an insouciant V, round the eddy. At last he sees the expected dimple, raises his rod tip sharply, and is fast to a good trout.

The nervous rod bends, and the line rips through the water as the fish shoots round the pool, flashing red and orange as it turns. Between runs, the trout shakes its head and bores for the bottom. Stripping in line slowly, the angler brings the fish close to the surface; then, holding the rod high in his right hand, he guides the subdued fish over the lip of the submerged landing net. Reaching into the net, he grasps the fish's lower jaw between thumb and forefinger, carefully unhooks the bedraggled fly from the corner of the trout's mouth, and holds up the fish so the sunlight gleams on the red-spotted sides, orange fins, and moss-agate back of one of the most beautiful fishes that swim.

Tapping the 11-inch brook trout on the head with his knife handle, he slides it into the oilskin-lined pocket of his fishing jacket.

Walter M. Lauffer, Ohio Natural Resources

↑ There Are Many Ways to Catch a Fish, or a Nap

They may not be biting on Ohio's Big Walnut River near Sunbury, but the fisherman above is enjoying the kind of day many wives suspect of angler husbands. Still fishing, such as this, does not necessarily require the skill of fly or bait casting.

← "It Was That Long!"

Too bad it got away. The biggest nearly always do!

William H. Lattimer, courtesy South Bend Bait Company

↓ No Alibi Is Needed Here

Wes Hamlet displays his world-record, 37-pound Rainbow trout, caught in Lake Pend Oreille, Idaho.

104 J. M. Rottier

 Washington Star

Anglers Swarm along the Potomac River Gorges when the Shad and Herring Annually Run

Early spring is the season when hickory shad and herring move up the river to spawn. Rocks and rapids a few miles northwest of the Capitol building give Washington fishermen their chance with spoons and snag hooks.

John Craighead

He Caught the Fish but Used Neither Hook nor Net

Frank Craighead demonstrates the art of "guddling" or taking fish without tackle. The guddler cautiously gropes under a log or rock until he feels his quarry. Then he eases his hand forward and clasps the victim near the gills to pull him out of the water. The fish is a fresh-water sucker, a bottom feeder.

The angler wades ashore, rests his rod against a low hemlock branch, and fills his pipe. The climbing sun's heat brings forth the resinous scent of evergreens and the fragrance of mountain laurel. Looking up at the sky, the fisherman releases a puff of blue smoke from between his teeth. It is the beginning of a good day. He is happy.

Nature Pays Dividends to Angler

Fishing takes one to the best places at the best time of year. The angler sees the first yellow-green spring flush of the waterside willows, uncovers the first violets, and watches the evening dance of May flies. He casts his lure to the edge of the lily pad's green disks where white blossoms unfold to the summer morning. He matches his fly to the burning colors of autumn. And even in winter the ice fisherman skating over the frozen lake may glimpse the tracery of bare black branches etched against the yellow sky.

The first settlers of this country found little time for sport fishing. They fished for the pot, and netted and speared fish by day and by torchlight as they shot the deer and turkey that abounded in the heavy forests.

Fish, like game, seemed inexhaustible. A hundred kinds swam in the rivers and lakes and along the coast. Every spring the river filled with hordes of migrating fishes swimming in from the sea to spawn—Atlantic sturgeon, herrings, shad, and salmon. Practically every Northeast coast river held its stock of salmon. The Connecticut received an enormous annual run, and even the Hudson knew the leaping silver fish.

When with increasing population came dams and water pollution, the sensitive salmon were the first to go, but the hardier shad have, incredibly, persisted to this day in the Hudson, and each spring a remnant of the once-great hordes returns to swim past the skyscrapers of New York to cleaner spawning grounds upstream (page 43).

In those days, every stream and rill on the

William Belknap, Jr.

Although the Lake Is Artificial, the Fish and Grins Are Real

These proud fishermen display a catch of whopping largemouth black bass taken in Lake Mead, which was formed by the Colorado River when it backed up behind Hoover Dam—highest in the world—on the Arizona-Nevada line.

Northeast coast contained that most American of fish, the brook trout. Let quibblers say he is not a trout but a char (a little matter of the mouth's bone structure), but the countless anglers who have seen him flash in the clear waters of a pool know him as a trout.

Early Americans Used Horsehair Lines

By the middle of the 18th century, rod fishing for trout was fairly widely practiced. Tackle came from England or was built here on the old models. Rods were formidable weapons of solid wood, from 15 to 18 feet long, usually fashioned of ash, hickory, or lancewood, in three or four sections. The butt, shaped like a billiard cue, was sometimes hollowed out for storage of the other sections.

Though the reel had been mentioned in English angling literature as early as 1651, most American fishers used no running line, but fixed their twisted horsehair line directly to the rod's tip.

Not until about 1830 did Americans do much fishing with the fly. Then they used a brass winch to hold the braided horsehair line that tapered to one or two hairs carrying a "leash" of three flies. The flies followed the classic patterns used in England for centuries. The first book in English on angling, dated 1496, listed 12 flies; 10 of these patterns are still in use today.

In 1845 the first useful American fishing manual was published; from then on, books on fishing appeared in the United States with increasing frequency.

Angling is easily the most literary of the sports. A collection at Harvard contains more than 10,000 titles. By far the largest number of fishing books were written in English, beginning with the above-mentioned *Treatyse of Fysshynge Wyth an Angle,* printed in 1496 at Westminster by Caxton's successor, Wynkyn de Worde.

Ever since, angling and fine bookmaking have gone together, and some of the volumes on fishing are among the finest examples of the

108

A Skillful Angler, Mrs. Kenneth E. Aikins, Keeps Her Line Taut as a Game Bass Fights for Its Life at Bellwood Lakes, Nebraska

How to Cast a Plug—Something New in High School Instruction

The Bait Casting Club of Woodrow Wilson High School, Washington, D. C., lines up in the school gymnasium for a lesson in the fine art of planting a lure under the nose of a desirable fish. In many families, the younger members inherit their devotion to the sport.

109

Carl Mansfield, courtesy South Bend Bait Company

Shades of Huck Finn—It's Saturday Morning in Spring

No school today. Barefoot young America sets off for the favorite fishing hole, equipped with cans of worms, cut-branch rods, and grocery-cord line.

printer's art. Such books are frequently of a high literary order. The best of them contain essays on the joys of angling, lyric descriptions of the countryside, and voice the reflections of the contemplative angler. It is not for the outmoded fishing instruction that Izaak Walton's *Compleat Angler* has gone through some 300 editions since its first appearance in 1653.

Some of the bags of fish taken in those days seem incredible now. An angler counted it a poor day if he took less than 30 or 40 fish, and catches of 100 trout were not uncommon.

As the population grew, the lumberman's ax rang louder in the thick virgin forests of America. The shading and water-retaining trees disappeared, river temperatures rose, and silt from farm land washed into the rivers. Large settlements dumped waste into the rivers, and pollution added its share to depopulate the warming clouded waters of trout.

While fishermen in the northeast part of the new country fished for trout, pickerel, perch, and salmon, southern anglers caught bluegills, crappie, catfish, and another kind of "trout," as some southerners called the black bass.

Black Bass Always Intrigued Americans

This American fish first became known to science in 1802, when the French naturalist Lacépède published a description based on drawings and a preserved specimen sent from the vicinity of Charleston, South Carolina.

Unfortunately for scientific accuracy, this first specimen had a mutilated dorsal fin, with some of the spines torn off. From this, Lacépède named the new genus *Micropterus*—"small fin"—though anyone who has ever caught a bass knows it has a large—and prickly!—dorsal.

Originally the black bass inhabited most of the inland waters of the United States east of the Rocky Mountains, with the exception of New England and the seaboard of the Middle Atlantic States. There were two major species, smallmouth and largemouth, with the smallmouth inhabiting clear, rocky-bottomed streams and lakes, and the largemouth favoring shallower, weedier waters.

The earliest bass fishers angled as many still do, with a long pole and live minnows, crayfish, or worms for bait. But the fast rushes and spectacular leaps of the hooked bass suggested tackle with more scope, and in 1810 a Paris, Kentucky watchmaker named George Snyder made the first Kentucky multiplying reel.

This reel had a wide spool that was quadruple multiplying—that is, it revolved four times for each turn of the handle. The angler wound his bait nearly to the rod tip, and on the cast the weight of the bait drew line directly from the fast-spinning reel.

Other watchmakers soon followed Snyder's lead, among them the famous early makers Milam and Meek, and the Kentucky reel was rapidly refined until it became the finest baitcasting reel in the world.

The early multipliers, of polished German silver, with hand-cut gears, ivory handles, and agate or garnet bearings, ran as smoothly as the watches their makers turned out. Occasionally one was fashioned of solid silver. Sometimes, instead of the purring click that warned when a fish was taking out line, makers fitted little bells that on one reel at least were tuned to musical fifths. Truly a fisherman's harmony.

Such reels were not cheap. They cost $50 or more, even in the days when a dollar was a potent unit of currency; but they lasted for several lifetimes. Many are still in use today.

As trout fishing fell off, bass fishing grew more important, and the bass was introduced into the other parts of the country. The hardy game fish took hold almost wherever planted and multiplied rapidly.

The Potomac River and adjacent water systems in Virginia and Maryland, originally empty of bass, offer a striking example of the bass's adaptability to new waters. In 1853, thirty bass were carried in the water tank of a locomotive from Wheeling, West Virginia, to Cumberland, Maryland, and placed in the old Chesapeake and Ohio Canal that connected with the Potomac. In a relatively few years' time, this small planting had increased so prodigiously that the Potomac, Shenandoah, and neighboring streams afforded some of the best smallmouth bass fishing to be had in the country.

Before 1870 anglers fished for black bass with rods 12 to 16 feet long. In the seventies James Alexander Henshall began to publish articles on the black bass, about which he made the famous statement, "Inch for inch and pound for pound, the gamest fish that swims." Dr. Henshall advocated a "short" single-handed rod of 8 feet 3 inches, for use with the Kentucky reel.

Gunsmith Revolutionizes Rodmaking

This rod, like most others, whether for bait or fly, was made of solid wood, although a revolutionary method of rod building had already appeared in the United States. In 1845, Samuel Philippe, a gunsmith of Easton, Pennsylvania, made a fishing rod of bamboo split into strips, planed to shape, and glued up into a solid unit. The split-bamboo construction seems to have been first employed in England, but Philippe was the first to make, independently, such a rod in America.

Philippe's first rods were made up of three strips, but they would not cast true; so he changed to four-strip construction, making a rod square in cross section. At least one American maker still uses that construction today.

Stradivarius of the Fishing Rod

The most common modern construction, six strips in hexagonal cross section, was brought to perfection about 1870 by Hiram Leonard of Bangor, Maine. The name of Leonard on a rod is like that of Stradivarius on a violin. Thomas and Payne, who worked in Leonard's early shop, later set up on their own and became equally famous. These form the great triumvirate of American pioneer rodmakers, though others equally skilled have followed in the tradition that has made American split-bamboo rods the world's best.

Builders who made

Fine Tackle Makes Fine Fishing. Skilled Craftsmen Display Their Art

Halved bamboo canes (left) destined to make hexagonal split-bamboo fly rods, must be "mismatched" before they are split into segments that will be glued together to form the rod. "Mismatching" staggers the bamboo nodes so that no potentially weak spots adjoin in the finished product.

A dry fly treated with silicone (upper right) sits high on the surface of the water. Silicone fly dressing provides permanent waterproofing and thus eliminates repeated oiling of flies.

One of the final stages of rodmaking is rod-winding—careful attachment of line guides, wrapped with fine thread. 112

National Geographic Photographer B. Anthony Stewart

Camp Otter, New Hampshire, Produced This Prized Catch

"Long Tom" Currier, well-known sportsman and guide, shows a group of admiring friends a prime land-locked salmon, big enough to be mounted with pride. It was taken in the First Connecticut Lake, the headwaters of the Connecticut River. Other trophies of the region adorn the walls.

hexagonal split-bamboo rods took a whole culm, or cane, of bamboo, split it into halves, quarters, and eighths, cut out the partitions that wall off the hollow tubes at the joints, filed off the outer nodes, then with a hand plane shaped narrow tapering strips into equilateral triangles in cross section. Glued together, the strips made one tough, springy, 6-sided stick. Few modern rodmakers still plane the strips by hand. Milling machines now turn out strips to micrometric tolerances, though in other steps of the process the best rods are still largely the product of hand work.

Most American fishing was still done with live bait or artificial flies, but in 1834 there had appeared an entirely new lure that soon accounted for phenomenal catches. The story goes that a Julio Buel, while eating his lunch on the shores of a Vermont lake, dropped his spoon into the water. As it sank, turning from side to side and catching the light, a large fish struck at the flashing spoon.

Buel saw the light, too, and on his return home soldered a fishhook to the polished bowl of a tablespoon. So was the "spoon bait" born, a lure that has become standard for salt-water trolling and for fishing in general around the world.

For the most part, Americans went on fishing with live bait and the fly, using a surprisingly full assortment of tackle for so new a country. The *American Angler's Guide* of 1857 could call attention to the fact that Americans were beginning to gain considerable experience in the manufacturing of all articles of tackle. Many craftsmen acquired a skill in their design and construction that started a tradition.

An exception was the making of hooks. These were then, as now, to a great extent imported from England. The *Treatyse* of 1496 gives directions for making hooks from sewing needles, by heating and bending, slicing barbs in the points, and retempering by quenching in water, but even before Walton's time hooks could be had ready-made.

Don Horter from Northern Consolidated Airlines

In Alaska Anglers Sometimes Fly Hundreds of Miles to the Best Fishing Waters

The airplane is the common means of transportation, and is widely used by anglers. Here two noted devotees, C. W. Davis, an executive of the tackle-making Shakespeare Company, and Frank Dufresne, of *Field & Stream,* tie into a couple of big ones before the engine of their plane has cooled.

English fishhook manufacture grew directly from the needlemaking industry, and through hundreds of years of experience the English hook makers learned many tricks and short cuts that enabled them to make fine hooks very cheaply.

For centuries England, and more lately, Norway, have nearly monopolized the fishhook industry of the world between them, England specializing in sport-fishing hooks and Norway making hooks mainly for commercial fishing.

As for the artificial baits mentioned in the *Angler's Guide,* English anglers used artificial minnows of oiled and painted silk, as well as a metal minnow fitted with fins that caused it to spin around the wire trace on which it was threaded. Fishing with this "Devon" minnow is called spinning, as opposed to fly fishing, and is done with a long two-handed rod and a free-running reel.

In the United States another accident, similar to that attending the birth of the spoon lure, brought an entirely new type of artificial bait into being. One day in the summer of 1898, James Heddon sat on the banks of clear, slow-flowing Dowagiac Creek in Michigan. He had been whittling a piece of wood, and now he tossed it into the water and watched it float away. Suddenly the water erupted with a great splash, and the stick disappeared, to bob up again in the agitated water. A big bass had struck the piece of wood, then spat it out.

Profiting by this experience, Jim Heddon whittled torpedo-shaped cedar baits by hand, thrust a metal bottle cap over the head, and attached hooks. He fished the baits by casting them out and retrieving in jerks; the bottle-cap collar caused the bait to dart and wobble. He caught bass, big ones, and many of them.

Then Heddon set up in business, turning out the world's first top-water wooden minnows, and later making diving and sinking models. Today, most "plugs" are made of tough molded plastic. Since then, American lures have been mainly wobblers; the British still prefer revolving baits.

To cast these plugs, rods grew shorter, and eventually the single-handed 5- or 6-foot bait casting rod as we know it today was evolved.

Only one more thing was needed to make the complete bait-casting outfit, and William Shakespeare, Jr., also of Michigan, brought that out in 1897—a level-wind device for the bait-casting reel. This consisted of a metal line guide that moved from side to side and spooled the line in even coils as the bait was wound in. Plug casting with this Midwestern short rod, level-wind reel, and silk line became the accepted method of fishing for bass.

Two Hundred Bass in One Afternoon

Like the earlier trout fishers of the East, bass anglers of the early days took fantastic bags of fish. One writer records a catch of 214 to one rod in an afternoon. Happy days!

Fly fishermen angled for bass with floating cork and feather "bugs." They also found that bass would take a bright fly, and a whole family of gaudy new flies was developed. The unsophisticated brook trout of the northern wilderness had always taken a bright fancy fly readily, as well as imitations of natural insects.

By the eighties and nineties, the series of brilliant fancy flies for trout and bass had grown out of all proportion to reason or fish-getting qualities. Some people invented these lures, as they should more properly be called, to indulge their artistic whims, and named the new pattern for a friend or favorite fishing place.

A scarce book, published in 1892, *Favorite Flies and Their Histories,* by Mary Orvis Marbury, contains exquisitely colored lithographs of most of the flies then in common use. Even at that time it is significant that the correspondents who sent in their lists of favorites from all round the country generally chose the soberer, more natural-appearing flies as the most taking.

Today there are about 500 "standard" patterns tied in the United States, but any practical fisherman will usually use half a dozen patterns at the most in his home area.

Peculiarly American flies that appeared somewhat later were the bucktails and streamers. Tied to imitate a minnow rather than an insect, these long tapering flies were tied of feathers or deer hair and were particularly effective for the landlocked salmon in Maine lakes.

Brown Trout Imported from Europe

To replace the brook trout that was disappearing from many American streams, the brown trout was imported from Europe in 1884. The new arrivals throve in water no longer cold enough for the brook trout, but they were finicky feeders and harder to catch. Not for them the gaudy lures of the bass and brook trout; when rising to the fly, they would take only good imitations of natural insects.

As Americans moved west, the early fishing conditions and methods of the East were largely repeated. Pioneers, busy clearing land and making a living in the wilderness, fished for food and not for pleasure, until they too had secured the immediate future and could begin to angle for sport.

The Midwest abounded with black bass; its relatives the sunfish, crappie, and bluegill; rock bass; walleyes; the pike, similar to its European cousin; and the great solitary pike, the muskellunge.

The deforestation cycle repeated itself: the hardwood forests of Maine and the northeastern United States had long since been cut over, and now the men with calked boots and stagged-off trousers moved west, to fell the heavy woods of central Michigan. In the clear cold streams of this region dwelt the Michigan grayling, a salmonid fish with a huge dorsal fin. But he did not last long; sawdust coating the gravel spawning beds and voracious introduced trout soon decimated the ranks of this dainty fish, until today it is believed extinct.

When settlers reached the Rocky Mountains, they found a whole series of new trouts —rainbows, cutthroats, and later the goldens— hard fighters and leapers, too, some of them. On the northwest Pacific coast rivers were alive with five varieties of salmon. Unfortunately, though some salmon came to the spoon or spinner in salt or brackish water, most would not take a fly.

A Briton, investigating what is now British Columbia, advised his government to leave the region to the Americans, as "the salmon will not rise to the fly."

Fishing Platforms for Striped Bass

Meanwhile, the principal game fish angled for in the Atlantic remained the striped bass. Fishing stands, platforms with iron railings, were set up on rocks and headlands along the coast, and anglers cast into the boiling waters for the sporting striped fish, which often ran to more than 40 pounds.

In 1865 a sporting club was founded on Cuttyhunk Island off the Massachusetts coast. This tiny island had been the site of the first white settlement on the New England coast, when Capt. Bartholomew Gosnold landed there in 1602, eighteen years before the Pilgrims set foot on Plymouth Rock. The Cuttyhunk Club built 23 fishing stands around the

117

Brown Trout Was Imported from Europe, Replaces Brook Trout

THE brown trout (*Salmo trutta*) was endemic in Europe, but has been widely introduced into various streams and lakes of North America, where it is locally abundant in some cool lakes and in many trout streams. This trout does not belong to the rainbow or the cutthroat series of trouts (page 127). Instead, it may be recognized by its brownish color dorsally, dark brownish spots and few scattered red spots along its sides. The brook trouts (page 100) have red spots also, but differ in having very tiny scales, more than 200 in the lateral line, whereas *Salmo trutta* has about 115 to 150 scales in the lateral line.

Brown trout have been introduced into many brook trout streams, accidentally and on purpose. This has caused many anglers to regard the brown trout as a predator and as undesirable. However, as civilization advanced, deforestation progressed and erosion silted streams, formerly productive trout streams have been changed ecologically so much that brook trout no longer are able to survive.

Brown trout are about the only trout that can live in these warmer streams. It grows rapidly and is a highly desirable introduction where it no longer competes with native trout. Although it is an important game fish, it is not so delicately flavored as the eastern brook trout.

This trout is similar to all others in regard to its feeding. It is predaceous, living on aquatic and terrestrial insects, crawfish, and worms; when it reaches over a pound or two in weight, its food consists mostly of small fishes.

The brown trout commonly reaches a weight of 5 to 10 pounds, a much larger size than the brook trout. The maximum size is probably a little over 20 pounds.

Trout as a group have been caught by sportsmen since America was first settled, and, almost from the beginning, methods have been used to maintain or build up the supply of game fish.

During the past two decades, it was realized by those interested in angling that our fishing ills could not be solved merely by planting millions of eggs or fry in a stream.

Consequently, there has grown up in this country much enthusiasm in what is called lake and stream improvement. This movement is directed at fish-habitat improvements such as reforestation and the installation of shelters, dams, and current deflectors.

More study has been given, also, to the environmental factors most important for the production of fish: suitable water supply and adequate spawning conditions for desirable species; sufficient and proper food; suitable resting places and shelter.

Kodachromes by W. A. Stickler

Black Bass and Muskellunge Are Favorite Game Fish of the Midwest

Hundreds of Midwesterners spend their vacations fishing the copious lakes and streams of their regions and take some fine catches. At left below are eight strapping black bass (page 99) caught in northern Minnesota. At right is a nearly man-size muskellunge (page 96), landed with light tackle on Big Fork River.

118

← Michigan Trout Are Kept Alive in Water Pen Amidships

Michigan has a fishing industry of over $5,000,000 value and protects it carefully. Each year the State plants more than a million legal-size trout and liberates a few giant brood fish at the end of the hatchery season.

Brown and rainbow trout (pages 117 and 127) are dipped into the Au Sable's South Branch here by a Department of Conservation crew. The fish were reared from eggs at one of Michigan's 12 hatcheries and were transferred to the planting boat from a tank truck at a bridge crossing. The battle for fish conservation is being intelligently fought but is not yet wholly won.

↘ An enterprising Michigan tackle dealer uses a giant fly to advertise his shop. Michigan has over 6,000 lakes, which thousands of anglers visit annually.

© National Geographic Society

119

Kodachromes by Andrew H. Brown,
National Geographic Staff

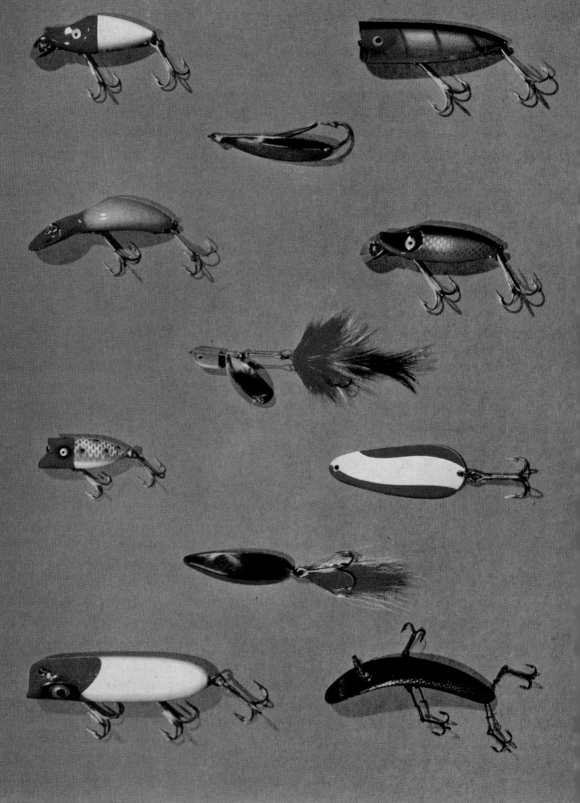

120 Ektachrome by National Geographic Photographer Willard R. Culver

The Origin of the Use of Lures Is Lost in Prehistoric Eras

Before 200 B.C., artificial bait was mentioned by the Greek poet Theocritus, and archeologists have unearthed primitive lures. Since 1848 they have been commercially manufactured in the United States, each with a specific name and use. In the left column, from the top, are the midget digit, tadpolly, threadline lure, and bass oreno. In the middle column are the Johnson spoon, Bunyan fly and spider, and another Johnson spoon. In the right column are the chugger, river runt, dardevle, and flatfish. All these lures are used for fresh-water game fish.

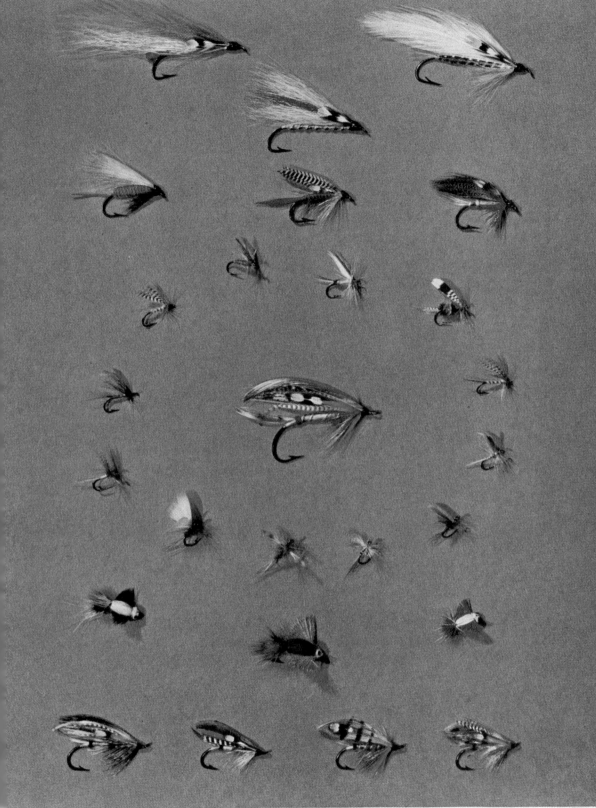

121

Ektachrome by National Geographic Photographer Willard R. Culver

Today the Manufacturing of Flies Is a Skilled, Precision Art

Flies are painstakingly made to simulate the food of fish. The general classifications, "wet" and "dry" (that is, sinking and floating) flies, are subdivided into over 300 patterns. The top three above are streamer flies favored in New England for trout and landlocked salmon. Next are steelhead flies from the Pacific coast. In the top center semicircle are wet trout flies, and in the lower semicircle are dry trout flies. In the second row from the bottom are floating bass bugs. At center and bottom are flies for Atlantic salmon.

122

Sunapee's Golden Trout Is Exclusively a Product of New Hampshire

The **Sunapee golden trout** was scientifically named by Dr. Tarleton Bean in 1888 as *Salvelinus aureolus*. It occurs only in Sunapee Lake, New Hampshire. This beautiful trout is one of the chars, to which belong our brook trout and the Dolly Varden. Some specimens are said to reach 15 or 20 pounds.

A biology class at Colby Junior College (above) is learning to identify the trout by counting fin rays and scale rows. The trout is named for the autumn color of the male, which at other times matches the female's silver-gray. The Sunapee region residents call the fish "white trout."

123

Kinship with the Water and Fishing Characterized American Children for Generations

Long before Mark Twain's Tom Sawyer and Huckleberry Finn, and ever since, the children of the United States have grown up to know the fun and adventure to be found on its beaches, lakes, and streams. The Michigan boys above have abandoned the fishing rod temporarily to experiment with a minnow net. The boys below, with their home-built but seaworthy craft, could belong to any generation. Long, slow summer days have taught boys the pleasures and contentment of fishing that they will probably spend much of their adult lives in an attempt to recapture.

124 Paintings by Walter A. Weber, National Geographic Staff Artist

The Sturdy Carp (Second from Top) Is a Nuisance to Other Fish Life

A CLOSE relative of the American shad and the sea herrings, the **hickory shad** (top, right—*Pomolobus mediocris*) ranges from Maine to Florida and averages two to three pounds. Though not a game fish, the 1,219,000-pound annual catch is commercially important.

Originally endemic in Asia, the **carp** (top, left —*Cyprinus carpio*) has been introduced widely into North America and now occurs from coast to coast and in parts of southern Canada.

Seeking aquatic insects on plants in streams, ponds, and lakes, the carp "root up" the bottoms, destroying vegetation. When abundant, they so muddy the water that it becomes unsuitable for many native fishes. Because of this, the carp has a bad reputation among sportsmen. Carp themselves are very hardy and can live in drying-up ponds after other fish have perished.

Weights of 35 to 40 pounds are frequent, but the average is 10 to 15 pounds. Over 19,000,000 pounds were marketed in a recent year.

Below are two species of catfish (page 66): the **flathead catfish**, or mudcat (top—*Pilodictis olivaris*), and the **northern black bullhead** (bottom pair—*Ameiurus melas melas*).

Because of its large size and excellently flavored flesh, the flathead catfish is important to anglers. It commonly grows to a weight of 40 pounds and has reached 5 feet in length and 100 pounds. European catfish reach 10 feet.

125 Painting by Walter A. Weber, National Geographic Staff Artist

The Populous Sunfish Family Has Many Varieties and Names

SUNFISH are a continuing problem to ichthyologists, because of the often close resemblance of one species to another, their wide introduction, and their interbreeding. Most species are between 3 and 8 inches long.

The **yellowbelly sunfish** (top, left pair—*Lepomis auritis*) occurs from Maine to Florida and in the Gulf drainage to Louisiana. An important game fish, it prefers quiet waters in lakes and in streams.

The **pumpkinseed sunfish** (top, right—*Lepomis gibbosus*) ranges widely in eastern North America and has been introduced into western North America. It is an excellent pan fish, though too small for commercial importance.

The **red sunfish** (left, center—*Lepomis miniatus*) occurs in the southern Mississippi Valley from Illinois and Ohio to Louisiana, northern Florida and Texas.

The **bluegill sunfish** (right, center—*Lepomis macrochirus*) ranges widely on the Atlantic coast south of New York and in the Mississippi Valley from southern Canada to the Gulf. It is largest of fresh water sunfishes.

The **warmouth sunfish** (bottom pair—*Chaenobryttus coronarius*) ranges from the Great Lakes to the Gulf coast and in Atlantic coast streams from Pennsylvania to Florida. It reaches a length of eight inches and occasionally grows to greater lengths.

126

Lake Herring, Close Relative of the White Fishes, Is Popular Smoked Fish

NO ONE but an experienced ichthyologist could recognize the numerous races of lake herring, or shallow water cisco (top, above—*Leucichthys artedi*). It occurs in the Great Lakes basin, upper Mississippi Basin in Wisconsin and Minnesota, and is reported from the Hudson River drainage and St. Lawrence River. This species has been broken up into 22 subspecies or races, each of which is restricted to certain lakes within the range of the species.

All of the lake herring are cold-water fishes and do not do well in warm-water lakes. They do not respond well to sport-fishing methods and are not first-class game fishes. Important commercially, their abundance has declined during the past two decades. The most recently recorded catch was 22,068,000 pounds. Ciscoes reach a length of a foot and a weight of eight pounds and are excellent when smoked.

The **mooneye** (bottom, above—*Hiodon tergisus*) ranges in the western and southern tributaries of the Hudson Bay drainage to the St. Lawrence River, southward to western Maryland, northern Alabama, southern Arkansas, westward to eastern Kansas, northward to Manitoba and Saskatchewan. Food of the mooneye consists of small crustaceans, minnows, and insects. It is of little value as a game or food fish but does serve as a forage fish. It is most numerous in large lakes and streams and reaches a length of over a foot and a weight of a little over two pounds.

Opposite are four famous trout. At the top is the **cutthroat trout** (*Salmo clarkii*), a choice game fish of western Canada and northwestern United States. The coastal cutthroat trout (*Salmo clarkii clarkii*) occurs in the coastal lakes and streams from Alaska to California, whereas its close relative, the Yellowstone or Montana black-spotted trout (*Salmo clarkii lewisi*) is found in the Columbia River Basin in Idaho and the northern Rocky Mountain States. Some which have migrated to salt water and grown to large size are called "steelhead cutthroats."

In clear, cold mountain streams this trout is abundant. Cutthroats rise to the fly during the warmer seasons or will take a small spinner. In spring a fly cast over a deep pool, near an overhanging bank or among eddies in rapids, is almost certain to be struck. Averaging from 7 to 12 inches, it does most of its fighting below the surface and puts up a lively battle.

Second from the top is the **eastern brook trout** (page 100). The **golden trout** (third from top—*Salmo agua-bonita*), of California, was named for Agua Bonita Falls (now Volcano Falls) in Volcano Creek (now Golden Trout Creek) under the supposition that the first specimens came from there. Actually, the species was found originally only in the headwaters of the South Fork of the Kern River, south of Mount Whitney, a high mountain area to which it was confined by impassable falls. These beautifully colored mountain trout, which occur in pools and rapids, may be taken in any sort of weather with artificial flies or on hooks baited with insects. The golden trout reaches a length of nearly a foot, but the usual length is about eight inches.

The **rainbow trout** (bottom—*Salmo gairdneri*), of the Atlantic and Great Lakes drainage systems, was transplanted first from streams in northern California and later from Oregon and Washington. In the Great Lakes region they are the most migratory of the trout.

The rainbow, or steelhead, is one of the most sought-after trout in North America. Wet and dry flies, along with spinners, are popular artificial lures. The usual size of rainbows in many of the western streams is about 8 to 12 inches.

WALTER A. WEBER

127   Painting by Walter A. Weber, National Geographic Staff Artist

WALTER A. WEBER

128

Painting by Walter A. Weber, National Geographic Staff Artist

129

The Grass Pickerel Is a Predatory Nuisance

MUD, or **grass, pickerel** (above—*Esox vermiculatus*) ranges from the southern half of the Lower Peninsula of Michigan, southern Ontario, southern Wisconsin, southward from upper Mississippi Valley from Nebraska to Pennsylvania to the Gulf coast from Texas to Alabama. Throughout its range the grass pickerel is rare or absent in the foothills and mountainous area.

This species lives in lakes and in the still waters of streams. It prefers the shallow margins, living in the weedy waters over muddy bottoms. It is a small species, often mistaken for the young of the larger species, and has all the predaceous habits of its larger relatives, feeding mostly on fishes.

As a sport or game fish, the grass pickerel is not important because of its small size, seldom reaching a length of a foot. Through errors in identification, it has been introduced into certain streams of the Pacific drainage where it does much damage, but is not caught as a game fish.

A close relative of the grass pickerel is the much larger **pike, northern pike,** or **pickerel** (top, opposite—*Esox lucius*), ranging from Alaska to Labrador, southward to New England and westward throughout the Great Lakes drainage system, the Ohio Valley to Missouri and eastern Nebraska. It has been introduced into certain lakes of northwestern United States.

This species prefers sluggish streams, weedy waters of lakes, and deep rocky lakes. It dwells in open water, along the shores of lakes and by the banks of streams. It is a predaceous fish, feeding largely on other fishes but occasionally on frogs, small ducks, mice, or rats, and even muskrats. The old claim that pike lose their teeth in late summer has been investigated, and there is no truth in the myth.

Northern pike breed in the early spring as soon as the ice melts. They ascend small streams and occupy flooded grassy margins of the streams or may move over such areas of lakes, where they deposit their eggs on the vegetation, to which the eggs adhere. Hatching occurs in about two weeks. The fry feed for a couple of weeks on insects or water fleas and then become piscivorous, feeding on newly hatched suckers and minnows.

The northern pike is of commercial importance, with the annual catch amounting to some 193,000 pounds. As a game fish it is especially important, reaching 54 inches in length and a weight of about 35 pounds. The best lure is a flashy spinner or spoon, and live minnows are also excellent. This species may be speared through the ice by using live bait or artificial lures.

The **yellow perch** (lower left pair, opposite—*Perca flavescens*) was endemic in Lesser Slave Lake of the Mackenzie system, Hudson Bay drainage eastward to Nova Scotia, Great Lakes basin westward to the Dakotas, Kansas southward to northern Missouri, Illinois, Ohio, and western Pennsylvania, and in the Atlantic coastal streams southward to North Carolina. This species has been introduced into numerous lakes of the western United States, but introductions into southern areas have not been successful. It prefers lakes, ponds, and the quieter parts of streams. It is carnivorous, feeding on small fishes, thin-shelled mollusks, insect larvae, crawfishes, worms, freshwater shrimps, amphipods, and isopods.

The yellow perch is one of the favorite game fishes of the northeastern part of the country. Commercially it is very important, a total recent catch amounting to 4,809,000 pounds. It reaches a length of a foot and a weight of about two pounds, but averages less than one pound.

The center pair opposite are small-mouth black bass (page 99).

130 Paintings by Walter A. Weber, National Geographic Staff Artist

Landlocked Salmon (Above) Has Made Maine a Fisherman's Mecca

THE **sebago** (above—*Salmo salar sebago*) is one of the races of the landlocked salmon of the Atlantic drainage region. It was derived from the sea-going Atlantic salmon (page 34) because either it lost its desire to migrate to the sea or some obstruction prevented it.

The sebago salmon was so named because it lived mostly in Sebago Lake, Maine. It is also found in other northern New England and southeastern Canada lakes.

The sebago salmon is important as a game fish, but has disappeared from many streams, as a result of industrialization, erosion, pollution, and dams. The last recorded annual commercial catch was only 1,000 pounds.

Early records indicate that sebago salmon reaches a length of 39 inches and a weight of 35½ pounds. Today a 3- to 5-pound fish is large.

Two representatives of the bass family (below) are also important as game fish. The **white bass** (top—*Lepibema chrysops*) ranges in the Mississippi River system, Great Lakes drainage except Lake Superior, and the St. Lawrence River southward to Texas and Alabama.

The **yellow bass** (bottom—*Morone interrupta*) ranges from southern Minnesota to Indiana southward in the Mississippi drainage to the Gulf States. It has been taken in the Chicago drainage canal and may soon spread to Lake Michigan, although it is a southern fish.

Both white and yellow bass reach an average length of a foot and a weight of three pounds. White bass has some commercial importance, the last recorded annual catch amounting to 811,000 pounds. But both species are important largely as game fishes.

These species belong to the family Serranidae, most of whose members are important marine fish.

131

One Form of the Sleek, Hard-fighting Grayling (Above) Has Disappeared in America

MONTANA grayling (above—*Thymallus montanus*) is a relative of the salmon and trout, occurring in Montana in the Madison and Gallatin Rivers. Another form, the Michigan grayling, became extinct in the 1930's, and the Montana grayling has been introduced into certain Michigan streams to replace it.

The third form, or Arctic grayling, ranges in the Mackenzie River, in Alaska and other streams tributary to the Arctic Ocean.

Once abundant, the grayling has gradually decreased, partly because it is at the extreme southern end of its range and even a little deforestation alters its habitat unfavorably. Reaching 18 inches, the grayling puts up a thrilling fight when caught.

Three varieties of minnow (below) are among the more colorful of fresh-water fishes. The **golden shiner** (top, left—*Notemigonus cryso-*

leucas) ranges from Canada to the Gulf and occurs in weedy lakes, quieter streams, and ponds.

Small golden shiners are important in feeding bass and trout in rearing ponds and as a bait minnow. In certain sections it is a palatable pan fish, reaching nearly a foot in length.

The **northern creek chub**, or **horned dace,** (center and top, right—*Semotilus atromaculatus*) ranges from southern Canada to the Gulf coast. It prefers small, clear creeks and is one of the most abundant minnows. Its large size, 6 to 12 inches, makes it excellent bait.

The 4-inch **eastern redside dace** (bottom—*Clinostomus vandoisulus*) ranges along the Atlantic drainage from the Potomac system southward into the Savannah River.

The brilliant color of this little fish makes it an attractive aquarium specimen. However, it is also used as bait by anglers.

132 Kodachrome by Andrew H. Brown, National Geographic Staff

Trout Fishing in Inland Waters Is Man's Most Contemplative Sport

As the world has become more industrialized, the lure of the trout stream has increased, partly for the sport and partly for the serenity of the surroundings. Here two fishermen visit the Au Sable River in Michigan.

island. Anglers employed a boy to "chum" the waters round the stand by throwing in bits of cut-up lobster.

For this fishing, Capt. Lester Crandall, who had been manufacturing lines at Ashaway, Rhode Island, since 1824, made a hand-laid twisted linen line of small diameter, and soon fame of this light and strong line, ideally suited to salt water, spread far beyond the little island on the Massachusetts coast. Before long "Cuttyhunk" line became the world's standard for deep-sea sport fishing.

In 1879 and 1881, two plantings of striped bass were made in San Francisco Bay, thus introducing this game fish for the first time to Pacific waters. The fish multiplied beyond all expectations and today it is found all along the west coast from the State of Washington to the vicinity of Los Angeles. Round the San Francisco area, it is the pre-eminent surf-casting fish. Along the west coast, too, it is protected as a game fish, but not on the Atlantic coast, its original home, where commercial netters annually take a tremendous toll.

The building of the railways in Florida that finally reached to the lower Keys at the turn of the century opened that fabulous fisherman's wonderland to anglers. In Florida's inland and offshore waters swam more than 600 varieties of fish; this was more than a fifth of the entire fish fauna of North America then known.

Tarpon Fishing Begins in Florida

The great silver herring, the tarpon, first caught on rod and reel in Florida's Indian River Inlet in 1884, became the focus of a new cult of angling, its devotees hotly disputing with salmon and bass enthusiasts the merits of the leaping tarpon as the supreme game fish.

Camps sprang up on both sides of Florida coast. Some were reached from railhead by stagecoach and sailboat. The fame of Florida fishing for tarpon, snook, wahoo, and a dozen other gamesters spread, and anglers even came from England expressly to try this new kind of fishing.

Florida was doubly blessed because the flat peninsula had scores of inland lakes, whose brown-stained cypress waters harbored some of the world's biggest largemouth bass. So hefty are these bronzebacks of Florida and adjacent areas, that the annual fishing contest of *Field & Stream* for some years has maintained a separate bass division for Florida and portions of adjacent States; otherwise, fishermen from these places always took first prize. No one else had a chance of approaching remotely the record fish from these waters.

A major American contribution to the art of sea angling had its beginning in 1896, when the first tuna to be caught on rod and reel was taken off Santa Catalina Island on the California coast. Two years later, Charles Frederick Holder founded the Tuna Club on Catalina, and the rules for tackle lengths and weights set up by this club became the model for subsequent attempts to regulate the new sport of big-game fishing for giant pelagic fishes, such as tuna, swordfish, sailfish, and marlin.

The real flowering of big-game angling came with the invention, shortly before World War I, of the slipping clutch reel. With this type of reel a hooked fish could strip line directly from the slipping reel spool, the reel handle remaining stationary. An adjustable drag was added later so that the angler could put as much brake on the running fish as desired.

When Holder began his tuna fishing in 1898, reel handles spun like a buzz saw when a fish made a run, and the angler had only his thumb to use as a brake, a dangerous business with big fish.

From the fine old club at Catalina the sport of taking big deep-sea fish on rod and reel spread all over the world. The center in our country today is off Florida and in adjacent Bahama waters, where every year thousands of anglers take sailfish, white and blue marlin, wahoo, and other roamers of the open sea.

Many world records have been set in the Gulf Stream waters off the tiny islands of Bimini and Cat Cay, about 55 miles east of Miami.

Floating Flies Introduce New Cult

Just before World War I, the dry fly came to this country from England. From time to time early angling literature said something about fishing a fly on the surface, but the first mention of the dry, or floating, fly, as we know it, was in Pulman's *Angler's Vade Mecum,* published in England in 1851.

In this delicate style of fishing, a floating fly was cast upstream and allowed to float down over the feeding fish like a natural insect. The method received its great impetus when England's F. M. Halford began in 1886 to publish his series of monumental books on the new art.

Halford eventually evolved a whole school of dry-fly angling, with a very full set of flies, meticulously tied to imitate exactly the various species of flies found on the crystalline slow-moving chalk streams of southern England.

These famous Hampshire streams such as the Test and Itchen well up through the chalk subsoil and flow, limpid and gin-clear, through lush water meadows. Thick beds of weeds

134 U. S. National Park Service

Like Musicians, Fishermen Must Practice to Keep Their Skill

There are no fish in the Reflecting Pool at Washington's Lincoln Memorial, but members of the National Capital Casting Club may be seen there every week end, practicing and instructing hopeful young Izaak Waltons. Bait and fly casting tournaments also are held at the pool.

and water plants grow in "islands" in these rivers and form a haven for a rich growth of insects, shrimp, and other trout foods.

In such streams, brown trout grow fat and choosy, feeding only when a definite hatch of insects is on. The slow current permits the trout to inspect the fly in a leisurely manner, and the angler has to be skilled in his presentation of a fly that must be an excellent imitation of the natural ephemerid to deceive these well-fed sophisticated fish.

American conditions were different. Our streams were for the most part fast brawling rivers, dashing down over rocks and boulders at such a pace that the trout had to make up his mind quickly or the morsel of food was snatched away. It was argued that the dry fly would not do for the rough American waters, as they would not float long enough for the trout to look them over.

In 1914, George M. L. La Branche, one of the really great American anglers, wrote an epoch-making book, *The Dry Fly and Fast Water,* which opened the eyes of Americans

to the possibilities of superior sport on their water. The rage was on.

The English fisherman fished only the rise, casting a fly to the individual feeding fish; within the first two or three casts he usually either caught the fish or "put it down," so that it stopped feeding. La Branche taught the American dry-fly fisherman to fish the water, since in the absence of definite heavy hatches of flies there were fewer natural rises.

So the American cast constantly and kept his fly on the water, floating it as La Branche had taught, even though for a few inches or feet only, in every likely lie that might hold a trout. For such fishing the dry fly had to be tied of the stiffest of cock hackles, waterproofed with oil or wax, so that it would remain afloat in broken water.

Fishing vs. "Poaching"

Following the English pattern, there sprang up an American school of purists who fished with nothing but the dry fly (even when conditions were not appropriate) and who looked

National Geographic Photographer John E. Fletcher

These Fishermen Were Honest, So the Truth Serum Was Not Used

Each year the Junior Chamber of Commerce of Detroit Lakes, Minnesota, holds an angling contest, winding up with weighing of catches and presentation of prizes. The "truth serum" is recommended for anglers whose prize-winning fish got away.

upon any other kind of angling as little short of poaching! These enthusiasts surrounded the method with an aura of mystery and difficulty. Actually, dry-fly fishing, once the elements have been mastered, is one of the easiest styles of fly fishing.

In England this fishing snobbery began to die out after G. E. M. Skues brought out his works on nymph fishing (using a sunk imitation of the nymph, or larval stage, of the May fly), and gradually the narrow attitude died down on this side of the Atlantic too. The result is that today, though admittedly the dry fly is the most delicate and sporting way yet devised to take fish, few anglers would deny that there are other methods just as taking and nearly as pleasurable.

Dry-fly fishing brought about a revolution in rod design too. Fly rods grew shorter, stiffer, and "quicker," because of the need to dry the fly by making constant false casts and to drive the fly upstream against a breeze. The need for a faster-actioned rod caused rod builders to modify their tapers and to abandon the old Calcutta cane entirely, using instead the stiffer Tonkin bamboo from China.

Originally, all split-bamboo rods had been built of Calcutta cane, which supposedly came from India or Burma. How and why the new material, first tried about fifty years ago, came to be called "Tonkin" is anyone's guess, as it does not come from Indochina but grows only in a small area on the border of Kwangtung and Kwangsi Provinces in China.

Still another typically American item of tackle appeared increasingly from the nineties onward: the steel fishing rod. Earliest attempts to make rods of this metal consisted of rolling sheet steel into a tube. Later, rods of solid fencing-foil blades were made, and finally appeared the drawn seamless steel tube.

Scientific Progress Benefits Fishermen

Excellent rods are now made of steel, solid and tubular, and are sold in enormous quantities, particularly for bait casting and light salt-water fishing. The material is a bit heavy

William Berkeley Payne, courtesy South Bend Bait Company

A Lady Braves a Boiling Stream to Net a Speckled Beauty

In ever increasing numbers women are taking to stream and ocean and sometimes successfully challenge men in the angler's art. Knee-deep in boisterous Fishing Creek, near Frederick, Maryland, Mrs. Luis Marden smiles in victory as the brook trout tempted by her dry fly is safely landed.

© London Times

↑ Britain Preserves a Shrine to the "Compleat Angler"

Here, on the Dove River, Izaak Walton, a rambler for the last 40 years of his life (1593-1683), frequently visited Charles Cotton, a brother angler. Dovedale, the limestone glen, divides Derbyshire and Staffordshire. It passes for the "Happy Valley" of Dr. Johnson's *Rasselas*. England's National Trust owns or protects several thousand acres hereabouts.

Easy Does It →

Real sportsmen throw back undersize catches. To remove the hook with the least damage, the fish should be grasped gently but firmly and the hook eased from the mouth. The process is demonstrated on a small trout from New Mexico's Red River fish hatchery.

National Geographic Photographer
Justin Locke

and harsh for really satisfactory light fly rods.

With the passage of years, advances in technology placed many new substances and devices in the hands of American anglers. In 1939 the Du Pont Company introduced a new synthetic fiber to the world. At first used to make women's stockings and to replace bristles in toothbrushes, nylon, waterproof and almost impervious to wear, soon found its way into the manufacture of fishing lines and leaders. In the latter field it virtually drove silkworm gut from the market.

In fly fishing it is the heavy line, and not the weightless lure, that is cast. The double taper flyline, with a heavy belly tapering to fine points at each end, had been in use for years. With a double taper a long line is more easily and delicately cast, and the fly lands lightly.

American tournament casters, ever striving for greater distance, conceived the idea of building a thick heavy section of line near the end; in casting, this weight pulled the lighter line after it. Thus was developed the "torpedo head," or "tadpole taper." Multiple taper lines have been refined to the point where seven or more tapers are woven into a single line, following very careful study of their action in casting. With such lines the world's record cast for single-handed rods has increased to undreamed-of distances—183 feet at the present writing.

Shortly before World War II a form of angling new to this continent arrived from Europe. Called threadlining by the British, who originated it a generation ago, and light casting by the French, who are its most ardent and advanced present-day exponents, the method falls somewhere between fly fishing and bait casting. The original threadline rods are usually of split bamboo, seven to 7½ feet long, fitted with a reel that differs from all other fishing reels in that the drum, fixed at right angles to the axis of the rod, does not revolve. Instead, the light nylon monofilament line slips off the open end in loose coils as the lure is cast, much as sewing thread might slip off the end of a spool.

Thus there is no fast revolving spool to overrun and cause backlash, that tight tangle known to all bait casters, which occurs when the angler's thumb allows the spool to run faster than the outgoing line. This equipment became known as "spinning" tackle in the United States.

With such tackle it is possible to cast much lighter lures than with a bait-casting outfit. The usual lure is a small weighted revolving spoon.

Until the advent of threadlining, the fly rod was perhaps the deadliest all-round angling implement ever invented. Yes, though some rough-and-ready fishermen regarded the fly rod as a dilettante's apparatus, not to be relied on when one wanted to *catch fish,* the long rod in the hands of an expert could probably do more execution among all kinds of fish than any other.

But now the threadline rod has moved to first place as the universal fishing tool, for with it one can fish bait, cast spinners, artificial minnows, and even dry flies. Because of the nearly invisible line, it is like fishing with a leader 150 feet long. Threadlining has a place on big waters, for bass, pike, or panfish, and even trout, but its constant use may depopulate small streams.

Fishing-rod makers constantly seek ways to make rods stiffer and stronger without increasing weight. A long time ago someone found out that by heating bamboo it could be stiffened and, incidentally, turned a handsome brown shade, lighter or darker according to the amount of heat treatment.

In 1942 the Orvis Company of Vermont developed a method of impregnating bamboo with Bakelite or other plastic and began to make split-bamboo rods treated in this fashion. Such rods certainly were stronger and stiffer for their diameters than a rod of untreated bamboo.

The Shakespeare Company in 1946 started a rod-making revolution by introducing the glass fishing rod to the world. Incredible as it may seem, this usually fragile but tough substance may turn out to be the ideal material for fishing rods.

Fishing Rods Made of Glass

The Shakespeare rods are built of long fibers of glass around a soft-wood center. These are wrapped in cellophane tape and bonded into a single unit with heat. Such construction approximated closely the structure of "Nature's glass," bamboo, with its hard outer fibers embedded in softer pith. Other makers now build glass rods by rolling a tube of glass fabric round a mandrel, to produce a hollow rod.

Glass has many unquestioned advantages for fishing rods: it is unaffected by moisture; it is exceedingly flexible and tough, being almost impossible to break in normal use; and it never takes a permanent bend or "set." Yet, though most bait-casting rods and threadline spinning rods in this country are now made of glass, fly-rod experts have not yet fully accepted it.

Nearly three fourths of all fishing rods made in the United States today are of glass.

No other angler in the world today is better equipped than the American fisherman. By constant refinement his split-bamboo

National Geographic Photographer Robert F. Sisson

"Suckers Will Do when the Catfish Aren't Biting"

This boy-fish-dog scene could occur along most any running stream in the country. Two bony suckers are
the trophies on the banks of northern Montana's Milk River, tributary to the Missouri.

rods have grown lighter through the years
until today they average about half the weight
of the traditional British rods.

His bait-casting reels, though lacking the
polish and bejeweled hand finish of the early
Kentucky masterpieces, cast far better than
did those early prototypes, thanks mainly to
light aluminum alloy spools that sharply
reduce backlashes.

His salmon rods are single-handed and light,
mainly because he fishes from a boat, rarely
having need to cover large rivers from the
bank, as in Britain.

His lures, such as the South Bend Bait
Company's Bass-Oreno, have become angling
classics.

No other country can approach the quality
and design of his big-game deep-sea tackle.

After this last war, American hook manufac-
turers began to fill a large part of the demand
for hooks, though we still have much to learn
before we can equal the superlative English
and Norwegian products.

American Anglers' Favorite Fishes

With all this equipment, what do most
Americans fish for, and how? By far the most
popular fish, because of their abundance and
savory qualities, are the so-called pan fish—
the bluegill, crappie, sunfish, yellow perch,
rock bass, and calico bass. Sixty to eighty percent of all American anglers, according to the
region, fish for these with cane poles and
live bait.

Next most angled-for fish would probably
be the bass, largemouth first, then smallmouth;

with walleyes, pike, and pickerel following. Then follow the trout and land-locked salmon, with the muskellunge in solitary majesty at the end. In some areas, as many as one fourth of all fishermen may use artificial fly or bait-casting lures of one kind or another for these.

Fly fishing for trout is strongest in the New England States, Pennsylvania, Michigan, the Rocky Mountain States, and in some west-coast areas. Nearly all States have some fly fishing, and Florida is now the center of a new angling fad for taking bonefish, tarpon, channel bass, and other sea fish on the fly.

Bait casting, the most typically American mode of angling, is done everywhere, but the short rod and multiplying reel now flourish best in the Southern and Southwestern States, where warm waters permit fish to feed the year round and growth is correspondingly more rapid. Down there, bass and pan fish grow to legal size in half the time needed in colder northern waters. Bait-casting enthusiasts in Florida even use bass tackle to take huge tarpon up to 100 pounds.

Virgin Fishing Grounds Disappearing

Little virgin water remains within the bounds of the continental United States. The automobile and its attendant network of roads have opened up the last wilderness areas. In few other countries in the world can the fisherman pack up his tackle and drive 200 miles or more to his fishing place and return the same day.

This extreme mobility of the fishing population poses a serious conservation problem. In other, older countries, streams, lakes, and coasts feel fishing pressure only from local inhabitants. The American fisherman has a continent at his disposal, which is wonderful—while it lasts.

In a few favored States and areas, fishing, through scientific management by enlightened State and Federal agencies is even better than it ever was. But such spots are few; on the whole, fishing has declined through deforestation, water pollution, introduction of competing species, and overfishing.

What then is the future of angling in the United States? Fish conservationists are not too pessimistic. Fishing, they say, will have to get worse before it can get better. Only when people actually begin to feel the pinch of poor fishing will they awaken to the need for stronger conservation measures.

There is no simple road to better fishing. The old idea of stocking hatchery-reared fish to be caught by anglers within a few days is a poor and partial answer. And it is too expensive. Today, to place a single fisherman's one-day catch of trout in the stream costs the State more than the license fee paid by the

angler who catches the fish. Because of this, trout fishermen may in future have to pay a higher license fee than other anglers.

Year-round Season Improves Some Fishing

Smaller bag limits and closed seasons do not now, as they once did, seem to be the whole answer. Indeed, in some large southern waters it may be better to permit year-round angling, so as to reduce the number of fish that compete for food and so increase the size and quality of the catch.

Conservationists have discovered that an acre of water, like an acre of land, can produce only a certain amount of animal life. Generally, the figure is about 100 pounds of fish per acre. Hook-and-line fishermen take only about half the "standing crop" in big waters like lakes, while in a small, heavily fished trout stream a substantial number of the larger fish is taken out by anglers each season.

With a rapidly increasing population, the United States is no longer a pioneer nation, where unlimited wild lands abounding in fish and game lie just over the horizon. To provide better fishing for everybody, there must be a combination of stocking, water improvement, closer regulations, and an increase in fishing water.

The use of water reservoirs as fishing places has been, by and large, overlooked in this country of past abundance. But it is significant that some of the largest trout caught each year in the British Isles come from the water supply of the great industrial city of Birmingham. We are coming to realize that many reservoirs, with careful management, can furnish superlative fishing to large numbers.

Hand in hand with these things go the education of the fisherman. Fewer and fewer Americans cling to the primitive belief that a man must bring home a huge string of fish to prove he is a good fisherman.

Everyone goes fishing to catch fish, but most anglers realize that sooner or later the catching becomes less certain unless common sense and intelligent management are combined. American fishermen today are determined that the future shall hold not only good fishing but also better fishing for everybody.

"And if the angler take fish; surely then is there no man merrier than he is in his spirit."

A Shark Walker Revives a Captive →
in Florida's Marine Studios

Grabbing a fin and shoving, the diver restores vitality to an exhausted shark captured at sea and transferred to the oceanarium in Marineland, Florida. Fresh sea water flowing across the gills puts oxygen back into the blood stream (page 156).

Marineland, Florida's Giant Fish Bowl

By Gilbert Grosvenor La Gorce

With Illustrations by Luis Marden, National Geographic Staff

Tiger Shark, Jet Bomber of Marineland's Oceanarium, Scatters Fish and Turtles

Sharks still carry the primitive cartilaginous skeleton used by fishes before Nature apparently perfected hard bones. As relics of a distant age, however, they remain terribly efficient. Few fish or men care to face them. Restless tiger sharks are always on the move. Certain ones are born alive. Razor-sharp teeth of some species move into line as they are needed. One snap of this monster's jaws could crush a sea turtle's shell.

MAN has amused and instructed himself by watching fish in aquariums since ancient times. But not until our own age has it been possible to stand a few inches from the predatory tiger shark, the vicious barracuda, and the malicious moray eel and watch them under conditions that simulate their natural habitat.

Today at Marineland, between St. Augustine and Daytona Beach, Florida, 10,000 fish live in the world's only oceanarium, not separately as in aquariums, but together in two huge tanks. Connected by a flume, the tanks are carefully planned and maintained to approximate conditions of marine life in the open sea. Through 200 portholes along the sides and beneath these giant "fish bowls," the scientists and visitors observe the drama of undersea life.

In the clear, blue-green water, pumped from the ocean at the rate of five million gallons a day, swim silver tarpon, undulating rays, lumbering turtles, and a myriad of school fish from the coral reefs and spawning grounds of the Gulf Stream.

Here, too, are bottle-nose dolphins, or porpoises as they are commonly called. Known and beloved by mariners, these friendly, air-breathing, warm-blooded mammals were first introduced into prolonged captivity here at Marine Studios. We shall meet them personally later on, as we make our tour of this simulated ocean's floor.

Strolling into the Marine Studios, we follow bluelighted corridors that contour the perimeters of the tanks. Through tempered glass ports, we peer into a kaleidoscopic world of sunlight and shadows. Sea fans and shells,

If the Shark Looked Out of His Tank, He'd See These Girls Looking In

Marineland's rectangular tank, which holds many varieties of ocean life, has 97 portholes. Almost every time a chartered bus drives up, scores of boys and girls pile off and rush up to the glass windows. Before their eager eyes swim lordly silver tarpon, dangerous barracuda, tropical reef fish, and many others. High-school biology students earned credit for attending class on this field trip.

graceful waving plumes, and brightly darting tropical fish reflect the filtered rays of a brilliant Florida sun. Cavernous man-made rock grottoes, a 7-ton replica of a coral reef and the barnacle-encrusted remains of a sunken vessel, complete with rusting anchor, provide natural ocean bottom surroundings.

Divers Hand-feed Some Fish

Suddenly, out of the haze beyond the wreck, appears the Martian figure of a deep-sea diver. In the stream of air bubbles cascading from his helmet swims a school of bumper fish. Near by a 400-pound jewfish, sensing the diver's progress, moves backward a few inches beneath the shattered timbers of the ship's hulk that is its domain.

Then into our view glides the shadowy figure of a tiger shark. A 12-foot-long mass of

sinewy muscle circles briefly to survey the scene. Involuntarily the diver steps back, holding his wire feeding basket filled with chopped mullet before him to help ward off a possible attack. We watch, electrified. The tableau holds for seconds before the great monster flips his powerful tail and disappears into the central gloom of the tank, leaving a swirl of bubbles in his wake.

"Several times a day a staff diver must make the rounds of the two tanks, inspecting his charges and feeding many of them by hand," a staff announcer explains.

"Look there!" he urges. "At the base of the rock grotto . . . see him? That's a moray eel."

The thick-bodied, sharp-toothed creature ribbons its way out of one hole and quickly slithers into another, leaving only its voracious

Porpoise, Mammal That She Is, Gives Birth to Fully Developed Young

Four baby porpoises have been born alive at Marineland. This captive, unable to bite the umbilical cord as most warm-blooded animals do, severs it with a quick, jerky whirl. Baby enters the world able to swim, but has to depend on mother for milk and protection.

head protruding. Morays, we learn, can inflict nasty bites. The diver skirts this fellow warily, continuing his rounds.

"Isn't that a cabbage head?" someone in the crowd asks.

← Porthole Spectators Appear as Framed Portraits

Marine Studios' 18-foot-deep rectangular tank swarms with fish. Common jack and a Bermuda chub (tail out of picture) partly mask a sandbar shark (center). Black angelfish (lower right) swim toward the dark, rusted anchor. Below them, a scorpion fish lies motionless on the tank's sandy floor. Yellowtails swim just above the shark. A black margate moves near the surface. Sheepshead are striped (lower left). The girl at the lower right porthole seems to wear a fish as her hat.

The announcer explains that several species of fish are vegetarians. Cabbage and lettuce heads are placed daily in the 100- by 40-foot rectangular tank to supply needed forage for these non-fish eaters.

In this tank the spectrum is reproduced in ever-changing pattern on fish forms, beautiful and grotesque. Our gaze follows the schools of common jacks or crevalles as they pass at varying levels, massed in herd instinct. We try to spot others as the announcer calls them out.

"Those are angelfish . . . here comes a parrotfish, with sheepshead just below it . . . these are triggerfish, with a school of young blues next in line."

Near the water's surface, clouds of beady-eyed shrimp snap backward as they swim in little spurts. Since many fish prize them for their flavor, they have short lives in the tank.

Porpoises Are the Star Performers

Porpoise feeding time at Marineland is a major performance. There are 22 species of porpoises in Atlantic and Pacific waters, the most common in this vicinity being the gray bottlenose dolphin (the inshore porpoise), *Tursiops truncatus*. In the 75-foot-diameter circular tank are also specimens of the deep-sea long-snouted dolphin, or spotted porpoise, *Stenella plagiodon*.

"It takes about two weeks to tame sufficiently a newly captured porpoise," a Studios scientist explains. "It will then begin to accept food from the attendant's hand."

The inshore porpoises are captured in nets strung in channels between points of land, where the animals feed in tidewaters. The new arrival is carefully transported by sling to the flume, its body kept dampened to prevent its skin from cracking and to maintain the proper body temperature while out of its natural element.

"Although frightened at first," our informant continues, "none has ever attempted to bite or otherwise attack the collecting crew."

Offshore specimens are captured with a tailgrab, an ingenious and harmless lariat. Only a few miles at sea, the collecting crew sails one of the powerful sea skiffs on a porpoise hunt. The frolicsome animals appear, sooner or later, surging along at the boat's prow. It is a tricky maneuver for the collector to thrust the mechanical lasso, with its forcepslike jaws, over the small of the porpoise's body just above the tail. A hempen line, threaded through the "iron," automatically forms a double loop. The staff is quickly withdrawn, and the line is snubbed and secured. Then the roped porpoise tows the boat over the ocean. Eventually wearying, it is finally drawn alongside for careful transport to its new home in the oceanarium.

Porpoises Are Exhibitionists

Flippy tows Pat Dale and Duke, the trainer's dog, the first ever to ride a porpoise-powered surfboard. Flippy, only porpoise to perform this trick, wears a harness like a dog's.

Pig-faced Spotted Whip Ray, Flapping on Batlike Wings, Appears to Fly Through Water

Rays often feed on clams and oysters, cracking shells with crushers in their mouths, and expelling the fragments like boys spitting melon seeds. Akin to sharks and sawfish, they have cartilaginous skeletons, and some species carry poisonous barbs on tails, using them with deadly accuracy against enemies. The cabbage "growing" on the Oceanarium's floor was planted for certain vegetarians, among them angelfish (page 235) and triggerfish (pages 229 and 257).

The high level of porpoises' ability to learn has been recorded by scientists at this unique marine biological laboratory. Being air breathers, porpoises replenish their oxygen supply normally at least once every thirty seconds although they can stay under water up to seven minutes. Usually they rise to the surface at such intervals, clear the blowhole on top of the head, and expel the air in their lungs before the next intake. In addition to learning to accept food from the attendant's hand in the water, they learn to leap high into the air to grasp the fish from the outstretched hand.

Porpoises are natural clowns. They love to tease other specimens in the oceanarium. Frequently they nip at the tails of little fish that hide in the rocky crevices. Occasionally they will devour one whole, for porpoises feed only on selective species of fish they can swallow without chewing. Their teeth are capable of inflicting damage, but they reserve these tactics for each other and, on occasion, for annoying some of the sharks.

Deadly Strength and Swift Speed

When aroused, porpoises become tough adversaries, ramming the sides of their finny opponents until death ensues. They are extremely powerful. Often one will shove a loggerhead turtle up and down and around the tank until the 200- or 300-pound creature develops an expression of silent desperation.

Porpoises in the oceanarium have weighed over 450 pounds. Their seemingly effortless speed has been clocked at 35 miles an hour in the open sea.

In this tank the Studios staff has witnessed the successful births of four baby porpoises. As a mammal, the mother nurses her baby for nearly a year before the little one learns to eat fish. But even new babies are able to swim along with the others. The female shields her offspring with her body to protect it from

148

The Author Needed No License to Catch This 31-pound Permit

Esteemed as a game fish, the permit fought an hour before coming to Mr. La Gorce's net. He was hooked between Caesar's and Angelfish Creeks in the Florida Keys. Right: Diver Floyd Adams frames his face in the jaws of a sand-tiger shark that threatened him in a Marineland tank.

possible attack by males or by the bigger sharks that might favor young porpoise steak.

For the past two years, experiments have been conducted at Marine Studios to determine the extent to which one of these animals could be trained. Mr. Adolph Frohn, an experienced animal trainer, undertook the task at the direction of Mr. W. Douglas Burden, President of Marine Studios, who is also a Trustee of the American Museum of Natural History, New York. Mr. Burden and Col. Ilia A. Tolstoy were the co-designers of Marineland, first opened in 1938.

"I'll ask Mr. Frohn to put Flippy through his paces for you," said the vice president and general manager of the Studios, William F. Rolleston. "We are proud of this animal."

"Flippy!" Mr. Frohn called. The young fellow, weighing about 200 pounds, had spotted us as we approached his tank. He thrust his head out of the water and swam to his trainer's outstretched hand. After patting him for a moment, the trainer slipped him a morsel of fish.

"I use the feeding incentive system," he told us. "It works well with all animals."

Command Performance of Flippy

Flippy then went through his repertoire: rolling over and over at the command; surging out of the water to grasp a rope and ring a bell; retrieving a thrown stick; backing up, head out of water, at each successive wave of his trainer's hand; and then expertly catching a thrown rubber ball, which he promptly returned to his master.

One trick was a supreme show of confidence and trust on the part of the animal. Mr. Frohn suspended a canvas sling over the tank, then lowered it beneath the surface. At his command, Flippy swam obediently onto the sling and lay there motionless. Mr. Frohn then hoisted the sling clear of the water. The porpoise remained absolutely still, except for the intermittent opening and closing of the blowhole atop his head. The trainer said that he didn't expose him too long to the sun because porpoise skin sunburns quickly.

Marineland is visited by thousands of people annually. There they can see the marine life of the Gulf Stream in all the color and much of the natural struggle that characterize it in the sea itself.

This Diver Caters to 10,000 Fish →

Marineland divers spend their working hours under water feeding and inspecting their voracious charges. Here a green moray eel hungrily eyes the dead mullet in the diver's gloved hand. Other fishes are a lookdown (upper left), Bermuda chub (upper right), and two angelfish (lower left).

Flippy Spears the Hoop at His Trainer's Command

Adolph Frohn spent two years teaching this friendly bottlenose dolphin, or porpoise, his bag of tricks.

Mr. Frohn applied the accepted technique of first winning his pet's confidence through feeding rewards. Now 4½-year-old Flippy obeys visual commands implicitly. His growing repertoire includes rolling over and over, blowing a horn, and retrieving a tossed stick and placing it in his master's hand. He can leap up and pull a bell cord or yank a lanyard raising a pennant.

The porpoise trustingly allows himself to be hoisted out of water in a canvas sling. Once he playfully leaped aboard a skiff into his trainer's arms.

Flippy was netted south of Daytona Beach in a section of the Intracoastal Waterway, a favorite feeding ground of inshore porpoises, which ride the flooding and ebbing tides to prey on school fish.

Some people rate the porpoise's ability to learn as close to that of the chimpanzee, which scientists consider the smartest mammal next to man.

Kodachrome by Luis Marden, National Geographic Staff

150

A Porpoise Leaps for Fish as a Trout Rises to a Fly

Porpoises at sea have been clocked at 35 miles an hour. Powerful flukes at the end of the tail give them speed. Unlike the vertical tails of fish, the porpoise's propellent blades are horizontal like those of its cousin, the whale.

Largest captives exceed 450 pounds. One of them can kill a shark by ramming its sides and damaging vital organs.

Porpoises, which lack external ears, can readily detect water-borne sounds; and so, when the dinner gong rings, they herd below the pulpit, look up, and, gathering momentum in water, erupt into the air, each one politely taking his turn at snatching a morsel.

Ten-foot leaps highlight the six shows a day. The mammals seem to walk on water as thrashing tails propel them up to the feeder's hand. Attendant Mitch Lightsey has permitted them to grasp fish held in his mouth. Not a feeder has been bitten. Friendly by nature, the porpoises gauge their jumps so as to hurt no one. But visitors standing in too close sometimes receive showers of sparkling sea water.

152

Porpoises Crowd the Pitcher's Box in a Ball Game Played with Mullet

Kodachrome by Luis Marden, National Geographic Staff

Fielders Show Flashing Speed Retrieving Fish Tossed to the Outfield

Kodachromes by Luis Marden, National Geographic Staff

Young Dolphin Catches the Ring
and Hurls It Back

Playful *Tursiops truncatus*, the gray dolphin or inshore porpoise is warm-blooded, just like man, his fellow mammal. An air breather, he surfaces approximately every 30 seconds to inhale, though he might remain submerged seven minutes. He was born in water, not from an egg, but alive like a baby.

Pitching the inner tube is a favorite pastime. If it is thrown from a group, this performer returns it to the tosser's hands.

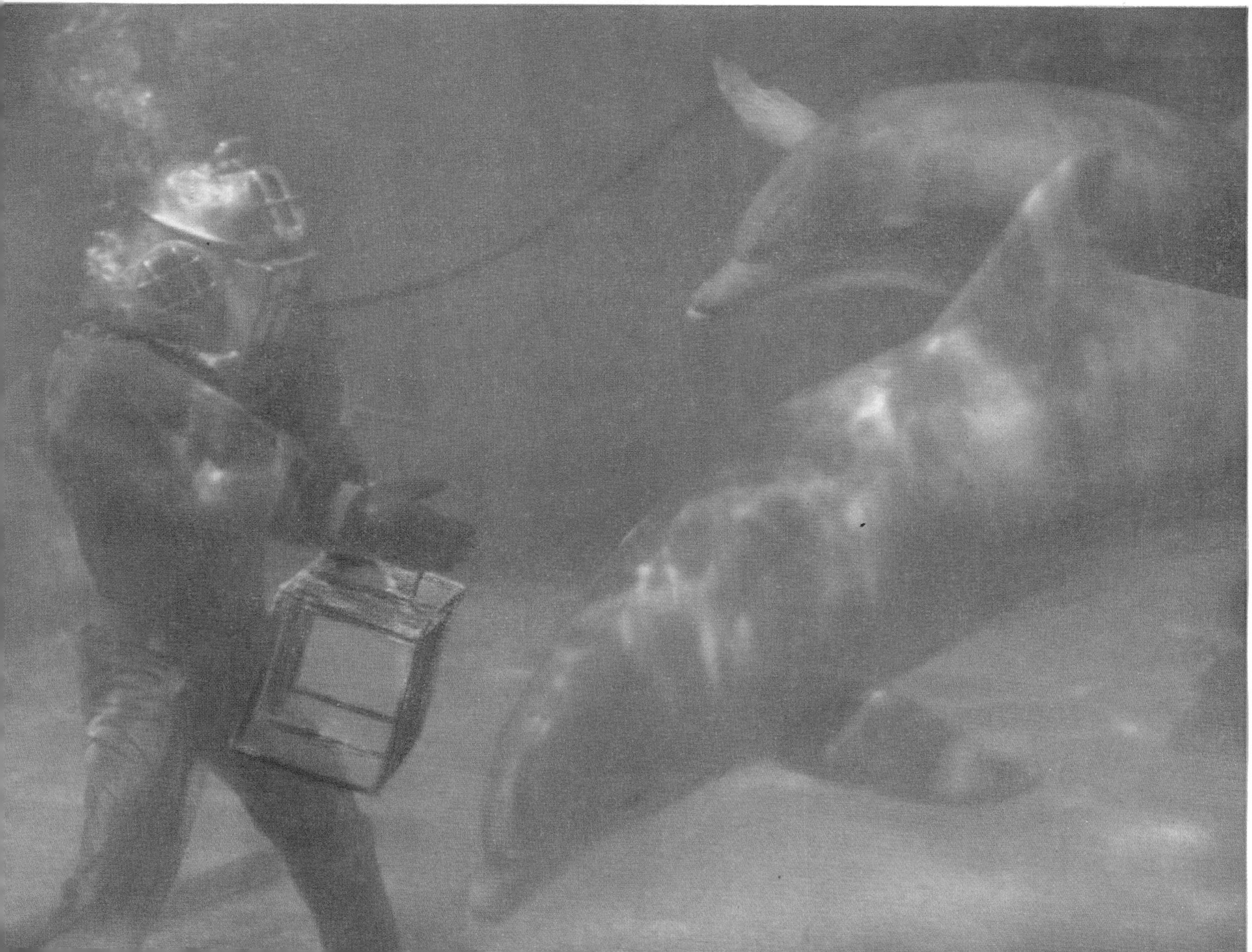

Sad Looks Reflect the Diver's Empty Feeding Basket

Marineland has greatly increased the world's store of knowledge about marine life. Its walled-in pools, refreshed daily with five million gallons of sea water, represent an approximation of the ocean itself; winter temperature in the tropical tank is a constant 70° F.

The Marine Studios' collecting crews catch *Tursiops*, the inshore porpoise, by stretching nets across tidewater channels. *Stenella plagiodon*, the deep-sea porpoise noted for frolicking around ships, is captured by boatmen, who thread a noose just above the tail with the aid of a harmless, forcepslike device. Within two weeks captives become tame enough to accept food from hand.

Here Florida sunshine floods the diver's bubbling helmet six feet below the surface of the circular tank. These porpoises, fed by hand in water, sheer off because the fish supply is exhausted.

Kodachrome by Luis Marden, National Geographic Staff

155

A Newly Caught Shark Gets a Stretcher Ride

Florida's warm seas teem with an apparently inexhaustible supply of marine life, but replenishing Marineland's oceanariums with fresh faces requires a constant struggle.

Sharks are caught in thousand-yard nets or on half-mile baited trotlines and transported by barge in a live well.

Equipped with an oxygenization pump, the barge has an entrance port cut below the waterline. Specimens are introduced to the live well without removing them from their natural element.

← This fish out of water accepts his fate quietly because he suffers a failure of oxygen. He goes into a shallow connecting tank, his sanctuary until he regains strength.

↓ Shark walking, like baby sitting, is a recognized job at Marineland. Comatose captives are towed by the fins to insure a steady flow of oxygenized water through the gills. Using this form of artificial respiration, diver Floyd Adams revives two tiger sharks. This job may require as much as two hours.

Kodachromes by Luis Marden,
National Geographic Staff

Some Curious Inhabitants of the Gulf Stream

By John T. Nichols

Curator of Recent Fishes, American Museum of Natural History

WE THINK of tropical seas as the home of a gaudily colored assemblage of fishes. In a sense, this first impression is correct. Active, short-bodied, elastic-scaled, spiny-finned, bright-colored species here occupy the center of the stage.

As a matter of fact, tropical shore lines are the great metropolis of the world's fish life. The snakelike moray (page 233), one of the most degenerate of true fishes, threads the hidden passages among the coral over which blue angel (page 235) and red, green, or particolored parrotfish (page 229) are swimming.

Out on the open sand, spotted flounders lie, matching their background so as to be well-nigh invisible; or little gray gobies move about like shadows, eager to escape detection.

Countless varieties of fishes are hiding in every patch of weed. Schools of silversides, anchovies, and herring dart through the stretches of open water.

It is their function, in the scheme of things, to feed on the minute organisms so abundant in sea water, to multiply prodigiously, and in turn form a basic food supply for a great variety of larger fishes.

To do this and at the same time contribute something to the forces of evolution, however, their numbers must be conserved. Their silvery sides render them difficult of observation by hungry eyes below, and they are available only to the quick and the keen.

Enormous Diversity of Sea Life

Over the heat equator warm air is constantly rising. Heavier, cooler air from higher latitudes flows steadily in to take its place, and, deflected by the earth's rotation, becomes the easterly trade winds. Before these far-famed winds, millions of waves, reflecting the clear deep blue of the ocean depths under their white crests, go dancing to the westward.

The whole surface of the tropical Atlantic moves, drifting toward the coast of America, is caught and turned about in the Gulf of Mexico, and shoots out past the Keys and the east coast of Florida as the Gulf Stream.

Since many young marine fishes and other animals regularly drift in ocean currents, it is easy to see what an enormous quantity and diversity of life the Gulf Stream must carry.

Furthermore, such waters, when they enter the Gulf, have already flowed under a tropical sun for many miles. The Gulf of Mexico is not a place for them to lose calories, and Gulf Stream water has a higher temperature than the 79° found, in general, at the surface of the open ocean on the Equator.

By no means all fishes whose haunts are on and among tropical reefs are brightly colored, but there are a great number of active species which wear red, green, yellow, blue, orange, etc., and which are marked in the boldest patterns, frequently with black.

Good examples are the rock beauty and the blue angelfish. Several parrotfishes, butterflyfishes, and others of similarly attractive appearance belong to this class.

Naturalists have offered in explanation that the reef itself was as full of color as a garden of varied flowers, wherein the very brightness of the fishes rendered them inconspicuous. To most observers, however, a coral reef as a whole appears rather monotonous in tone. The many varied fishes swimming about give it the principal note of high color, and these are not only easily seen but readily identified.

Immunity colors, they have been called most appropriately. The idea is that a wide-awake, active fish on a coral reef has so many avenues of escape from its enemies, so many projections to dodge behind and holes to hide in, as to be practically immune from attack. It can afford to be as conspicuous as it likes.

Be this as it may, the striking patterns are a great convenience to the ichthyologist, who has to separate one species from another; for nowhere else does one find so many different, but closely related, species living side by side, each doubtless differing from the others in habits in some way, be it ever so slightly.

A Hooked Bass Seldom Escapes

Many are food fishes of importance. They have leathery mouths, so that when once hooked they are not easily lost. Though well formed and by no means sluggish, they are solitary and sedentary, as contrasted with the equally abundant predaceous family of snappers, for instance.

E. R. Sanborn

When Odd Fellows Get Together

The porcupinefish (above) can inflate itself into a large ball, bristling with spines, and thus confuse its natural enemies. The hogfish (below), sometimes called the capitaine, is beautifully colored and an excellent food fish. Many of the strange variations in the shape and defense equipment of undersea creatures are Nature's ingenious provisions for self-protection.

The porcupinefish, closely related to the familiar swellfishes, used to be hollowed out by the Japanese, when the fish was inflated, for use as lanterns. The hogfish, one of the most beautiful of tropical fishes, derives its uncomplimentary name neither from ugly appearance nor from greed but from the hoglike shape of its snout.

Always lurking on the lookout for smaller fishes to come within striking distance, and sometimes associated in considerable numbers at favorable localities, they do not range about, hunting in schools, like the snappers.

The colors of this group are varied and sometimes extremely beautiful, in none more so than in the small rock hind (page 231), whose home is in the bright lights of the coral reef. But the plan of coloring is such as to lower, not raise, the visibility of the fish. Contrast, for instance, the color plans of the rock hind and the bizarre rock beauty.

These groupers, rockfishes, and hinds, furthermore, have the power of undergoing complete color changes almost instantaneously. The color tone becomes lighter or darker and the markings become bold or fade and disappear. Such color changes can be seen to advantage in individuals kept in an aquarium. There is no doubt that in the fish's natural environment it adapts its color to the bottom over which it swims, and, further, that inconspicuousness may aid in its getting a full meal at the expense of its smaller associates.

The fish life of warm shores is one of contrasts. In contrast to the big-mouthed sea basses, there are species, usually sluggish, with very small mouths, depending for their subsistence on the great abundance of small sea animals found about tropical reefs and ledges or seaweeds. To capture such small creatures does not require great agility.

The Strange Sea Horses

The sort of life they lead has probably been taken up gradually, through long periods of time, and many of them have meanwhile acquired remarkable and some-

F. G. Lancaster

Twenty-four Baby Sharks Were Removed from Their Mother's Abdomen

Unlike most fishes, most kinds of shark do not lay eggs but develop their young within their bodies. A mother shark caught off the west coast of Andros, in "the Mud," as the shallow sponge banks are called, was found to have been bearing two dozen babies. Young sharks are usually able to care for themselves at birth.

times quite unfishlike characters of form and structure. None is stranger than the little sea horses (page 228), with body encased in rings of bony mail, horse-shaped head set at right angles, and prehensile tail to grasp the seaweed where they are hiding, body floating upward erect in the water.

The male sea horse receives and carries the eggs in an abdominal pouch situated under his tail, until they are hatched and the young large enough to fend for themselves.

Sluggish, small-mouthed species frequently have hard nipperlike teeth, as many of the small animals which they eat are shelly.

Since it is difficult for them to evade larger predaceous fish, they are variously protected against attack, mostly being colored more or less in resemblance to their surroundings. The trigger-fishes have a stout dorsal spine which locks erect, as well as a very thick leathery hide which must be of some protection. The gaudy colors of the queen trigger-fish (page 229) are an exception among such forms.

A somewhat related flat-sided filefish scarcely swims about at all but drifts with the tides, more or less head downward, and can be easily captured in the hand. It is so striped as to be readily overlooked, however,

among the eelgrass which is drifting with it.

The swellfishes (page 248) have the power of suddenly inflating the body with water or air until they assume an approximately globular form several times the normal diameter. Such a performance must be disconcerting to any enemy about to seize one.

The porcupinefish, in addition to doing this, has the body everywhere covered with long, sharp spines which project in every direction like the quills of a hedgehog.

The trunkfishes, instead of being protected in this way, have the body encased in a bony shell, like a turtle. In the East Indies there are rectangular species, but ours are all three-cornered, beechnut-shaped. They go by various names—cuckold, shellfish, and so forth. The cowfish (page 183) is a species with two hornlike spines projecting from its forehead. They are excellent eating, cooked in the shell like a lobster.

Forked Tails Promote Speed

Most marine animals which swim especially swiftly and continuously have a forked tail fin. This shape of tail avoids the space immediately behind the axis of the body where the streamlines following the sides (of a moving fish) converge. A rounded or pointed tail

Ralph Bowden

A Wahoo Comes Aboard near Bimini

The mate of the yacht *Alberta* boats one of the gamest fighters of the warm seas. The wahoo, which is excellent eating, may reach a weight of more than 130 pounds. The vertical stripes on the side of the fish disappear soon after death.

which would occupy such area would be a drag.

Whales and porpoises, though they move the tail up and down instead of from side to side, have a forked tail-fin, only it lies in a horizontal instead of a vertical plane. The wide-ranging members of the mackerel family and other more or less related marine fishes have a forked tail-fin set on a firm, narrow base; and the freest swimming sharks (mackerel sharks and the man-eater) have acquired a tail of the same shape, though the ordinary shark tail is weak and unsymmetrical.

Fresh-water minnows almost invariably have a forked tail fin since the waters which they must traverse are considerable in relation to the small size of the fishes themselves.

In the blues and greens of the waters through which it swims, the yellowtail's bright-yellow tail probably makes a shining mark, though its colors otherwise are well calculated to give it a low visibility.

There is a tendency for fishes which swim deep down under the blue or green sea, and yet within the range of surface light penetration, to be red in color. A great many are not, but a larger proportion are red here than elsewhere, frequently a bright striking red all over.

It seems almost a pity that the light in which they live is so green that the color, red, must appear an intangible neutral gray! Perhaps it gives them a useful inconspicuousness down there, or perhaps it absorbs a maximum amount of the dim, strongly blue-green sunlight, which is in some way beneficial.

The Shark Is a Living Fossil

Ages before modern fishes, of which we now find such countless variety in tropical seas, had been evolved there were sharks which differed comparatively little from those of the present day. Intermediate forms have become antiquated and dropped out, but the primeval shark is still with us. Especially in the Tropics they occur in great abundance.

Prowling singly along the edges of the reefs, over the shallow flats, or through offshore stretches of open water, they hunt largely by sense of smell and congregate in numbers wherever food is abundant.

When a whale is being cut up at sea, it is astonishing how quickly the slender, offshore blue sharks gather to the feast, it would almost seem from nowhere.

By far the most abundant sharks are the

ground sharks (*Carcharhinus*). There is probably no tropical or temperate coast line where one or more species of this genus do not enter the bays and inshore water at the proper season to give birth to their young.

Though relics of a bygone age, as far as bodily structure is concerned, sharks, of all fishes, have the most highly developed reproductive system. Some lay a few large eggs, each one protected by a horny shell; but usually the egg stage is passed within the body of the parent fish, and the young are born well grown and able to fend for themselves.

The black-tip shark (*Carcharhinus limbatus*) is a small species of ground shark, females of which are taken with young in the Bay (Florida) in April. They are frequently hooked by tarpon fishermen who erroneously call them "mackerel shark." They are usually between 5 and 5½ feet in length, and the young, about three to six in number, are 2 feet long, or a little less, when born.

We have data concerning another ground shark, *Carcharhinus milberti*, the sand-bar shark, which gives birth to its young in Great South Bay, New York, in midsummer. The mother sharks are a little larger than those of the black-tip species, measuring 6 or 7 feet. The young, however, are of about the same size, but there are more of them in a brown shark's family, eight to eleven having been recorded for this species. Some kinds of sharks which grow much larger have a proportionately larger number of young.

Rays Are Flattened Sharks

In contrast with its conservative treatment of sharks in general, evolution has made unusual and interesting creatures of the rays, which originally were nothing but sharks flattened to lie on the bottom face down.

The skates which are abundant in northern waters are just this. Their breast fins have become fused with the flat sides of the body to form a disk, undulated at the edges as they swim, while the elongated tail, no longer used in locomotion, drags behind.

The sting rays are a more or less intermediate stage in which the tail has become a whiplike lash, with one or more jagged defensive spines at its base to ward off enemies. Finally the eagle rays, still flattened, have become free-swimming again, the corners of their disks pointed like the wings of a bird and used like wings to "fly" through the water.

161 National Geographic Photographer Robert F. Sisson

Voracious Sharks Bite at Almost Anything

Operations of the National Geographic Society-Woods Hole Oceanographic Institution-Columbia University Expedition to study the Atlantic's underwater mountain range were hampered by sharks who bit at the underwater instruments used. Here one is bagged by the crew.

162   Luis Marden, National Geographic Staff

Here Each Coral Dweller Selects Its Bed

An open air tidal fish pen at Bimini's Lerner dock flashes with life as the electric-blue markings of the queen triggerfish (insert) and other species catch the light. At dusk the triggers patrol their chosen spots, savagely chasing away intruders. With darkness movement ceases and the fish lie flat in the sand or among rocks and coral, as shown in these flash photographs. The larger fish take the best beds, and weaker rivals are banished to outlying "slums" to sleep crowded six deep against the wire fence of the pen. Having no eyelids, fish sleep with eyes wide open.

The Lerner Marine Laboratory has achieved world fame among scientists since its establishment in 1948. Clues to such problems in abnormal growth as cancer are sought by scientists in probing and analyzing marine life.

Man-of-War Fleet Attacks Bimini

By Paul A. Zahl, Ph.D.

Associate Director, Haskins Laboratories

IT WAS late January, and from the Gulf Stream, flowing northward between Bimini Islands and the Florida mainland, an enormous fleet had cast itself with full force against the nearest shore.

As far as the eye could see, the invaders were strewn by thousands upon the sand, stranded by the ebbing tide. In the surf a myriad more were being tossed and battered by the breakers. Bimini had been stormed by a vast armada of one of the most curious "dreadnoughts" on the high seas, the Portuguese man-of-war (page 234).

Tentacles Inflict Tormenting Burns

These long-tentacled creatures (*Physalia pelagica*) belong to that group of aquatic animals known commonly as jellyfish, technically as coelenterates. These include the glamorous corals and sea anemones. Among our planet's most primitive inhabitants, their unique adaptations to the ruthless environment of the sea give them special status in the realm of Nature's fantasies.

I had only a textbook knowledge of this strange blue creature, and so, after a preliminary tour of the littered beach, I hastened back to the Lerner Marine Laboratory for collecting buckets and jumbo-size tweezers.

Returning to the beach, I approached the stranded men-of-war with caution. Some of them were still alive. Dropped into a bucket of sea water, they immediately reacted to the familiar environment and, despite the limited space, actually began to lower their tentacles in an instinctive search for prey.

While gathering and manipulating the specimens, I could not avoid an occasional light hand contact with the tentacle tissue. For a few minutes I would feel no distress, but gradually a painful burning sensation would set in. For hours it kept me uncomfortably aware of the tentacle poison's virulence.

Down on the beach that morning I had noticed some small Bimini boys hopping from one man-of-war to another, each time causing the air-filled organism to explode like a damp firecracker. Had my hands been as thickly calloused as their foot soles, I too should probably have felt no stinging aftereffects!

In the laboratory I transferred the specimens which I had in my buckets to large tanks filled with running water. Through the glass walls I was able to observe the heavily armed men-of-war in complete detail.

Hoists Sail, Lowers Fishing Lines

The Portuguese man-of-war consists essentially of a thin-membraned bladderlike chamber crested on top by a narrow ridge of air sacs. These form a "sail" which can be raised or lowered at will, enabling this armless, legless, and finless marvel to travel before the wind. The sail with its underlying hull may be as long as nine inches and as wide as five. It shimmers a diaphanous blue in the sunlight, with splotches of reds, delicate pinks, and lavenders.

That portion of the hull which lies in contact with the water surface is thick and jellylike. In it are the digestive and reproductive tissues. From it extends a great pack of trailing blue tentacles which in the sea are completely submerged. Their amazing elasticity enables them to descend into the salty depths as far as 50 feet, hanging there as a silent lure to unwary fishes and small marine invertebrates as well.

A Thousand Hypodermics at Once

No attempt is made to seek out prey; in fact, the tentacles are capable of only two motions, up and down. But if a fish merely brushes one of the tentacles, a thousand harpoonlike hypodermics, microscopically lining these long streamers, are instantly discharged to pierce its body, each injecting a tiny drop of poison.

The minute hollow threads do not withdraw, but cling. As the fish struggles, it gets only more fouled up and thus receives additional hypodermic broadsides until it is paralyzed. The tentacles, like elevators, lift the catch to the man-of-war's eating tissues for digestion. Then down again they go, for more lethal angling.

Floating shiplike, the Portuguese man-of-war inhabits many of the globe's tropical seas. It thrives in the Gulf Stream, where, during certain brief periods of the year, countless

Luis Marden, National Geographic Staff

A Free Loading Remora Rides a Gray Shark's Fin

Remoras, or shark suckers, cling to the big fish to snatch morsels of his meals. Their powerful suction discs make no impression on sandpaper-like sharkskin. This five-foot gray shark in a Bimini Island pen is about to eat a stunned grunt, floating belly up. Contrary to popular belief he does not have to roll over to gobble a meal. About three-quarters of a shark's brain are devoted to the olfactory sense. He smells his prey, sometimes stalks it briefly, but frequently swoops down on it the instant it is spotted.

thousands suddenly appear riding high and proud on the warm swells.

Storms Wreck Man-of-War Fleets

Storms and onshore winds are their foe, and a persistent blow may drive great fleets before it, wrecking and piling them up, as here in Bimini, on whatever beach, near or far, may loom ahead. Stranded, the men-of-war quickly wilt and die as masses of ugly blue slime, or jelly, familiar to anyone who has trod Caribbean shores.

Portuguese man-of-war mass invasions occur in the Bimini area only occasionally, usually in late winter. They constitute no particular hazard, so long as one avoids them in the water!

Except for a narrow entering channel, North Bimini's harbor bay is surrounded by a tightly strung necklace of islets, sand bars, and shallows.

In view of this seclusion from the sea, I was astonished that midmorning of *Physalia* D-day when people came running into the laboratory to announce incredulously that the bay, too, was being overrun by Portuguese men-of-war.

Men-of-War Have Submarine Consorts

I grabbed buckets and dip nets and a few minutes later my small boat was whining out into the bay in pursuit of the wind-blown and tide-swept invaders of peaceful Bimini.

Sure enough, they were there. The strong incoming tide was carrying hundreds of them through the sea channel and into the bay.

With one hand on my outboard tiller and the other firmly clutching a long dip net, I

Luis Marden, National Geographic Staff

Like the Dog, Porpoises Have Warm Blood and Breathe Air

Gentle and intelligent, the bottle-nosed dolphin or porpoise thrives in captivity and shows little fear of man. This small one needs little running start to jump for breakfast; a few strokes of her powerful tail kick her out of the water. Porpoises belong to the toothed whale family, mammals whose ancestors chose an aquatic existence. They outswim most fish, but can remain submerged no longer than three minutes. Usually they surface for breath every 30 to 45 seconds, even during sleep.

sputtered from one man-of-war to another, netting vigorously and depositing each catch in a water-filled enamel pail.

Not for sport was I zigzagging about the bay like a nervous water bug. I was after a fish known as *Nomeus gronovii*, alone reputed to live in close association with the Portuguese man-of-war. In fact its common name is "man-of-war fish," because it is seldom found except among the poisonous tentacles of the man-of-war.

Although zoology textbooks refer in wonderment to this strange relationship, actually little is known about it firsthand. Here in the clear waters of placid Bimini bay was the chance of a lifetime to make some ringside observations on the nature of this enigmatic alliance.

I found what I sought. Hovering with ap-

parent impunity among the treacherous man-of-war tentacles were *Nomeus* fishes, brilliantly mottled with blue and silver and with forefins almost winglike in size.

Some men-of-war harbored only one of these submarine consorts; others two, three, up to 15. Most of the fish were two to three inches long, but one relatively giant 8-inch specimen also found its way into my net.

Artful Dodgers Among Deadly Tentacles

I was very curious to know how such fish can survive a life among deadly tentacles. Do they have a natural immunity to the poison? Why have they chosen so strange a habitat? Does the Portuguese man-of-war protect them as a lure for other creatures? On what do they feed? On crumbs, perhaps, from the master's table?

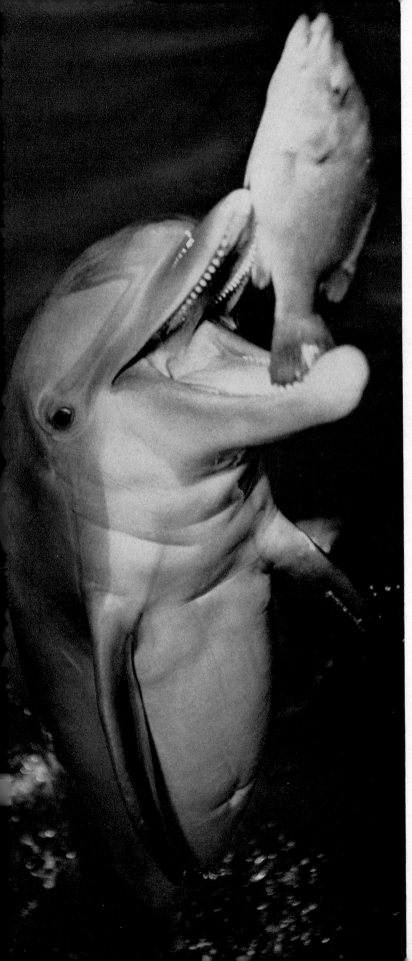

In partial answer to some of these questions, which have remained debatable since the days of Agassiz, I found, for one thing, that the *Nomeus* fish is decidedly not immune to man-of-war's poison.

Whenever I caught a man-of-war and its associate fish together in the same net haul, the latter would become panicky, flap against the tentacles, and invariably get stung. I would drop the entire catch into a pail of water, and within a few minutes all the fish would be dead!

On the other hand, if the net under a man-of-war was maneuvered so as to catch only its fish, these could survive indefinitely.

Clearly, *Nomeus* has a reliable, almost miraculous technique for avoiding any direct contact with the poisonous curtain which surrounds its bower. It's as if a man should live his life in a maze of high-tension wires whose touch would mean quick death.

The idea has been advanced that *Nomeus* may actually feed on the poisonous man-of-war tentacles. But we found no signs of tentacle tissue in the stomach contents of the fish, and now I knew from personal observation that the fish itself is highly susceptible to the poison.

One sea dweller that does apparently possess a natural protection or immunity is the loggerhead turtle. A skipper with years of experience in Gulf Stream waters tells me he has seen such tur-

Porpoise Accepts a Fish with a Thank-you Grin

The umbilical indentation marks this marine creature as a true mammal born attached to his mother. Scientists believe his predecessors anciently walked on land, since vestigial hind-leg bones are buried deep in the flesh of some species. The bottlenose carries 80 to 94 teeth but seldom uses them to chew; it swallows fish in one gulp.

Luis Marden, National Geographic Staff

Sea Turtles, Flippers Trussed, Lie Upside Down on a Sailboat Deck

Bahamas fishing boats sail silently up to surfaced large turtles and scoop up small ones in dip nets. Native swimmers seize, ride, and noose the larger ones, then immobilize them by laying them on their backs and tying the flippers.

tles prey upon men-of-war. A turtle will close its eyes, he declares, and gulp the man-of-war whole. Still swallowing, according to the captain, the turtle swims off with man-of-war tentacles streaming out of its mouth like weird holiday bunting.

Problems of the Parasite

Once having accepted a particular man-of-war as its food provider, does a *Nomeus* remain faithful to that individual? This struck me as an especially intriguing problem in natural history. When one large specimen in my dip net escaped overboard, I thought I saw it make a beeline for the organism from whose underside it had just been snatched. I doubt the significance of this observation, however, for that particular man-of-war also happened to be the closest at hand.

Consider in this regard, too, the thousands of these satellite fishes left safely behind in the surf when their masters are tossed ashore during a blow.

Do these thereafter live independent lives? Or do they seek out other men-of-war with which to join up? I believe the latter, although there is still no strong evidence to support my opinion.

The fascinating biological problem of parasitism and animal cooperation, in all its multitudinous forms, is these days a major field of experimental biology. New facts of interest and usefulness are daily being uncovered by people trained in science working at such marine laboratories as the Lerner station on Bimini, where bizarre sea organisms conveniently throw themselves at the island or obligingly live almost at the laboratory door.

Bimini Has No Cars;
Its Only Highways
Are Narrow Walks

North Bimini, a slender strip of land five miles long and a few hundred yards wide, contains all the inhabitants of Bimini's three main islands. King's Highway (left) parallels Bimini bay: Queen's Highway (right) extends along the beach facing the Gulf Stream. Only pedestrians, bicycles, handcarts and wheelbarrows use these concrete walks.

The author first sighted Bimini's Portugese man-of-war fleet when the tide washed the invaders up on the beach at right. Later they moved through the harbor entrance (top center) into the bay.

Buildings of the Lerner Marine Research Laboratory (lower left) face the shallow bay. Dr. Michael Lerner's pier is marked by wire-enclosed fish pens (upper center). A fishing yacht leaves the pier.

Legend says the aging Ponce de León landed on South Bimini (upper left) in vain search for the Fountain of Youth!

168

Hunter and Hunted Move Through Crystal Waters off Bimini, Westernmost of the Bahamas

This remarkable aerial photograph shows a large school of migrating tuna, who move north to their summer waters off Long Island, Maine, and Nova Scotia in May and June, as they pass Bimini. The school's estimated travel speed is five to seven miles per hour. The fishing yacht, G. A. Bass's 30-foot *Sambo*, is attempting to maneuver into position ahead of them so baits, one to one-and-a-half pound mullet, can be offered. But they might not be taken, and if the anglers are unsuccessful after ten minutes of trolling, they look for another school. Migrating tuna travel close to the surface and can be spotted easily by a boat lookout or, even better, a light plane having marine radiotelephone connections with the boat.

Courtesy of G. A. Bass

169

 Luis Marden, National Geographic Staff

Insects, Fleeing Light, Crawl Down These Cloth Funnels to Their Death

Several insects new to science have been discovered on Bimini. Dr. Mont Cazier, entomologist, here examines specimens at the Lerner Marine Laboratory. These Berlese funnels are filled with insect-bearing earth and leaf mold. Overhead lamps, burning constantly, drive light-shunning insects down into lethal fluid at the funnel tips.

A mere 55 air miles east of Miami Beach, Florida, Bimini is a tiny cluster of low-lying palm-studded islands enclosing a shallow bay through whose lucite-clear waters one may see quilled sea urchins, pearly-lipped conchs, and gaily colored starfish lazing on the white sand bottom. The only populated isle is a splinter of land five miles long and but a few hundred yards in width.

Happy Hunting Grounds for Scientists

To the west, Bimini faces that great aorta of Western seas, the wondrous Gulf Stream. To the east stretches the generally more quiet and shallow area known as the Great Bahama Bank.

Since Ponce de León landed there in 1513, Bimini had a humble history, save in the era of prohibition in the United States; its inhabitants were victims of a not overrich soil and an isolation from primary trading areas. Today its citizenry consists mainly of about 700 Bahama negroes living in the quaint village settlements of Alice Town and Bailey Town.

From the British Government office at Alice Town, a Nassau-appointed and most cooperative white Commissioner directs the civil administration.

In recent years a group of American and Canadian families have erected spacious modern tropical homes on the tiny island, and several small hotels afford visitors comfortable accommodations.

During winter, spring, and early summer, sports fishermen from many parts of the United States, seeking sun and prize catches, dock their yachts at one of the wharves, anchor on the bay side of Alice Town, or fly over from south Florida resorts. Gathering on the docks of Bimini, they swap tall sea tales and conjecture on the probable location of big marlin and tuna schools they hope to catch on the morrow!

Sea Creatures Aid Cancer Research

Conspicuous to the Bimini visitor is the sustaining and valued influence of Dr. and Mrs. Michael Lerner, internationally known big-game fishermen. In 1948, in collaboration with Dr. Charles M. Breder, Jr., distinguished biologist and marine authority of the American Museum of Natural History, they designed, had built, and equipped a modern marine laboratory on Bimini and presented it as a field operation station to the American Museum.

Here to the Lerner Marine Laboratory come scientists to carry on their researches in basic biology. More and more the technical facilities of the laboratory have been devoted to

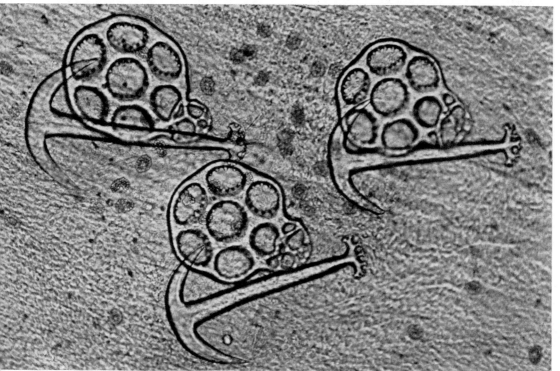

Paul A. Zahl

Nature Duplicates Anchors on the Sea Cucumber's Skin

The ugly *Synapta* is best described by its common name of sea cucumber. These undersea animals have microscopic hooks, here magnified 150 times, projecting from the skin The hooks, looking like old fashioned anchors, enable the creature to cling to anything it touches. Principal claim to fame of the sea cucumber is that some carry in their intestines a tapered, almost transparent fish about five inches long.

cancer research. Nearly half of all the investigations carried on since the laboratory's opening have been concerned with the cancer problem in one form or another.

Among the agencies that have contributed to cancer study at this laboratory are the Damon Runyon Fund, the American Cancer Society, and the United States Public Health Service.

Workers in this field have finally gone back to Mother Sea, for it was in the ocean that the earliest forms of life on this planet probably originated and the biochemical patterns of all living things were laid down.

The dread disease, found not only in humans but in fish, plants, birds, and amphibia as well, poses essentially a fundamental biological problem in growth. Simple organisms taken from the sea constitute excellent material for the study of growth, both normal and abnormal; and because these creatures multiply so rapidly, answers to technical questions can be obtained in hours compared with the years sometimes required in research with human subjects.

Infinite Variety of Marine Life

Life teems in the waters around Bimini, and the research biologist finds a rich source of organisms on which to experiment, from huge oceanic fishes all down the biological ladder to invisible bacteria. Bimini touches the migration routes and haunts of giant pelagic fishes, such as bluefin tuna, blue and white marlin, sailfish, wahoo, a variety of sharks, and other fast swimmers of the open ocean.

In the marbled blue and green waters of Bimini bay are found an almost infinite variety and number of brightly colored reef fishes, crustaceans, sponges, corals, and all sorts of microscopic life.

The laboratory building and its adjoining residence for visiting scientists are spacious and attractive. They stand on several acres of land straddling the narrow neck of North Bimini. At its front door is the tidal, shallow bay and, only a hundred yards to the westward, the blue Atlantic.

The laboratory is specially equipped for marine and cancer biology. It has aquarium rooms, dissecting, dehumidifying, and refrigerating rooms, constant-temperature ovens, microscopes and microtomes, a photographic darkroom, and much additional technical gear for the study of life processes.

On the staff of the laboratory are experienced native collectors who man a fleet of boats and gather whatever specimens the scientists require for observation and experiments. Small and larger sea organisms are placed in aquariums where sea water circulates freely and constantly through a nonmetallic piping system.

Concrete pools on the grounds hold yet larger specimens. Oceanic fish are kept in large numbers in the spacious tideswept wire "pens" at the Lerner residence dock and are the constant delight of Bimini visitors.

Under the directorship of Dr. Breder and Dr. Bishop the laboratory has become one of those places of which scientists dream, for here qualified investigators can work in the remote quiet and isolation of a small tropical island, yet are only 25 minutes by air from the facilities of Florida's Greater Miami area.

When the man-of-war invasion ended and the hot sun dried up the blue heaps of beach-strewn jelly, I found other absorbing subjects for my daily collecting trips.

Long "Ears" Give Sea Hare Its Name

On the far side of Bimini bay, opposite the Alice Town section, are shallows which, whenever the tide is low, turn into mud flats and tide pools. Here abound forms of marine life no less striking than the Portuguese man-of-war.

The sea hare, for instance, is a mollusk which during evolution has lost all signs of an external shell.

A mass of greenish-yellow jelly about the size of one's fist, the sea hare is decorated in ugly elegance with black leopardlike spots. At one end are two conelike flaps of skin which look ever so much like rabbit ears; hence its descriptive name.

When disturbed, the creature is able to discharge a jet of mysterious purple fluid that diffuses eerily through the surrounding water.

Whether this is a "smoke screen" in which to hide from enemies or a toxic material with which to poison them is not yet clear. I hazard a guess that the latter is the case, for when sea hares were placed in a small aquarium containing fish, sponges, and coral, all but the sea hares died forthwith!

As I sloshed through mud and pools left by a receding tide, I saw brilliant orange-colored sponges all about; some were brick-red, with tiny chimneys through which they continuously "breathed" water.

Enormous black sponges may be several feet across. When overturned, they reveal themselves to be squatters' quarters for a dozen non-sponge species.

Marine Gardens Like Contrary Mary's

An ugly-looking brittle star extends one of its legs through a hole on a sponge's surface and then, sensing danger, quickly slithers it back. Worms with a thousand tiny feet coil

and attempt to retreat unseen into some hidden crevice.

The disappearing worm looks for all the world like a purple posy from Contrary Mary's garden. Its stalk is a tube coated with sand, out of which extends a most gorgeous display of purple fronds, actually the worm's gills.

One may see a garden of such fronds and stoop to admire it, when suddenly it disappears. All the worms have simultaneously swished their gills down into the protection of the tubes.

The reaction occurs at such lightning speed as to suggest that the garden may have existed only in one's imagination.

In wandering about Bimini's shallows, one must be careful not to step on sea urchins, for the common Caribbean species is a pincushion of deeply purple spines.

Nor may the urchins be picked up by hand, for needle-sharp spines can readily pierce one's skin, causing extreme pain and sometimes even infection.

Then there are the ugly sea cucumbers, whose name is their best description. Their principal claim to distinction is that, like the Portuguese man-of-war, they have a curious consort. Often living in the sea cucumber's intestine is a tapered, almost transparent fish about five inches long!

Of such is composed the countless variety of warm sea life.

My personal pet among Bimini's creatures is one that looks like a worm but is actually closely related to the sea cucumber (page 171). It is about as thick as one's thumb and perhaps 12 inches long; but when disturbed it may stretch to be over a yard long and even break into several fragments, each of which, reportedly, may become a new individual!

Having picked up the creature, you find that getting rid of it is quite another matter. You shake your hand, then grab at the worm with the other hand, but the creature's skin seems to possess a sticking power of remarkable tenacity.

Curious, I made microscopic preparations of the worm's skin. There, magnified 150 times, was the answer. Thousands of tiny spicule structures, shaped like ships' anchors, extended through the outer surface of the skin, each ready to attach itself invisibly to whatever material the worm touched.

The Governor of the Bahamas, Maj. Gen. Robert A. R. Neville, escorted by Dr. Lerner, visited the laboratory one day. General Neville, clearly an English gentleman of few words, took a look at the worm's tenacious anchors under the microscope and breathed but two passionate words: "Most extraordinary!"—which well describes Bimini's family of grotesque sea children.

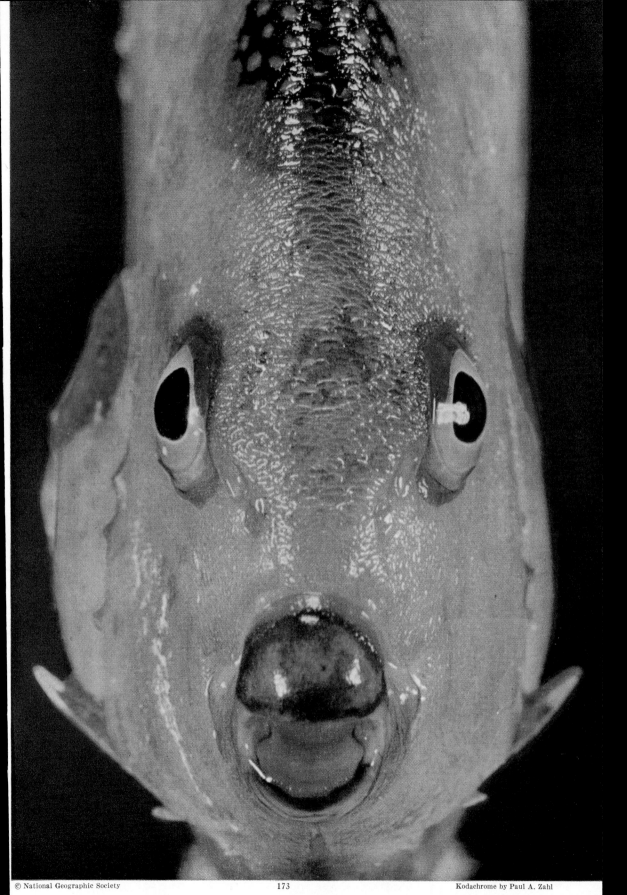

The Small Mouth of the Angelfish (P. 235) Limits Its Diet to Tiny Invertebrates and Vegetation

Kodachrome by Paul A. Zahl

174

Thousands of Portuguese Men-of-War Litter the Bimini Beachhead after Involuntary Invasion

Strong west winds of late January blew ashore a huge armada of the big impressively armed Portuguese men-of-war (*Physalia pelagica*), related to jellyfish. Blue floats of casualties cover the sands; these slimy "dreadnoughts" cannot live out of water.

Wary of Poison Tentacles, the Author Probes Men-of-War. Right: A Convoy of Eleven, and One Wrecked on the Beach

With long, streamerlike, poison-laden tentacles, Portuguese men-of-war catch fish and other creatures of the sea. Hidden by the water, such "fishing lines" dangle below the flotilla at upper right. Bladderlike floats, veering in the breeze like sails, alter the drift of the fish, but gales pile them up on shore in countless numbers. In the summer the Portuguese man-of-war has been known to drift as far north as Cape Cod.

Kodachromes by Paul A. Zahl

175

Poisonous Tentacles of the Men-of-War Entangle Two Careless Victims

Little schoolmaster fishes, brushing against clinging tentacles armed with batteries of stinging cells, were quickly killed. One (lower right) is about to be hauled up and digested. The other rests on the bottom (center).

177

Kodachrome by Paul A. Zahl

Nomeus Fishes Live amid Dangling Death, Somehow Steering Clear of Harm

In a strange alliance, these little 5- to 8-inch fishes find protection under the sinister Portuguese man-of-war, and probably share its prey. They are not immune to the poison, but avoid touching the tentacles.

178 Kodachromes by Luis Marden, National Geographic Staff

For Research Purposes, Big Fish Are Penned in Blue-green Bimini Bay

Built beside the long pier, numerous tidal pens hold a variety of ocean fish for scientific study. The Anchorage, the Michael Lerner residence (upper left), faces the Gulf Stream.

Opposite page: At the pens, Dr. and Mrs. Lerner (left) and Miss Francesca LaMonte, noted ichthyologist, watch a big cobia (center), ocean triggerfish, parrotfish, and horse-eye jack. Sharks and barracudas, being well fed daily in these open-air aquariums, rarely eat other inmates.

180

Filefish (Above) and Pipefish (Below) Are Valued as Neither Food nor Game

In the world of fishes, there are scores of species for which man has found no practical use at all. Two of them, the filefish (page 261) and the pipefish (page 58) are characterized by small mouths, which in the case of the pipefish is at the end of a long snout. Small-mouthed fish usually depend upon vegetation, tiny crustaceans and marine worms for sustenance. Large-mouthed fish are apt to be voracious and carnivorous.

There is as much diversity in the internal structure of fishes as there is in such external characteristics as mouths, shapes, and colors. The digestive apparatus, for example, differs among fishes, in general correlation with food types.

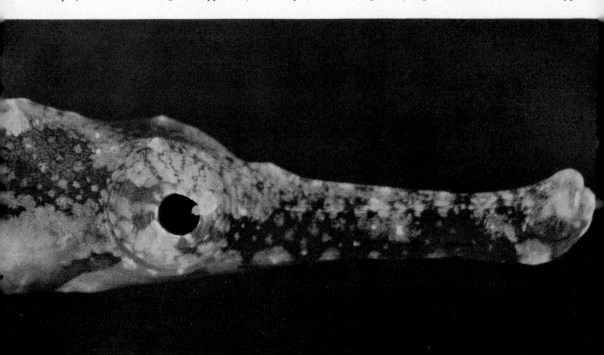

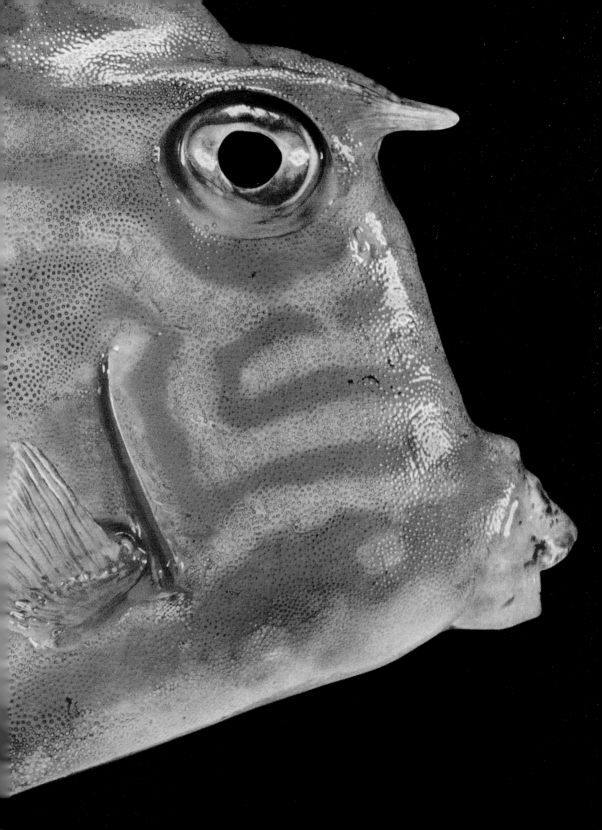

181

Horned Brow Gives the Cowfish a Bovine Look

Like other trunkfishes (page 235), cowfishes are slow and sluggish. They are bottom feeders, sometimes a foot or more in length; both sexes have a horn or spine over each eye. The body is encased in a bony box of little 6-sided plates, which are modified scales; only eyes, jaws, and fins are free to move. They are a good food fish, and are often cooked by baking them in their shells.

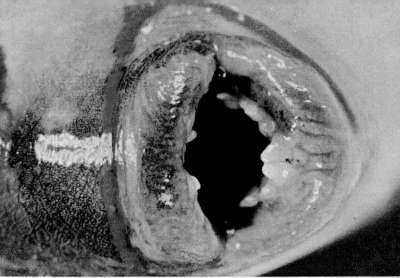

Nightmare to Crabs Is the Queen Triggerfish, with Pitiless, Staring Eye and Voracious Maw

Balistes, the queen triggerfish, or turbot, feeds partly on crabs, which flail with their claws when seized. Note the wide separation between mouth and eye. If the eyes were closer to the mouth, they would be in danger of being scratched out by crabs. In fact, the fish will not tackle a crab whose reach exceeds the distance between mouth and eye.

Another peculiarity is a long, sharp spike, the first spine of the dorsal fin. When alarmed or picked up, the fish immediately raises this spike upright. At its base is a lock which prevents it from being forced down. But, strangely, a smaller spine somewhat to the rear of the large one does unlock it; the two have a tendon connection. Push down this trigger and the larger spine falls flat.

Teeth of this rapacious fish can inflict a severe wound upon the careless handler.

Below are three trunkfishes (page 235), whose heavy shells make them slow swimmers and weak fighters.

Kodachromes by Paul A. Zahl

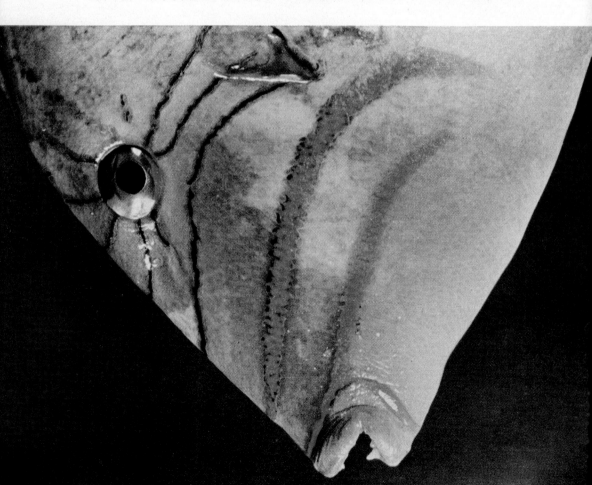

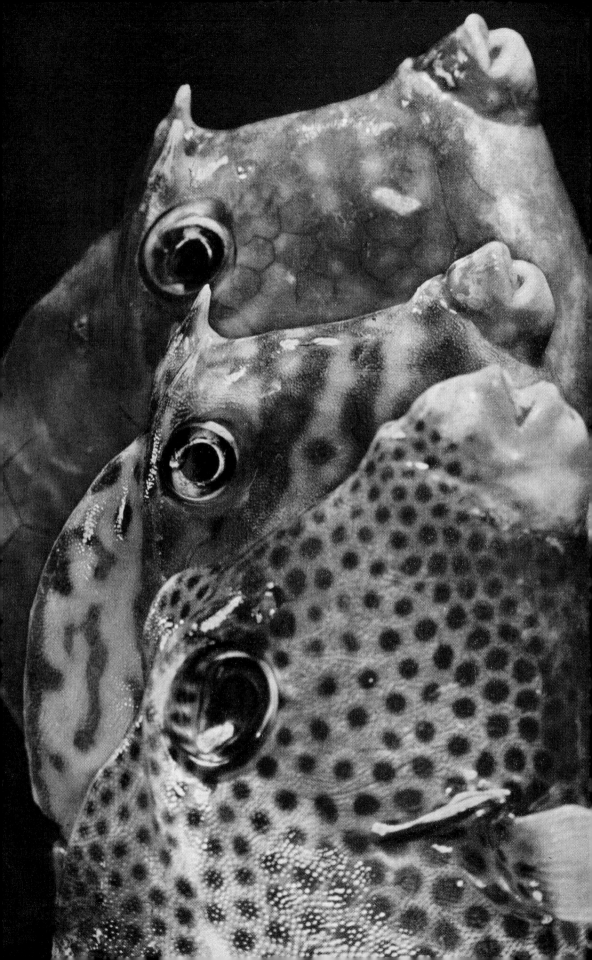

184

Bright Colors Dominate the Shallows of Bimini Bay

An underwater tableau shows an angelfish, lavender disappearing worm, sea anemones, corals, and sponges.

"Petals" of the disappearing worm are its gills for getting oxygen from water. Disturb the owner and they whisk back into the case; hence the name.

A white sea anemone's partly extended tentacles resemble those of the brainlike coral directly under the angelfish (above).

Kodachromes by Paul A. Zahl

185 Kodachrome by Paul A. Zahl

The Sargassum Fish Drifts Through Tropical Seas with Seaweed

The sargassum fish *(Histrio histrio)*, a member of the frogfish family, is named for the floating seaweed called sargassum, in which it is found in the tropical Atlantic. It climbs through the seaweed frog-fashion with its armlike fins.

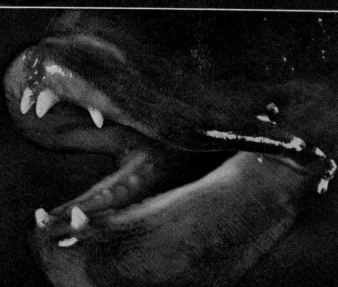

Mouths, Jaws, and Teeth of Fishes Vary Greatly, Ranging from Scissors to Piglike Snout

THE needlefish (upper—*Strongylura*) is characterized by its extremely elongate jaws, armed with long, sharp teeth, which give it another common name, **houndfish.** Predaceous and carnivorous, some species of houndfishes reach a length of more than three feet. The species shown inhabits the warm waters of the western Atlantic. The fish held in its mouth may be the sergeant major (page 228).

The needlefish has a peculiar habit under proper conditions of jumping over small objects floating at the surface. This is attributed to playful frolicking.

The **blue-head wrasse** (middle—*Thalassoma*) is a common species in the West Indian regions, reaching a foot in length. Similar to other wrasse, it has the teeth at the front of each jaw enlarged and projecting forward beyond the others.

The **hogfish** (lower—*Lachnolaimus*) is another kind of wrasse, reaching a record length of three feet and a weight of 22 pounds. It ranges in the West Indies north to North Carolina. It is a market fish of small value; an annual catch of 15,-000 pounds was recently recorded.

The hogfish is abundant and popular through the lower Florida Keys.

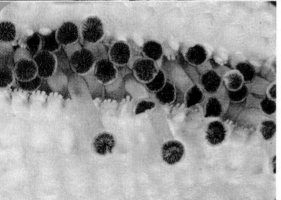

187

← Nature's Nonskid Tread—the Suction-
cup Feet of a Starfish ↓

Hundreds of vacuum-type podia, or feet, cling to rocks so tenaciously that it takes a powerful pull to dislodge the owner. Round spots along the short, broad arms of *Oreaster reticulatus* (close-up at left) are the suction-cup ends of the tube feet. Not all starfish are so equipped.

↓ A Cousin, the Brittle Star, Is Sometimes
Called the Serpent Star

Some species of the brittle star detach an arm if seized; the part comes off in one's hand. Then the creature grows a replacement. This kind lacks that useful gift for foiling its enemies.

Kodachromes by Paul A. Zahl

The Huge Batlike Manta Ray Provides Dangerous Sport

ONE of the giants of the sea, the **manta ray,** long popularly called the **devilfish** (*Manta birostris*), has been known to weigh a ton and a half and to measure 22 feet across "wing tips." It may be distinguished from all other rays by means of the cephalic appendages, two long earlike lobes that project forward from the front of the head. The cephalic appendages are partly curled and direct a current of water towards the mouth during feeding operations.

Manta rays have very tiny teeth in a narrow band in their jaws, and these teeth probably are nonfunctionable. Their food, which consists largely of planktonic crustaceans, is strained from the current of water directed by the cephalic lobes into their mouths. Their gill arches are supplied with sievelike strainers for removing their planktonic food.

Swimming movements are typical for all manta rays. The exposed tips of the pectoral fins curve upward and outward as the big ray moves along the surface of the sea. Manta rays show little or no fear of men or boats.

Recent studies of manta rays indicate there are several species occurring in the various oceans.

The present opinion of ichthyologists is that *Manta birostris* occupies the tropical western Atlantic, *Manta hamiltoni* the eastern tropical Pacific, and *Manta alfredi* the western tropical Pacific, including the Indo-Australian region.

These species are distinguished by differences in the color pattern and shape. All three kinds have the white shoulder patches. The problem of determining the different kinds is not a simple one because of the large size of this fish and difficulty of preserving specimens in museums.

Mantas from 10 to 18 feet between "wing tips" are common sizes. One specimen off Panama in the Pacific measured 18½ feet across the disk and weighed 2,310 pounds. It contained an embryo 45 inches wide, weighing 28 pounds.

In spite of this large size, manta rays are harmless creatures, avoiding dangers. But when harpooned they may upset small boats, because of their large size and long endurance, and the sport of harpooning them (pages 189-195) is one of the more dangerous deep-sea diversions. The great size of the fish and its violent thrashing, however, are not matched by a predatory or aggressive nature.

Devilfishing in the Gulf Stream

By John Oliver La Gorce

W HAT the rolling prairie of the Far West was to the buffalo in the olden days, when it roamed in countless thousands to and fro in search of seasonal pastures and salt, the ever-rolling Gulf Stream— that mysterious mighty, warm river which parallels the east coast of Florida—is to the fish legions of our semitropical seas.

Few fishermen realize that there are found in the Atlantic Ocean offshore between Miami and Key West some hundreds of varieties of fish—a grand total which constitutes about one-tenth of the entire marine fauna of the American Continent.

Unrelated Monsters of the Deep

To describe in detail the amazing variety of marine life along the Florida east coast would overflow a 5-foot shelf, and I shall venture into no such survey but confine myself to the experience of our party in hunting and capturing a manta or devilfish, one of the largest specimens taken in American waters in many years.

The devilfish and the octopus are frequently confused, whereas they belong to entirely different marine families. Indeed, their only association is in the fact that they live in the same waters! The devilfish, or *Manta birostris* of science, belongs to the giant ray family. It is a huge batlike creature which uses its powerful body propellers as a bird employs its wings in flying, with a waving, undulating motion that drives it along beneath the water at a remarkable pace.

Aside from its immense "wingspread," the outstanding feature of the devilfish, and the one from which it derives its satanic name, are the lobes, or, as they are sometimes termed, cephalic fins, which extend outward and upward from each side of its flat head like huge animated horns.

In the adult fish the paddlelike head fins are from 3 to 4 feet in length and from about 6 to 10 inches wide. Nature has fashioned them of a leathery muscle tissue which spells strength in every ounce.

When the giant ray dashes into a school of fish, the head fins are of great assistance in obtaining food. Like the arms of a boxer, they are in constant motion, whirling about and sweeping living prey into a yard-wide mouth with amazing facility as the giant hurls its body about in its natural element.

The remarkable strength and twisting movements of the head fins are responsible for the legends of this fish in olden times as a menace to mankind, whereas, unless attacked and in panic, the huge sea bat seeks to harm no one in going about on its "lawful occasions."

As a matter of fact, there have been reports of the devilfish's running foul of a ship's anchor chain. True to instinct, it clasps the chain by wrapping its tenacula arms about it, applies its tremendous strength, lifts the heavy anchor, and starts away with anchor, chain, and ship, to the amazement and terror of the crew. They cannot believe their eyes as their vessel suddenly begins to move through the water without a sail set or an engine's turning, when a moment before it was quietly moored to the ocean floor!

The octopus, although sometimes termed "devilfish," is of a different family entirely, an invertebrate, of the typical group of cephalopods—in simple words, the highest class of Mollusca, in which squids, cuttlefish, and octopuses are known.

In appearance the octopus is most repulsive. Its large, ugly head is topped with two diabolical eyes set close together. The fierce-looking mouth, armed with powerful horny jaws and shaped much like a parrot's beak, is also an object of terror. The grotesque head is mounted on a somewhat oval body from which radiate eight arms, usually united at the body base by a tough membrane. The arms, or tentacles, are provided with rows of disclike suckers with which it seizes and clings to its prey with uncanny tenacity.

Generally speaking, it will not give battle to man unless angered or injured, but when challenged will fight to the last, doing its best to pull its victim beneath the surface.

The Start for the Hunting Grounds

From the beaches of South Florida the run across the Gulf Stream to the nearest islands of the Bahamas is about 50 miles. We started from Miami Beach one afternoon, aboard the seagoing motor yacht *L'Apache,* with a 25-foot motor-driven fishing boat in tow bobbing along behind.

In the party of fishermen were the late

John Oliver La Gorce

A Giant Devilfish Tows Three Men in a Motorboat

This immense member of the manta, or ray family measured 22 feet from fin to fin and weighed more than 3,000 pounds. When photographed in the Gulf Stream off Bimini, it was towing the loaded 25-foot fishing cruiser at motor speed! The monsters are taken with harpoons, but the three in this one were not enough. A high-power rifle gave the *coup de grâce* after the fish had fought five hours, playing tugboat to the anglers over miles of open ocean.

James A. Allison, Capt. Charles H. Thompson, of Miami, an authority on the fish of the warm seas; Commodore Charles W. Kotcher, A. G. Batchelder, Carl G. Fisher, and the writer.

Favored by the northeastward surge of the ever-moving Gulf Stream, we made fine progress, and about dark cast anchor in the harbor of Bimini, the tiny island resting like a jeweled feather on a summer sea, the westernmost outrider of the Bahama group.

It was then an out-of-the-world spot peopled by Bahama negro families, who eked out a precarious existence by fishing, gathering conch shells, sponges, and, in a small way, cultivating sisal, a fibrous plant from which rope is made.

Of late years Bimini has bloomed and to-day affords several small but comfortable hotels, a fishing club, a few charming modern residences and shops, and the Lerner Marine Laboratory. There are seaplane connections with Miami Beach and to nearby beautiful Cat Cay.

Bimini annually attracts an increasing number of big game fishermen from the United States and Europe to hunt and capture the heavyweight fighters of the warm seas. The widely publicized fishing tournaments staged here and at Cat Cay annually produce new record catches of giant blue marlin, tuna, and such other varieties as fishermen dream of.

As we approached the island, a mile or two offshore, the clarity of the water permitted glimpses of the amazing marine gardens some 50 feet below the surface.

Because of the sand bottom and the glorious blue of the sky, together with the tropical sunlight and the changing cloud effects, the bewildering gradations of color to be seen in these waters challenge the skill of the artist, although he paint with the brush of genius.

For Years the Sea Fed the Biminites

For many generations the sea furnished most of the food for the native Biminites of ebon hue. They supplemented their meager larder, however, by raising indifferent patches of corn and peas and getting a few other such staples as fresh vegetables, flour, tea and salt meats when a supply boat arrived periodically from Nassau, 130 miles away.

Conch, the marine animal which inhabits the beautiful spiral shell, was then a staple article of food, of which the island folk consumed thousands each year. It was easily gathered from near-by tidal sand banks and made into chowder or eaten raw.

After we had received the official call of the Crown's representative, we had visits alongside from small shore boats, manned by dusky merchants. Each hopeful tradesman, with an ingratiating grin, offered for sale varieties of sponges, brilliantly colored conch shells, sea beans, and tortoise shell. The latter is obtained from the hawksbill turtle, frequently taken in Bahama waters.

It was like pulling teeth to go below and leave the beauty of the tropical night, with the soft, cooling touch of the ever-blowing trade wind, the shadowy grace of the coconut palms swaying and whispering in the moonlight on the near-by beach, while the surf, grounding upon the coral strand of the outer harbor, lulled with its crooning obbligato.

But wiser heads spoke of the need of a good night's rest to prepare for the battle royal which we hoped was in the offing. We regretfully turned in instead of having a try at the tarpon which could be heard jumping and rolling like playful puppies on the harbor surface a few hundred yards astern.

At sunrise next morning all hands turned out ready for the hunt. Our cook soon had a hot breakfast ready, after which we piled aboard our motor-driven fishing boat, upon which rods, lines, and harpoon gear had been made ready.

Making a course to sea out through the island channel, all save the steersman hung over the side to enjoy the amazing sights in the deep tidal pools. One would excitedly point to a squad of six or eight big tarpon lazily wallowing about far below, masters of their element, unafraid, and therefore ready to give running battle to anything except, perhaps, a tiger shark.

The Channel a Natural Aquarium

Another startled shipmate would call out that a 10-foot hammerhead or a nurse shark was rolling an eye at him from the harbor floor. Still another inland fisherman wanted to jump down among a school of hundreds of large and small mangrove snappers busily

191

Anthony V. Ragusin

"Say Ahhh!"

This youngster's head is dwarfed as he peers into the "jet scoop" mouth of a giant ray, or devilfish, hauled up on a Biloxi, Mississippi dock.

parading up and down a long stretch of coral shelf which afforded them instant hiding places upon the sudden appearance of hungry enemies. The clear water made the harbor channel a natural aquarium.

Over the bar and outside all hands were soon scanning the heaving swell of the Gulf Stream for big game, like the crew of a destroyer peeling their eyes for a periscope in a wartime danger zone.

Oddly enough, the noise of a propeller seldom frightens the large fish of the warm seas. If they are attracted by the trolling bait or are not disturbed by the approach of a natural enemy below water, one can not only get close up but will have little difficulty in keeping some of the surface-hunting fish in sight, once they are located and something of their habits is known.

After a bit, Captain Thompson called attention to a long, dark shadow not far below the surface, and the boat was turned toward the first sign of a quarry. It turned out to be a herring hog, a large species of porpoise. It was an adult about 7 feet long and weighed

Frightened Rays Take to the Air

Rays, or devilfish, when frightened, sometimes leap clear of the water, coming back to the surface with a deafening smack. The big fellow at top is taking the air off Cabo Blanco, Peru.

The remarkable shot of three rays jumping in formation was made by National Geographic Photographer Luis Marden off Panama.

Rays are batlike creatures that use their powerful body propellers as a bird employs wings in flying, driving through the water at high speed with a waving, undulating motion.

Despite legends to the contrary, most rays are comparatively harmless and will not attack man.

Top: Alfred C. Glassell, Jr.

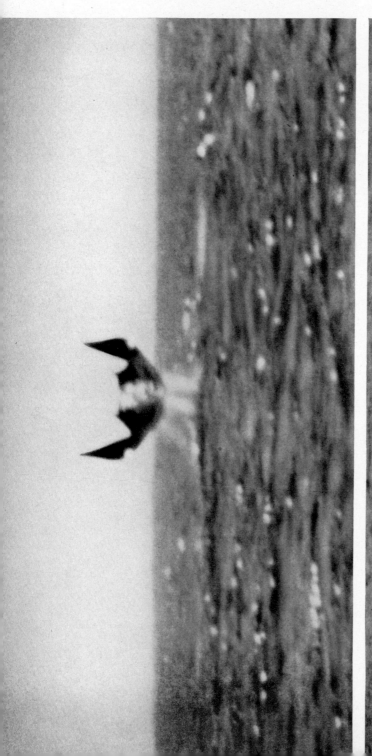

The Battle Over, a Cruiser Tows a Defeated Giant Ray into Pascagoula, Mississippi

One of the thrills of fishing is to be in a boat towed by a giant devilfish. This 20-foot monster pulled the boat and fishermen for miles through the Gulf of Mexico before the harpoons dispatched him.

Elmer Gautier

193

Luis Marden, National Geographic Staff

A Sting Ray, Trailing a Barbed Tail, Flaps Up to Be Fed

Rays, relatives of sharks and sawfish, prefer to lie concealed on the sea bottom. Waders may be painfully stabbed by a six-inch bony spear carried near the base of the whiplike tail. In the warm seas, rays feed on mollusks and crustaceans. This captive in the Lerner Marine Laboratory pens at Bimini today takes fish from the attendant's hands.

by Captain Thompson on the surface of the water about a quarter of a mile away. It was thought to be either a leopard shark, a killer whale or a battle royal between two big denizens of the deep. Anything can be expected in those waters!

The Real Business of the Day

It was our business, however, to have ringside seats at this battle, whatever it was. All hands then took hold of the harpoon line. Reversing the engine—not a very sportsmanlike procedure but decidedly effective in checking the porpoise—we brought him alongside without further loss of time, dispatched him, then turned our attention to the mystery now close at hand.

We were all excited at the thought of perhaps getting a harpoon into a big leopard shark, which will fight any and everything that swims, and, according to authorities on marine life, is one of several members of the shark family dangerous to man while in the water.

around 400 pounds. As this species destroys great quantities of food fish, we went for it with a harpoon.

When the proper position to strike was reached, a hand harpoon was thrown, which found its mark. Away the herring hog went at a fast clip. One of the less experienced fishermen of the party, who rated a little hazing, was given the harpoon line with orders to bring the big fellow alongside forthwith, and further advised to "keep the herring hog's head up and not let him drown!" The rest of us sat back to enjoy his strenuous but futile efforts to obey!

About twenty minutes after the strike, while the herring hog was still demonstrating no signs of tiring, a disturbance was observed

Our excitement was increased when suddenly Captain Thompson, who, having uncanny eyesight plus long experience with subsea life, suddenly exclaimed: "Stand by, men! It's the biggest devilfish I've ever seen!"

As we quietly circled near, it seemed to me that a big patch of the ocean floor was suddenly dark and moving off. I saw in the translucent depths a gigantic shadow which had the appearance of a prehistoric bird flapping its wings as it "flew" slowly along.

While we were coming up to the fish, which was evidently swallowing something it had killed and was paying no attention to anything else, the gear which we had used in harpooning the herring hog was made ready for action. At the right instant Captain Thompson let fly, and then things began to happen sure enough!

Not a man of us in the boat was ready for the extraordinary events that followed. The devilfish came topside as if hurled by a submarine explosion. One of its great curling, batlike fins flashed out, sending gallons of water over us and splintering the harpoon pole against the boat's side as if it had been a match stem. Then one of its 10-foot pectoral wings struck the water with a terrific impact, making a noise which might have been heard a mile away.

For a moment the monster seemed bewildered. That lost moment cost it dear, for the pause enabled us to throw another harpoon, which struck deep into its body. Away it started, taking our harpoon lines out at a pace which made us apprehensive, although a moment before we had thought there was a wide margin of line. All hands put their weight on the lines, and, as the boat was by this time moving on a more even keel, we took a wrap around a bow cleat and started for the horizon—giant fish, boat, and crew!

The Monster Lifts the Launch

Several times the devilfish hurled itself out of the water, and its huge body would come down with a crash like the explosion of a depth charge. Now and then it would sound for deep water in an effort to shake us off, and our lines paid out so near the ends that Thompson stood by with a hatchet to cut them in the event the bow should be drawn dangerously under water. This came uncomfortably near to happening more than once.

All of a sudden the lines slackened, and we frantically hauled in as the monster turned and dashed toward us, coming up almost, but not quite under our craft. Its great bulk lifted one side of the heavy launch well out of water and gave us a pretty stiff scare.

Captain Thompson let drive another harpoon, which found lodgment. Away it dashed again. With three harpoon lines, one in each side of the body, and another near the head, it was possible at times to drive the monster as one would a runaway horse, swerving it toward the shore of Bimini and into more shallow water by the process of pulling first on one line and then on the other.

The 3,000-pound Fighter Finally Tires

By this time the devilfish had towed us for several miles, and although losing blood, it was still going strong. Our next experiment was to throw out the anchor in the hope that this maneuver might further slow things up. But this expedient made little difference to the giant, for it continued to pull us along as if our heavy boat was but a birch canoe.

After an hour or so, during which the devilfish alternated between trying to pull the bow under water by a "power dive" or suddenly turning and endeavoring to come up under us, we maneuvered into more shallow water. The anchor began to take hold, and our giant became a little more amenable to reason, so that a number of times we were able to haul in slack and recoil our lines. Eventually we approached within 20 or 30 feet of the creature as it propelled itself along with its 12-foot wings, a little less powerful in stroke and somewhat slower.

These photographs, because of the refraction of light in the water, do not give a clear idea of this fellow's size. Therefore, it is somewhat hard to realize that our captive measured 22 feet across from the tip of one pectoral fin to the other and 17 feet 1 inch from the head to the end of its tail. It weighed more than 3,000 pounds.

Victory after Hours of Battle

Luckily, about this time a fast-sailing island sponge boat approached to see what the excitement was all about. We managed to make the spongers understand that we wanted them to go back to our yacht and bring us a rifle.

After another hour of skirmishing, the yacht's motor-driven dory came tearing out with an express rifle, and we were able to give our gallant foe the *coup de grâce*. Our use of a bullet to quiet the devilfish perhaps was not sporting, but under the circumstances it was the only solution of our problem.

Until then none of us was aware that nearly five hours had elapsed since we first tackled this Jumbo of the deep.

The Bimini fisherfolk were greatly interested in the capture, for devilfish were seldom seen close up, much less captured, thereabouts.

Nearly Wrecks the Wharf

By bringing into play a heavy block and tackle used for hoisting cargoes of sisal fiber, and after much breaking of ropes, fearing all the while, too, lest the then none-too-strong wharf collapse under the great weight of the fish, we finally succeeded in getting most of its body out of water so that it could be photographed and weighed on a large sisal scale. The limit of this scale was 3,000 pounds, and this was all we claimed for the fish, although we judged it weighed 4,000 or more.

It was a grand battle, full of thrills for each of us, although a little tough on the devilfish. We wanted the monster for scientific study, and upon our return to Miami it was mounted by a skilled taxidermist and exhibited in the then Allison Aquarium at Miami Beach.

© John Mahony

An Atlantic Sailfish Twists and Turns in an Aquatic Ballet

This big sail's jumping tactics show why his species is a favorite with deep sea anglers the world over. The giant dorsal fin from which the sailfish gets its name is here furled in a slot along the jumper's back.

Certain Citizens of the Warm Seas

By Louis L. Mowbray

Former Curator, Bermuda Government Aquarium

(Revised 1952 by L. S. Mowbray)

MAN'S most terrific wars against his fellows have some respite; they are but cataclysms in world history. But the battle of fish against fish, savage and to the death, is never-ending.

Along the edges of the warm waters of the Gulf Stream off Florida and the Bahamas, where in calm weather the lazy waves of the surface seem to symbolize peace, there is, nevertheless, a war among the finny legions below that never ends.

The battle for survival in the seas takes many forms and embraces many living things, from those of microscopic size to the largest of whales—the most enormous creatures on the face of the globe. The lowly plankton (pages 308-324)—the tiny animal and plant life which is carried within the ocean currents —is preyed upon by countless millions of fishes. Most numerous of the plankton hunters are menhaden and herring, though the principal food of the world's largest fish, the whale shark, is also this nutritious dish. However, it appears that even the patience of these usually harmless organisms can become exhausted at times, and they gang up and strike back at their oppressors.

Certain conditions make possible the abnormal reproduction of billions of microscopic organisms quite suddenly, though at long and irregular intervals. On occasion, these terrific concentrations of bodies in the sea have a catastrophic effect on the fauna in that particular area. This was true in the localities of Naples, Fort Myers, and Sanibel Island off the west coast of Florida, covering the period from November, 1946, to August, 1947.

A tiny protozoan, about one-thousandth of an inch in diameter in size, now known scientifically as *Gymnodinium brevis* (Davis), occurred in such vast numbers as to become visible in large brownish-red patches. Later it became famous throughout fishing circles as the "red tide." Such quantities of these tiny creatures were grouped together that the patches of "discolored water" were literally slimy. As this particular species is toxic in its effect, millions of food and game fishes perished as a result.

Scientists at the University of Miami Marine Laboratory have estimated that approximately 500,000,000 fish were killed during this period. Fortunately, no large concentrations of these protozoa have been observed since that year.

In 1882, vessels arriving at northeastern ports had steamed through miles of dead tilefish (page 27), an important food fish which inhabits the depths along the edge of the Gulf Stream. From the accounts received it was estimated that an area approximating 7,500 square miles was thickly strewn with the dead and dying of this species.

Wholesale Death Struck Gulf Stream Fish

Various reasons were advanced as to the cause of this gigantic marine tragedy. The most plausible was that a sudden influx of a cold current along the western edge of the Gulf Stream proved fatal to these warm-water fish. Had other species been affected, an earlier parallel to the "red tide" could have been suspected, but this was not the case. For several years it appeared that tilefish had been almost totally destroyed in those localities, but eventually they were rediscovered in great numbers in their former habitat. These examples show dramatically how Nature maintains a balance.

Nature has also devised many ways of protecting particular forms of life in the seas. Some are automatically protected by their size, like the sharks, rays, porpoises, and whales. Others, like the mackerels, tunas, and wahoos, are usually safe in their great speed. However, the many hundreds of other species of fishes must rely on their wiles or coloration to assist in their survival.

Most curious of all is the angler fish, which actually possesses a fishing rod. This strange fish is not equipped with fins for rapid movement or for swimming any great distance. Through lack of use, the tail has degenerated somewhat. The habit of slowly stalking its prey has modified the pectoral, or side, fins into little "hands" and the ventral fins into little "feet."

The approach of an angler fish to its chosen

A Huge Bluefin Tuna Is Brought Aboard

Each year fishermen flock to Wedgeport, Nova Scotia, to compete in the International Tuna Cup Match. This 600-pounder was taken by Captain Thorvald Sanchez of the Habana, Cuba, team in tournament competition.

victim is a lesson in patience, and its use of the "fishing rod" is a work of art.

Literally, there is an appendage, which may be raised or lowered at will, situated on the head of the angler fish between the eyes and the mouth. At the outer extremity of the rod is a filamentous growth, resembling a small worm, which is dangled frantically in front of a small fish to attract its attention. During this period the remainder of the body of the angler remains completely immobile.

If the attempt to attract the prey fails, then the stalk begins. It may be accomplished so inconspicuously that it may move only an inch or two in several minutes. Invariably the smaller fish are attracted closer by the moving "bait," and frequently the angler fish has to withdraw it rapidly to prevent damage. When the victim is enticed sufficiently close, the angler's huge mouth can suck it in from several inches away. In the anglers from the very deep sea the "bait" is luminous.

Old wrecks afford a partial refuge to myriads of the young of larger fish. In consequence, many species gather at these spots either for protection or to feed on the others. Well knowing this, the fishermen of Bermuda often create new fishing grounds simply by sinking old hulks in places easily accessible in all kinds of weather.

Still other fish take advantage of the protection afforded by larger species. The shark

A Pair of Heavyweight Scrappers

The retired, undefeated World heavyweight boxing champion, Captain Gene Tunney, USNR, loves sport fishing and annually makes the pilgrimage to Wedgeport, Nova Scotia, for the giant bluefin tuna run.

Richard B. Hoit

Teeth Like Knives Gave Cutlassfish Its Name

This form of cutlassfish, with its alarming expression, is called the hairtail. It is one of the strangest inhabitants of the open sea and is seldom taken by collectors or fishermen. When one is caught, it is often mistaken for a sea serpent because its greatly elongated body terminates in a hairlike tail.

sucker (page 231) holds on to sharks with a sucking disc on the top of its head.

A beautiful little red fish, known as amia, lives with the animal within the shell of a large West Indian conch (pronounced "conk"). While finding protection there, this little fish carries its eggs in its mouth!

Man Joins the Battle of the Sea

Into the battle of the many species in the sea steps man, who looks to the sea for food, recreation, and other benefits. Commercial enterprises extract millions upon millions of tons of marine products from the sea each year, to be used for human consumption or for such products as glue and fertilizer.

The sportsman also takes his share, though on a much smaller scale. Many of the followers of Izaak Walton fish entirely for pleasure and release their large fighting catch alive, to grow and fight another day. Others fish for the fun of it and for the opportunity of obtaining a choice dish for the table.

Regardless of the more complicated phases of fishing, the sport as a whole has great appeal to most people. It affords a wonderful opportunity for relaxation and exercise, or it can provide terrific excitement, depending upon the species sought and the locality fished.

Who has failed to be thrilled at the spectacle of a huge marlin leaping to free the hook from its mouth, or the sight of fast-diminishing line on the reel when a tuna or wahoo strips it off? Those who have not been fortunate enough to have watched a large tarpon take a streamer fly, plug, or bait really have something to look forward to.

All the excitement is not confined to the hooking of the fish. Marlin have been known to attack a boat on rare occasions, and when that happens it is every man for himself. A slashing marlin is a dangerous customer to attempt to subdue. Of greater frequency, and no less dangerous to the angler and guide, is the occurrence of a large tarpon leaping clear of the water to free the hook and landing in the boat or canoe in the process. Pandemonium, broken rods, smashed planks, and possibly fractured limbs result.

Tarpon fishing (pages 277-283) is a thrilling sport, provided that the angler is prepared to hook ten in order to land one. The tarpon can usually be induced to bite or strike a lure, but the hard bony mouth makes it difficult to set a hook, and it is usual for the fish to throw it clear the first or second jump.

Tarpon grow to over 240 pounds in weight and put up a wonderful fight in open water. However, as they are not considered good food, by far an ever-increasing percentage are set free by real sportsmen at the end of the battle. Many are kept as trophies, of course, and the huge silver scales which cover the entire body of the fish are distributed among friends as souvenirs. Tarpon have larger scales than any other flat-scaled fish, some measuring as much as four inches in diameter.

Huge Marlin Weighed a Ton

To encounter the really large game fish, it is often necessary to venture beyond the shallow bays and rivers into the open sea. There we find the huge marlin, or spearfishes, the broadbill swordfish, and the bluefin tuna. All three of these species have been captured by harpooning in excess of 1,000 pounds in weight. There is reportedly a record of a giant marlin, harpooned in error for a swordfish on or near the Grand Banks, which measured 18½ feet in length. The estimated weight was 2,200 pounds.

The three species of marlin found in the Atlantic are called by the

201

Fourteen Pounds, and All Fight

Dr. Robert Becker, of York, Pennsylvania, had a battle on his hands before he landed this record 14-pound bonefish at Castle Harbour, Bermuda. Pound for pound, the species is rated as tough a fighter as is found in salt water. When taken on December 29, 1950, the 34½-inch beauty above was the largest ever caught in the Atlantic on rod and reel. In Pacific waters the record is 16 pounds.

common names of white marlin, blue marlin, and black marlin. The latter appears to be very rare. The white marlin (page 216) is smaller than the others, but for its size it is a very much gamer fish to catch. Its favorite baits are squid or strip baits. Though found throughout the West Indies, Florida, and Bermuda, concentrations occur in season off Ocean City, Maryland.

The blue marlin is a fish of the deep waters, though it can often be attracted to the surface with a bait rigged to skip along the water, making considerable splash in its progress. This conspicuous movement entices the big fish to investigate, and then the angler often has the opportunity of yelling "Strike!" and

the battle is on. When hooked on rod and reel, the marlin puts on an amazing show, usually fighting on or near the surface.

One of the famous performances of the marlin when hooked, and the one which makes it a popular game fish, is known as "tail walking." The fish rises almost entirely clear of the water and, thrashing its tail the while, covers many yards in this position in an effort to shake the hook from its mouth. Often it will leap clear and splash back into the sea. This maneuver weakens the fish rapidly and may shorten the fight to as little as an hour on a 400-pound fish, though the battle will often last four or five hours.

The marlins, sailfishes, and swordfish have a somewhat long bill or spear protruding from

202

Porpoises Seem to Laugh with Glee as They Snap Up Mullet near St. Augustine, Florida

Porpoises pursue the mullet in shallow water near shore and dextrously catch the frantic prey as it jumps into the air. They belong to the same group as whales. Frequently, schools of porpoises hunting food in long lines patrol miles of open water offshore and clean it of fish for days.

Tuna by the Ton, Caught in Eight Days by a Single Fisherman, Hangs High at Wedgeport, Nova Scotia Dock

Dr. Michael Lerner of New York and Bimini, President of the International Game Fish Association, stands holding the rod with which he captured the 21 giant bluefins weighing a total of 3,677 pounds. Mrs. Helen Lerner, likewise a master fisherman, has numerous records to her skill and credit.

203

Union of South Africa Information Office

This "Fossil" Was Taken Alive in South Africa

The "East London" fish *(Latimeria chalumnae)*, belonging to the Coelacanth group, believed to be extinct before the end of the Mesozoic epoch some 50 million years ago, was captured in South African waters in one of the most startling discoveries of "living fossils" ever made. Apparent unusual characteristics of this fish are its scaling, its curious tail, the long fins—almost like limbs carrying fin rays, and the pair of bony plates under the floor of the mouth. This mounted specimen is five feet long.

the upper jaw; hence the name of the former of spearfish or marlinspike fish (shortened to marlin). The bills of the marlin and sailfish are rounded, but that of the swordfish is flattened considerably, giving it the appearance of its name—broadbill swordfish (page 217).

Few broadbills are captured by rod and reel in the Atlantic, though many are taken annually off the coast of Chile by this method. All the swordfish found in the markets of North America have been harpooned. There are many boats and men solely employed in the capture of these huge and delectable fish, because their flesh brings high market prices.

The sailfish (page 215) is more beautiful than the other billfish, though it is not quite the same game fighter. Its name is derived from the abnormally large saillike dorsal fin. More sailfish are caught off the stretch of water between Bakers Haulover, Miami Beach, and Stuart, Florida, on the edge of the Gulf Stream than in any other part of the world. Fortunately, the trend now is to release all sailfish alive unless the angler requires the fish for a trophy. In this way the species will not become fished out from that area.

Tuna Fight for 12 Hours

In the Pacific, the sailfish grow much larger and are better fighters. The largest approach the 300-pound mark in weight. The waters of the Galápagos Islands and off the port of Acapulco, Mexico, are the "hot spots" for these giants.

Far more numerous than the billfishes are the tunas. Better known than any is the giant bluefin tuna (page 212), which reaches a weight of 1,500 pounds or more. These huge gamesters are sought after the world over for food and for sport, though in catching a really large one there is far more work than fun. Battles with these warriors have lasted for more than 12 hours without the fish being finally brought to gaff!

Pliny, in the first century after Christ, relates that the multitude of tuna which met the fleet of Alexander the Great on one occasion was so vast that, only by advancing in battle line, as on an enemy, were the ships able to cut their way through the school. Long before the days of Christ the regular appearances of these tunas were known in the Mediterranean Sea. Yet in spite of that, and the fact that they still appear regularly on certain dates in many parts of the world, little more of their habits or whereabouts during the "disappearing" season is known now than 2,000 years ago.

Each year in mid-May, hundreds of the huge bluefin tuna migrate along the eastern edge of the Gulf Stream past the Bahamas. Some apparently come through the Caribbean Sea and around the west end of Cuba, and

Painting by Hashime Murayama

The Fast, Wily Bonefish Is Hard to Land

BELONGING to the family of ladyfishes, Albulidae, members of which range in all warm seas, bonefish (*Albula vulpes*) is related to the herring family, Clupeidae, and to the tarpons, family Elopidae. This species ranges along the sandy shores of all tropical seas.

The bonefish is not strikingly colored. It is mostly silvery, a little grayish dorsally and whitish ventrally. The characteristics that distinguish this species are the sleek streamline form, wariness and the unusual strength and agility. It is capable of swimming at tremendous velocity.

Bonefish occur in shallow waters, over sandy bottoms or over muddy bottoms. Among the Florida Keys, in the Bahama Islands and in Bermuda, bonefish are reported as abundant. On the west coast, they occur along the shores of southern California.

The bonefish is highly esteemed by sportsmen in Florida and in southern California. It is generally known as "one of the gamest fish that swims." Wily, vigorous, and tireless, its scientific name means "whitish fox."

The most successful baits for this fish are the segmented sea worms, the pileworms found among mussels and barnacles on wharf piles, and pieces of conch and hermit crabs. The latter live in the discarded shells of snails, using the shell as a house. However, to capture a bonefish requires skill and patience; the slightest disturbance or ripple startles this species, and it is lost to the sports fisherman.

The breeding habits of the bonefish are little known. After hatching from the egg, the larva passes through the leptocephalid stage, when it becomes a narrow transparent ribbonlike fish a few inches long.

At a length of an inch, the leptocephalid larva of *Albula* have six dark spots along the lateral line, six median spots above them, five dark saddles dividing the interspaces equally and other dark spots below the lateral line. At a length of two inches, a little black pigment appears along the outer rays of the caudal fin and along the side of the belly.

The bonefish does not appear in the markets of the United States. Although it is a good food fish, its flesh, similar to the shad and other herringlike fishes, contains innumerable small bones, hence its name.

This species averages about a foot to a foot and a half in length. The maximum length so far recorded is 38 inches and the maximum weight is 16 pounds.

Unlike its relatives, the herrings, the bonefish is not given to appearing in large schools. It is a bottom feeder, and its mouth is small and inferior under a piglike snout.

Bonefish feed largely on crabs, shrimps and worms, and can sometimes be spotted by fishermen by the mud they stir up as they grub for food on the bottom.

The speed and wariness of the bonefish make it one of the most challenging contestants for experienced anglers and also one of the most rewarding catches when landed.

206

An Aristocrat among Small Southern Fishes Is Sometimes Called Reef King

A MEMBER of the snapper family, Lutjanidae, the **muttonfish** *(Lutjanus analis)* ranges in the western Atlantic from Florida, the West Indies, and Gulf of Mexico southward to Brazil. During the summer when the warm Gulf current moves northward to Woods Hole, Massachusetts, it wanders that far north occasionally.

The muttonfish has several close relatives in American seas, most important of which are the **gray, or mangrove, snapper,** *Lutjanus griseus;* the **schoolmaster,** *L. apodus;* the **dog snapper,** *L. jocu;* and the **red snapper,** *L. blackfordii.*

This species is variable in coloration. The back may be dark olive-green, and the scales with light-blue spots form irregular oblique streaks in the young. In the large adults the blue spots disappear, the undersides become whitish or tinted with reddish, the head is bronze-olive, darker dorsally, a broad pearly streak extends from snout below eye to upper edge of the gill cover, and a narrow blue streak from eye to nostrils. The eye is bright red, and so are the pectoral, pelvic, caudal, and anal fins. The caudal is margined with black; the dorsal fin is yellowish. The black spot on the upper side is characteristic for this and a few other species of snappers.

The late Dr. W. H. Longley noted that muttonfish 12 to 14 inches long, when resting on the bottom, were invariably vertically barred, whether with or without cover, and when swimming changed to a pattern of oblique streaks. A large individual 18 inches long, it was observed, changed from the dark barred color phase to one of very faintly indicated bars when it started to swim.

This common species in the Florida Keys is a predaceous and carnivorous fish, feeding on small fishes such as grunts and on shrimp and crabs. It is a nocturnal feeder, like its relatives the gray snapper and the schoolmaster.

The life history has never been fully studied, but observations indicate that spawning occurs in the summer.

This snapper is a valuable food and game fish. It is taken by hook promptly when baited with small fishes, crabs, or cut bait. It should be fished for on rocky bottoms in about three to nine fathoms. When caught, it puts up a fair fight.

The muttonfish is of commercial importance. The U. S. Fish and Wildlife Service latest statistical report indicates a catch of 253,000 pounds valued at $44,000. Although the species averages only four or five pounds, it reaches a maximum weight of 25 pounds and a length of 27 inches.

Snappers in general comprise a large family of which there are several species. All of them derive their common name from large and quick mouths, and most of them also have fine, sharp teeth. Most snappers are schooling fishes in habit, but the muttonfish is an exception and schools only seasonally in some places and, in others, not at all.

Among fishermen the muttonfish, like other snappers, has a reputation for craftiness and for a darting, snatching response to bait, requiring alertness from the angler.

207

Grunts Probably Produced Shipwrecking "Song of the Sirens"

CLOSELY related to the snapper family are the grunts, which are named for their ability to make a grunting noise by grating their teeth. Most of the members of this large and widespread family are good food fish and are characterized by bright colors. Most of them also have large red or orange mouths.

The **margate fish,** *Haemulon album,* is one of the larger grunts. It has reached a length of over two feet and a weight of ten pounds, but averages one to two pounds. It ranges in abundance from Florida and the West Indies to Brazil, occasionally straying a little northward. This species has several very close relatives in the western Atlantic in the same genus, such as the bluestriped grunt (page 230), white grunt, and the ronco, or sailor's-choice.

The margate fish prefers to live around coral stacks, in gorgonian patches over rocky bottoms, and in old shipwrecks. This grunt, like the other members of the genus, feeds almost wholly at night and reaches two feet in length. The stomachs of specimens taken in the morning are usually filled with algae, mollusks, and marine worms. They also feed on small fishes and crustaceans, sometimes on jellyfishes.

The grunts are important not only as food but for their ability to produce sound. During World War II, subsurface listening devices developed for detection of surface craft, submarines, and the presence of mines also revealed a complicated background noise not attributable to ship traffic or activity ashore. Much of this noise was of biological origin, caused by grunts and other fishes. Subsurface listeners, as reported by Marie P. Fish, described these unidentifiable noises as from a mild beeping, clicking, hoarse croaking, crackling, and whistling to a grunting, hammering, and moaning noise, as well as mewing and a staccato tapping. Sometimes the noises sounded like coal rolling down a chute into a basement or the dragging of heavy chains.

Mrs. Fish stated that "Early in the nineteenth century at the mouth of the River Cambodia, Cochin China, Lieutenant John White of the U. S. Navy (1824) reported extraordinary sounds originating below his ship, imaginatively compared to the united efforts of a deep-toned organ, jingling bells, a guttural frog, and an enormous harp. The natives assured him that the melee of sound was produced by fishes."

No doubt the "Song of the Sirens" was produced by fishes and, if followed by a ship, might well lead to disaster, since some sound-producing fishes are in shoal waters. The loud rasping croak of the grunt may be produced under water or in the air. Martin Burkenroad held the mouth open of adult grunts and could see the upper and lower pharyngeal teeth rubbing together and producing noise. When he placed a cloth between the pharyngeal teeth of a living grunt, it no longer was able to produce noise.

The margate fish is a better game fish than most grunts. It often can get away with the bait, leaving the hook clean. The annual commercial catch of grunts is some 160,000 pounds.

Painting by Hashime Murayama

High-browed Lookdown Is Iridescent Beauty

THE lookdown (*Selene vomer*) and the moonfish (*Vomer setapinnis*), family Carangidae, look very much alike and are often mistaken in identity. Both species range from Cape Cod to Uruguay, but are common only south of Chesapeake Bay.

They may be recognized by their vertical "forehead" and deep compressed bodies, as well as their narrow tube-shaped caudal peduncle and deeply forked caudal fin.

The lookdown differs from the moonfish in completely lacking scaly scutes on the lateral line and having the first soft rays of dorsal and anal fins greatly elongated.

Selene vomer has two close relatives in the eastern Pacific: *S. brevoostii* and *S. oerstedii*; whereas *Vomer setapinnis* has but one: *V. declivifrons*.

When alive, the lookdown is bluish green, shading into bright silvery on the sides, and the back is dusky; the caudal fin is yellowish and produced rays, dusky. Its iridescence is considerable, reflecting a variety of colors.

Selene vomer should rightfully be called the moonfish, since the generic name, *Selene*, is a Greek word for the moon. However, since the word "moonfish" makes a better market name, it is currently applied to *Vomer setapinnis*.

The young of the lookdown are noted for their different appearance when compared with adults. The spiny dorsal fin in the young has the first spines greatly elongated, with long, fine threads several times longer than their owner. The body is covered with large, dark spots. As the lookdown grows, the dorsal spines become very short, and the dark spots disappear.

The lookdown is more of an open-water species than a reef inhabitant. It feeds on shrimp and other crustaceans, small fishes, and mollusks. Spawning habits are unknown.

An excellent and delicious food fish, the lookdown is rarely seen in the market. It is a small species, reaching a length of a foot and a weight of nearly two pounds, but it averages only seven to eight inches in length and a weight of a half to three-quarters of a pound. Its close relative, *Vomer setapinnis*, grows to the same size and weight, but is abundant enough to appear on the market, since 32,000 pounds were reported for a recent year. But its flesh is not of equal flavor to that of the lookdown.

The lookdown is reported to put up a good fight for a fish of its size. It is often caught near or under bridges, docks, and along the high banks of channels, to which places it goes to find protection.

Small spinning lures and streamer flies will bring eager strikes from the lookdown, which will also respond to live bait such as shrimps or to small cut bait.

In common with most all fishes that are familiar to many people, the lookdown has acquired many names over a period of years. Usually such popular names have been derived from physical attributes. In the case of the lookdown, its exceptionally long face has been responsible for the nicknames horsefish and horsehead. It has also been called bluntnosed shiner and silver moonfish.

The Great Barracuda Strikes Savagely with the Speed of a Torpedo

AS CURRENTLY recognized in a review of the barracudas by Dr. Leonard P. Schultz in his report on the Marshall Island fishes, 21 species are known in the world, and the only species that is circumtropical in distribution is the **great barracuda** (*Sphyraena barracuda*). It ranges in the western Atlantic from Florida and the West Indies to Brazil, and strays northward to Massachusetts in the summer.

It has three close relatives in the Atlantic, and there are three other American species in the eastern Pacific.

The great barracuda occurs wherever other fishes gather, those three to five feet long singly and the smaller ones in schools.

The food of barracuda consists mostly of fishes, although squid are eaten when available. This voracious species can be seen lying near schooling fishes which warily avoid it. At intervals the barracuda will dash suddenly into the school, probably catching a fish.

Barracuda may be caught by trolling. Live bait, a shiny flashing spoon or other artificial lure is used. This habit of attacking light-colored objects has caused the barracuda to attain a bloodthirsty reputation. Should an unwary fish leave its retreat, the barracuda shoots forward with courage and fury, at a speed so fast the eye can scarcely follow it in the water. The victim is caught in the jaws of the barracuda by its large knifelike canine teeth.

The great barracuda reaches a length of six feet and does not hesitate to attack man or fish his equal in size. There are numerous records of barracuda attacks on swimmers. The series of large knifelike teeth along both sides of each jaw make a clean, straight cut. Usually there is but a single strike by a barracuda whereas in attacks by sharks the prey may be completely devoured or badly mutilated by several attacks. The bite by a shark makes a curved edge; the cut by a barracuda is nearly straight.

When trolling in tropical waters, sportsmen commonly catch a fish and before it can be hauled into the boat a barracuda will bite out a chunk or get hooked in its attack on the already caught fish (page 247). Then before it is landed, another barracuda will bite a chunk out of the hooked one.

Barracuda are used for food throughout their range. However, large ones may have poisonous flesh, possibly resulting from the fish feeding on poisonous algae or marine invertebrates or on other fishes that have been feeding on these poisonous organisms.

Barracuda are of commercial importance, especially on the Pacific coast, a recent total annual catch being 2,542,000 pounds.

209

Painting by Hashime Murayama

Painting by Hashime Murayama

© National Geographic Society

Voracious Jacks Sometimes Called Murderers of the Sea

THE amberjack (top—*Seriola fasciata*) is closely related to four other species in the genus: *Seriola lalandi, S. dumerili, S. falcata* and *S. zonata*, all of the Atlantic. The yellow-tail, *Seriola dorsalis*, of the eastern Pacific, is another species. The correct identification of these fishes is very difficult, but a recent revision of them by Isaac Ginsburg indicates that *S. fasciata* loses the blackish streaks through the eye at about a length of a foot and that in other species it disappears at a size of only a few inches.

Amberjacks feed avariciously on fishes, shrimp, other crustaceans and squid. They are considered of some value as food, but are more important as game fishes. They live in bays, inlets, channels, and offshore, where they may be caught by trolling with artificial lure or hook-and-line fishing over the side of a small boat. Chumming them with pieces of mullet gives good results. They will then respond to such live fish bait as pilchard. Seldom approaching shore, the amberjack prefers to frequent depths in excess of 15 feet. They fight with speed and power.

The U. S. commercial catch of all the species of amberjack in the western Atlantic totals only 211,000 pounds. The International Game Fish Association lists as a world record 119 pounds 8 ounces for an amberjack caught in 1952 off Rio de Janeiro, Brazil.

The amberjack is more highly regarded as a game fish than it is as a food fish. However, its flavor when smoked has many devotees.

The **runner** (bottom—*Caranx ruber*) ranges throughout the West Indies and strays northward along the southern United States. It has several close relatives, among which the yellow jack (*Caranx bartholomaei*), the blue runner (*C. crysos*), and the common jack (*C. hippos*) are the most important

The runner inhabits open water. It is swift and restless. Small ones occur in great numbers and are preyed upon by the gulls around Dry Tortugas, Florida. The runner and other jacks are caught by hook-and-line fishing and by trolling with baited hooks or bright artificial lures.

The runner and other jacks are the terror of small fishes. The latter scurry in all directions to avoid the swift rushes of these voracious feeders.

The jacks are of considerable commercial value. Although the runner is not recorded in the United States Fish and Wildlife catch statistics, two other species are: the common jack or crevalle (*C. hippos*) amounted to 545,000 pounds, and the blue runner (*C. crysos*), 1,227,000 pounds.

The runner reaches a length of a little over a foot, whereas the common jack may attain a length of two or three feet and a weight of more than 20 pounds.

Members of the Mackerel Family Contribute Greatly to World Food Supply

BEAUTIFULLY colored, streamlined fishes, the **cero** (top pair—*Scombero-morus regalis*) and the **Spanish mackerel** (bottom—*Scomberomorus macu-latus*), family Scombridae, range in the western Atlantic from Cape Cod to Brazil. A close relative is the king mackerel (*Scomberomorus cavalla*). Inhabitants of the high seas, they are especially abundant in the western tropical Atlantic and Gulf of Mexico. The Spanish mackerel ranges eastward to the African coast.

These fishes occur in enormous schools near the surface of the ocean. During the summer months they appear as far north as Cape Cod. They feed chiefly on fishes and squid.

Spawning occurs offshore during the spring and summer months. The non-adhesive eggs are transparent and buoyant. They hatch in about a day.

Like their close relatives the tunas, the cero and Spanish mackerel have their fins fitting into grooves, thus cutting down resistance when swimming.

They are game fishes of great importance, almost equaling the dolphin for spectacular movements and jumping ability. Trolling with a bright spoon, bait cut from the white belly of a fish or with a small whole fish or squid, attracts them quickly. They strike with power and give a thrilling fight.

These fishes are rated as some of the best-flavored species in Europe and America. The flesh is oily and may vary in color from reddish to pink or whitish. As a pan fish they are excellent.

This group of fishes is of considerable economic value in the United States. They are caught by the fishing fleet, working out of our southern ports. The latest statistics indicate an annual catch for the cero of 2,000 pounds; for the king mackerel, 4,235,000 and for the Spanish mackerel, 9,874,000 pounds.

The International Game Fish Association gives a maximum length of 5 feet, 2 inches, and a weight of 73½ pounds for the king mackerel. The Spanish mackerel reaches a weight of 25 pounds and is the smallest of the local species, since the cero attains a weight of 35 pounds.

Mackerels in general are found all over the world in tropical and temperate oceans and many seas. They are so prolific that, although they are the prey of many other fishes, furnishing an important part of the diet of some, they remain abundant, still supplying a great percentage of the world's fish markets.

The flesh of the various species of mackerel has become a food staple in many areas. Combined with such giants of the family as tuna (pages 212, 213) and albacore (page 225), the amount of fish of the mackerel family consumed everywhere reaches huge amounts.

211

Painting by Hashime Murayama

212

The Ubiquitous Bluefin Tuna Is Consumed Largely after Canning

THIS giant mackerel is the largest member of its family and among the largest of all fishes. The largest **bluefin tuna** (*Thunnus thynnus*) on record, taken off New Jersey, was about 14 feet long and weighed 1,600 pounds. It is on record also that in one season a single fisherman harpooned 30 tuna averaging about 1,000 pounds. Though such enormous fish occasionally are caught, the usual size is well under 250 pounds.

The bluefin tuna is almost world-wide in occurrence, being found on both sides of the Atlantic and the Pacific. In Europe it ranges from Norway to the Mediterranean Sea, and off the African coast to the Cape of Good Hope. On the Atlantic coast of America, it ranges from Newfoundland at least as far as Florida. On the Pacific coast, the bluefin tuna is found from Washington to southern California.

Though the giant fish mentioned were not conquered with rod and reel, a fish weighing 977 pounds was landed off Nova Scotia. The bluefin tuna generally has been considered one of the world's gamest fish.

Sportsmen on the Pacific coast have long sought this "tiger of the California seas." It is only within comparatively recent years, however, that tuna fishing, as a sport, has gained in popularity on the Atlantic coast of America, where the largest fish occur.

Tunas are beasts of prey, and large quantities of food are required for their nourishment. They are a schooling fish, like all their relatives, and feed principally on other schooling fish. The tuna is one of the chief enemies of its relative, the mackerel, and also of the menhaden and herring. Neither are dogfish (sharks) spared, for whole dogfish, weighing as much as eight pounds, have been found in their stomachs. Tunas, in fact, feed on virtually all smaller schooling fish, and also on squid. It is probable that their local abundance and movements are governed in large part by the schools of fish on which they prey.

Of these large, powerful animals Charles F. Holder has said: "Weight for weight, they have double the fighting power of the tarpon. They are living meteors that strike like a whirlwind and play like a storm."

The tunas themselves are preyed upon by killerwhales, which are said to seize them by the nape, cut the spinal cord, and thus kill them instantly. The fish sometimes become stranded, presumably either while pursuing prey or perhaps while fleeing from enemies.

Although tunas have been highly regarded as a food fish in the region of the Mediterranean Sea and in California for many years, commercial fishermen on our Atlantic coast once considered them a nuisance, for they then had no sale value and were prone to follow mackerel and herring into nets, only to tear their way out again. Many years ago a few were harpooned for the extraction of oil. That industry failed to be profitable and was discontinued. Nearly the entire commercial catch is now canned.

Although a few tunas are harpooned, most are taken with purse seines or in pound nets.

213 Painting by Hashime Murayama

The Commercial Value of Yellowfin Tuna Amounts to Millions

ALLISON TUNA was described by Louis L. Mowbray in 1920 from a Florida specimen and named *Thunnus allisoni*. Some sportsmen insist that Allison's tuna is a distinct species, characterized by elongated dorsal and anal fins. Such a tuna also occurs in the Pacific Ocean in our tropical American waters and in the Hawaiian Islands. Ichthyologists and fishery biologists have concluded that the elongate dorsal and anal fins are merely old specimens of the well-known **yellowfin tuna** of both oceans.

This conclusion was reached after large series of all sizes were carefully measured and studied. It was found that the shorter-finned form gradually graded into the longer-finned form.

The yellowfin, when first out of the sea and alive, is brilliantly iridescent with a golden or bright yellowish stripe along the side of the body; yellowish fins (thus its common name); bluish-black back; and whitish underneath. Soon after death the bright colors fade, and the yellowish hues completely disappear.

The yellowfin tuna ranges throughout the tropical parts of the Atlantic, Pacific, and Indian Oceans, usually in waters from 60° to 85°. It is not especially abundant along the southeast coast of the United States, but acres of them occur in Japan, Hawaii, Indonesia, India, and in the open ocean where there is a meeting of different oceanic currents.

The yellowfin tuna, reaching 450 pounds, is a carnivorous and predaceous fish, feeding on fishes, especially flying fishes, sauries, sardines, and many other kinds. Smaller yellowfins feed on copepods, crabs, spiny lobsters, shrimp, and squid.

There is very little known about the spawning and migration of this tuna, but its entire life history and biology is being studied by the Pacific Oceanic Fishery Investigations under the able direction of the United States Fish and Wildlife Service, with headquarters at Honolulu.

Yellowfin tuna and the variety called Allison's tuna are magnificent game fishes. They are caught by trolling with feather jigs, bright spoons, and live bait. This species fights and jumps, and gives the sportsman a thrill. When light tackle is used, it takes about three quarters of an hour up to two hours to tire a big Allison tuna.

Yellowfin tuna are very important commercially. The usual method of catching them for the market is by means of large ocean-going tuna clippers capable of cruising 10,000 miles and staying out at sea for a few months.

The method of catching tuna is to chum them to the ship by throwing over the side live bait such as sardines or other small fishes. Barbless hooks are used on a short line over the side, and the tuna are rapidly flipped on the deck. A recent annual commercial catch of yellowfin tuna totaled 190,543,000 pounds—twice the poundage of any other species of tuna. The value was $30,999,000.

The record size of the Allison tuna is given by the International Game Fish Association as 265 pounds and 6 feet, 1 inch long.

It was caught in the summer of 1937 off Makua, Hawaii, with an 80-pound line.

Predatory Fish of the Atlantic Terrorize Smaller Fishes

Painting by Hashime Murayama

214

THE highly predatory Atlantic bonito (top—*Sarda sarda*) belongs to that eminent family of fishes, the mackerels. It lives mainly in the open sea, widely wandering in vast schools and approaching land only in search of food or for spawning. Its summer range is from Maine to Cape Sable, Florida; it is also found in the Gulf of Mexico and on the European coast from Scandinavia to the Mediterranean Sea. It sometimes reaches a length of 2 to 3 feet, and a weight of 10 to 20 pounds; but usually it does not exceed 6 pounds.

The flesh of the bonito often passes as Spanish mackerel, though it is far inferior to that fish in edibility. In the Chesapeake Bay region it is often sold as "Boston mackerel," that is, as the Atlantic mackerel (page 21—*Scomber scombrus*).

The late Professor G. B. Goode called the bonito a marvel of strength and beauty, one of the ocean's fastest swimmers. It is built on such fine streamline proportions and has such a polished-surface body that water resistance is negligible.

The Atlantic bonito is a fine, powerful game fish and puts up a good fight. The species is of comparatively little commercial value, however, and generally is taken more or less incidentally in connection with other fishing operations.

The **bluefish** (bottom—*Pomatomus saltatrix*) stands alone in its family. It is a gracefully shaped fish, which has as its nearest relatives the pompanos. It is a gracefully shaped fish, with a rather long head, large mouth, and being somewhat deeper than broad, with a rather long head, large mouth, and forked tail. Its color above is deep blue, which shades into green along the side, and the green shades into the silvery color of the belly.

The bluefish is widely distributed, occurring in the warmer parts of the Atlantic and Indian Oceans. On the Atlantic coast it ranges from Maine to or beyond Venezuela. The annual United States catch is 4,000,000 pounds.

Like the bonito, bluefish are highly predatory and form schools that follow and feed on smaller schooling fish. They are terrors among smaller fish. After they have fed to their fullest capacity, they continue the destruction, killing many more than they can eat.

A maximum length of 3 feet 9 inches and a weight of 27 pounds are known to be attained; but the general run of market fish range from about one to four pounds, the greater size occurring in the northern part of the range.

The Atlantic Sailfish Can Hoist or Furl the Sail on Its Back

RANGING throughout the tropical Atlantic and occurring in American waters from off Massachusetts southward to Brazil, the **Atlantic sailfish** (*Istiophorus americanus*) belongs to the sailfish and marlin family, Istiophoridae. The closest relative of the Atlantic species is the Pacific sailfish (*I. greyi*). The Florida sailfish (*I. volador*) has been considered by recent sailfish experts as only a color variety of *I. americanus*.

The Pacific sailfish ranges throughout the tropical Pacific and Indian Oceans.

In the American Pacific, *I. greyi* occurs from southern California to northern Peru. Sailfish are pelagic, or oceanic, species. They occur in the open ocean. They may be recognized by the high dorsal fin, known as the sail, and the long spearlike nose. They inhabit surface waters, feeding on small fishes, including flying fishes, and also crustaceans. The breeding places of sailfish are unknown. Very few larval sailfish have been taken by fishery investigators.

Of no commercial importance, sailfish are important big game fish. The baits most frequently used are strips of flesh taken from the belly of dolphins, mullet, mackerel, bonito, or whole needlefish. Artificial lures of a bright silvery color are used. Whatever bait is selected, it is trolled about five or six miles an hour.

Leaping from the water and trying to dislodge the hook when caught, sailfish sometimes fight for an hour before they are exhausted and turn on their side.

The average size of Atlantic sailfish caught is between 35 and 50 pounds, and any smaller than 25 pounds is a rarity. The largest reported from the Atlantic by the International Game Fish Association measured 10 feet 4 inches and weighed 123 pounds. It was caught by H. Teetor in the British West Indies. The largest Pacific sailfish was 10 feet 9 inches long, weight 221 pounds. This catch was made by C. W. Stewart in the Galápagos Islands.

The long bill of the sailfish is used as a club, with which it beats its prey into submission before consuming it.

Painting by Hashime Murayama

Hashime Murayama

216 Painting by Maynard Reece, courtesy of South Bend Bait Company

Marlins and Swordfish Are Aristocrats among Marine Game Fishes

SPEARFISHES are characterized by upper jaws that are prolonged into swordlike or spearlike protuberances. Best known among them are the **striped marlin** (above—*Makaira mitsukurii*), the **white marlin** (opposite, below—*Makaira albida*), and the **broadbill swordfish** (opposite, top—*Xiphias gladius*).

The striped marlin is found only in the Pacific, north to California, and reaches a weight of over 400 pounds. The white marlin ranges in the Atlantic from the West Indies to Massachusetts and is much smaller than other marlin, such as the striped and blue marlin.

The white marlin rod-and-reel record weight is 161 pounds, whereas that for the striped marlin is 692 pounds. The striped marlin is also much more given to making spectacular leaps out of the water, which the white marlin rarely does except when caught. But all marlins are game fighters and more important as such than for their strong and oily flesh. The resemblance of marlins to the sailfish (page 215) is striking, except for the larger dorsal fin of the latter.

The broadbill swordfish rivals the shark in both size and strength, sometimes reaching a weight in excess of 800 pounds, although most of those caught weigh less than half as much.

One authority says that it strikes with the force of 15 double hammers and with the velocity of a swivel shot.

Its stupidity in attacking ships and other objects is so great that Oppian tells us that "Nature her bounty to his mouth confined, gave him a sword, but left unarmed his mind."

In feeding, the swordfish uses its bill to thrash smaller fishes, which it promptly devours.

The swordfish is caught chiefly by harpooning, although a few accomplished sportsmen have taken it with hook and line. There are some of the thrills of whaling in swordfishing, since there is no slow baiting or careful waiting and no bother with nondescript bait stealers. The swordfish is a worthy antagonist, and many a vessel has limped into port leaking badly as a result of attacks by wounded swordfish. Occasionally a small boat is attacked and the sword rammed through its side.

The commercial swordfish catch in the United States is so inadequate as to furnish only about one eighth of the some 8,000,000 pounds annually consumed, the major portion being imported from Canada, Japan, Peru and Chile.

The largest broadbill swordfish recorded by the International Game Fish Association was caught off Chile and was 860 pounds in weight and 13 feet, 9 inches in length.

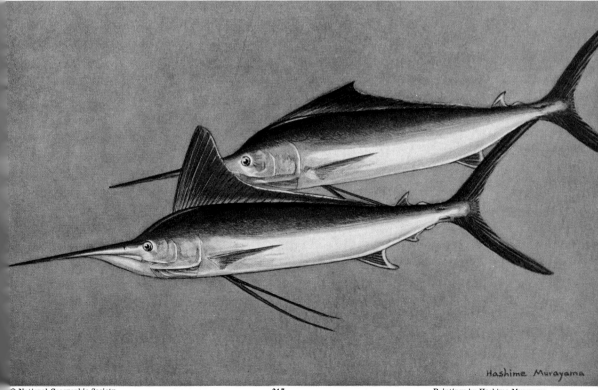

Hashime Murayama

Paintings by Hashime Murayama

Painting by Hashime Murayama

Groupers Valued as Food

THE large, prolific grouper family number species ranging from the 2-pound rock hind (page 231) to the giant jewfish that has reached 750 pounds.

The **red grouper** (upper—*Epinephelus morio*) and the **Nassau grouper** (lower—*Epinephelus striatus*) average 5 and 8 pounds respectively but have reached 80 and 125 pounds. The red grouper ranges from off Virginia throughout the West Indies southward to Brazil and strays northward to Massachusetts during the summer.

It is one of the most abundant species of the family, living in rocky places among corals or wherever it may find shelter. The larger individuals occur in deeper water. The red grouper, like the other members of the genus, is individualistic. It occurs singly, never in schools.

This species appears always to be hungry and is easily caught by hook and line. The best baits are shrimp, parts of crab, worms, and small fishes. Natural food consists of fishes, octopuses, and crustaceans such as shrimps and crabs. The red grouper is a game fish of some value.

The commercial catch of groupers in the United States makes the several species very valuable. In the most recently recorded year, 9,816,000 pounds were landed.

The Nassau grouper, or hamlet, ranges from North Carolina through the West Indies to Brazil. In Florida it is a common species in the coral-gorgonian belt but is infrequently found elsewhere.

At Dry Tortugas, Florida, the late Dr. Longley made friends with this grouper. He said: "One that I fed frequently usually appeared promptly upon my approach from under the coral heads and got underfoot or picked at my pockets, in which I had carried crawfish tails for it. It could scarcely be driven far enough away to photograph, and might easily have been captured with bare hands if it had not been so strong, hard, and slippery."

The Nassau and red groupers are noted for their ability to change colors and shades quickly from one phase to another. Although the color pattern mostly agrees with the environment, Dr. Longley observed a Nassau grouper which displayed a color pattern never seen at any other time when a red grouper came near it. In this distinctive phase the stripe through the eye, instead of being one of the darkest, became one of the lightest; the color on the side above the level of the pectoral was abruptly replaced by white marked with a few dark spots.

The Nassau grouper is valuable as a food and game fish. A voracious feeder, it may be caught readily on baited hook.

The weight of the red grouper is apt to vary greatly. Those offshore frequently weigh as much as 5 to 25 pounds, while those from inside waters more commonly weigh around 3 pounds.

Members of the Widespread Grouper Family Never Get Enough to Eat in Their Warm-water Range

OVER 130 kinds of groupers occur in all warm seas and are noted for always being hungry.

The **gag** (upper—*Mycteroperca microlepis*) ranges along our South Atlantic and Gulf coasts, southward from North Carolina, and is rare in the West Indies. It does not appear to be abundant in shallow waters, preferring deeper waters around the reefs where it is caught as a game and food fish.

This species feeds on other fishes, crabs, and shrimp. Dr. W. H. Longley saw a gag capture and swallow a fish one third its length. A length of three feet and a record weight of 50 pounds are attained, although the average is about 4 pounds.

All groupers are members of the sea bass family and are found all year along rocky shores in tropical seas, although some species roam as far north as Massachusetts under the influence of the Gulf Stream in summer.

The **black grouper** (lower—*Mycteroperca bonaci*) is one of those that normally range from Florida through the West Indies to Brazil and sometimes stray northward to Massachusetts.

The sea basses, Serranidae, of which groupers form a branch, are a varied family, with numerous representatives classified into about 60 genera and 400 species, all of which range in temperate and tropical waters. Closely related to the serranids are our fresh-water basses and sunfishes of North America. The two genera with the largest number of species are *Epinephelus* with about 100 and *Mycteroperca* with about 30 species. Ichthyologists have not yet discovered and described all the species in this large family.

The black grouper is beautifully colored. Its back is olive and grayish, sides marked with deep orange-brownish, eye reddish.

This grouper takes the baited hook readily and, like its other relatives, feeds on fishes and on crabs and other crustaceans. It is a food fish of considerable value, but is not recorded separately in the catch statistics of the Fish and Wildlife Service.

The black grouper reaches a length of three feet and a weight of 50 pounds, but averages much smaller. It is abundant around Key West, and it is a hard and fast striker.

Unlike some groupers (opposite), the black grouper does not frequent inside waters or come very close to shore. When hooked, it is a persistent fighter of considerable strength, requiring fairly heavy tackle.

219

Painting by Hashime Murayama

Hashime Murayama

The Legendary "Horror" of the Seas

THE common octopus of the Atlantic Ocean is *Octopus vulgaris*. It ranges in the western Atlantic from Connecticut to the Caribbean Sea and also occurs in the eastern Atlantic, preferring warm waters. This octopus has been reported from a depth of 220 fathoms, but occurs mostly along rocky shores above 100 fathoms. This species reaches a weight of about 50 pounds and a radial span of about 10 feet.

The common octopus is wholly predatory and carnivorous. Its prey consists of crustaceans and mollusks which it bites with a powerful, parrotlike beak. The conger eel feeds on the octopus.

The chief defenses of an octopus are its ability to hide in crevices and its great strength enabling it to remain fastened on rocks. In open water, the octopus has considerable ability for swimming by jet propulsion, and it is remarkably agile on rocky surfaces. In addition, the octopus is provided with an ink sac. When disturbed, the contents of the sac are discharged into the water, forming a dense blackish cloud designed to confuse and baffle the enemy.

In the Pacific occurs another octopus, *Octopus hongkongensis*, formerly known as *O. punctatus*, the latter a synonym. This too is a littoral species, living along rocky shores and seeking crevices and holes in which to hide. This species is much larger than the common Atlantic octopus, reaching a radial span of 28 feet and a weight of over 50 pounds. This octopus occurs in the North Pacific from Japan to Alaska southward to Baja California.

The octopus moves with its arms along the bottom of the sea, although some forms swim or float along the surface.

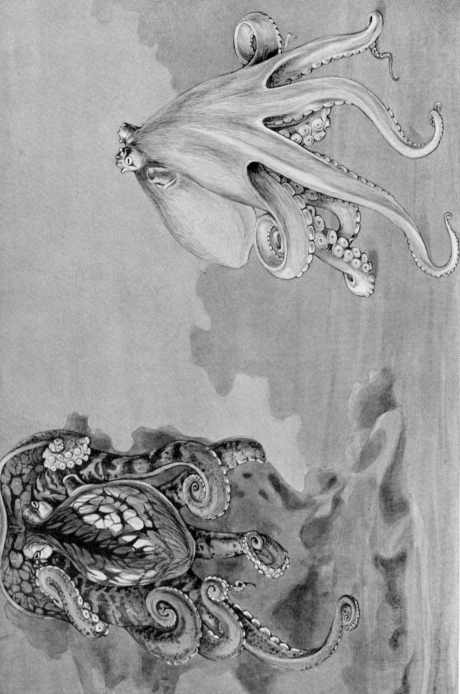

220

Painting by Hashime Murayama

Because of its abundance and habits, it forms a small fishery; 122,000 pounds were landed in a recent year along the Pacific coast of the United States. Since the octopus likes to crawl into holes to conceal itself, kegs open at one end are lowered into rocky areas and baited with fish. An octopus will remain in the keg when it is hauled to the surface. The common Atlantic octopus does not appear in the commercial fish statistics prepared by the U. S. Fish and Wildlife Service.

The Dolphin Has Been Used from Ancient Times as a Symbol in Heraldry and Art

THE dolphin, or dorado (*Coryphaena hippurus*) ranges in all warm seas. Although the dolphin has been described many times as a different species in several areas, most experts consider this fish to be a single species of wide distribution.

The dorado, Spanish name for the dolphin, is rarely seen in shallow waters. It stays mostly in the open sea or over rather deep waters off reefs, sometimes in lagoons or bays. The young, however, may occur in shallow water and have been found in floating seaweeds inshore.

Dolphins, according to the late Dr. W. H. Longley, are enemies of flying fishes. They flush them like quail, sometimes following and catching the flying fishes as they fall after a fumbling start or in full flight. On the other hand, young dolphins suffer greatly from the attack of terns and are one of the six species of fishes commonly found in the food remains on the Bird Key, Florida, breeding grounds.

The dolphin is noted for its terrific speed, which it acquires partly from its streamlined shape. It is an active, exciting fish often mentioned in stories.

This species is most gorgeously colored when first taken from its natural habitat. The dominating colors are purplish to bluish gold, vivid hues of lilac, sea greens, and emerald shades in pastel hues. The fish is especially endowed with the ability to change its beautiful iridescent shades very rapidly. However, the dolphin loses its colors shortly after it is caught and, when death occurs, it soon becomes plain grayish in color.

Dolphins are caught mostly by trolling slowly with hooks baited with fish or chunks of fish or with artificial lures such as plugs, spoons, feather jigs, or spinners. The lure is taken with great quickness, often accompanied by a leap. When once hooked, the dolphin puts up a remarkable exhibition of animated fury, repeating leaps of 10 to 20 feet, and displaying its rainbowlike colors in each leap.

Although the dolphin is an important big-game fish, it is not of great commercial importance in the markets of the United States. Recent U. S. Fish and Wildlife Service statistics list only 82,000 pounds annually.

The average-size dolphin is about 2 or 3 feet. The largest one yet recorded, from Waianae in the Hawaiian Islands, measured 5 feet, 8½ inches long and weighed sixty-seven and a half pounds.

In ancient times the Greeks used the word dolphin to identify a mammal of the porpoise family, and the porpoises of the Mediterranean are still called dolphins. A figure which Dr. C. M. Breder, Jr., identifies as a possible combination of the porpoise and the fish was early adopted as a symbol in heraldry and Christian art to represent diligence, love, and swiftness.

221

Painting by Hashime Murayama

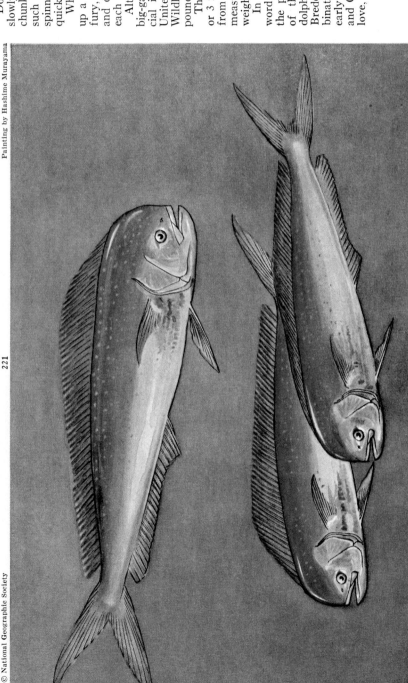

222

Spiny Lobster (Lower Pair) Can Walk Backward, Forward, or Sideways and Swim Backward

LIKE other rudderfishes, the **opaleye,** or greenfish (top—*Girella nigricans*), has incisorlike teeth and is herbivorous, feeding on algae. Compactly built and averaging only 10 inches, the greenfish depends upon fast swimming to escape its enemies. It is abundant on the Pacific coast from Cape San Lucas to San Francisco.

The **spiny lobster** (lower—*Panulirus interruptus*) is common from Point Conception, California, to Mexico, hiding among rocks, and in kelp, which furnishes protection and food.

The average spiny lobster weighs two or three pounds. In California the latest annual catch was 834,300 pounds.

The Prawn, Living in Depths Down to 1,600 Feet, Is Cannibalistic

THE crustacean family Pandalidae, or **prawns** (lower—*Pandalus platyceros*), two to three inches long, consists of shrimplike creatures frequently taken with shrimp from Unalaska to San Diego, California. Young shrimp are always males. At 1½ to 3½ years old they become females, probably remaining so for the rest of their lives.

The chief value of the ocean goldfish, called **garibaldi** (top—*Hypsypops rubicundus*), averaging 8 inches, is decorative. Close relatives strikingly colored occur in most warm seas. Visitors to Santa Catalina Island's Marine Garden spot them readily from the glass-bottomed boats. They have no importance as game fish.

223

Painting by Hashime Murayama

Painting by Hashime Murayama

224

Flying Fish Attains 35 MPH Speed in Take-off and Stays Aloft 2 to 15 Seconds

THE California flying fish (*Cypselurus californicus*) inhabits warm seas only.

As the 12-inch flying fish swims at high speed, the fins are folded against the body. On breaking through the surface, the large fore fins spread wide and serve as supporting planes. While the tail remains in the water, the body is supported in the air at an angle for distances up to 45 feet. The tail now vibrates violently sidewise, furnishing the propulsion to lift the fish from the water. As the "taxi" along the surface progresses, only the lower side of the tail is in the water. Tail action ceases when the whole fish is aloft.

The Sleek Albacore Is a Popular Canned Food under the Name of Tuna

ALBACORE (*Germo alaunga*) are closely related to the mackerels and, like the latter, have crescent-shaped tail fins that furnish strong propulsion and speed for swimming. They are distinguished by the great length of the pectoral fins, nearly half the length of the fish without the tail fin.

The 3-foot albacore, most abundant off the west coast, puts up a violent battle when hooked, and big-game fishermen in increasing numbers have recently taken to pitting their skill against it with light tackle.

All the fins of the albacore fit into grooves, making the entire fish almost perfectly streamlined.

© National Geographic Society

Painting by Hashime Murayama

225

226

The Spiny Lobster's Delicate Flesh Gives It a High Market Value

COMMERCIALLY important in the West Indies, Bahamas, Bermuda, and the Florida Keys, the **crayfish** (*Panulirus argus*), or **spiny lobster** (above), averages 10 inches in length. The **hawksbill turtle** (left below—*Eretmochelys* *imbricata*), ranging from Bermuda to Brazil, has an ornamental shell of wide commercial use. It is smaller, averaging 35 pounds, than the **green turtle** (right—*Chelonia mydas*), averaging 50 pounds and most valued as food.

227

Gigantic but Harmless Sunfish Love to Bask in the Sun

A FISH of the high seas but venturing close into shore, the **ocean sunfish** (top—*Mola mola*) occurs in all temperate and tropical seas of the Atlantic and Pacific Oceans.

The immense ocean sunfish is usually some 40 inches in length and is as long vertically as it is horizontally. Its chopped-off look has given it the nickname "headfish," since it appears to have no body at all.

The name "ocean sunfish" derives from its habit of lying motionless in the sun on the ocean's surface. It makes an excellent target for harpooners, who like to bring it in for display because of its odd shape and huge size.

Occasionally giant specimens are found. One was mounted in the American Museum of Natural History, New York City, measuring 10 feet in length by 11 in height and weighing over a ton.

The **opah** or **moonfish** (bottom—*Lampris regius*) is one of the most beautiful and graceful fishes in the ocean. It has been reported singly and in schools in widely scattered areas of the Atlantic and Pacific Oceans, and it has been taken as far northward as Yakutat, Alaska, on the West Coast and Nova Scotia on the East.

There is a single living species which reaches a length of about six feet and a weight of 600 pounds, but the usual length is 30 inches. The flesh is described as salmon-red, tender, and oily, with a delicious flavor.

Although desirable as food, unlike the bigger sunfish, the moonfish has almost as little economic importance because of its scarcity and irregular occurrence.

Sea Horse Is a Curiosity

THE American sea horse (left —*Hippocampus hudsonius*) is related to pipefishes (page 58). Occurring along the shores of most tropical seas, it ranges from Cape Cod in the summer southward to Florida and the West Indies.

The sea horse, averaging only three or four inches, is remarkable for its tail, which can be curled around stems of seaweeds. This is a great advantage, since it is a weak swimmer and could be swept into open water, exposing itself to predaceous fishes.

Another trait is the male's external pouch, which receives the eggs of the female. Male sea horses and male pipefishes belong to the only group of fishes that has the kangaroolike pouch for incubation of the young.

The **sergeant major** (below— *Abudefduf saxatilis*) occurs in the Atlantic from Cape Cod to Brazil, in the tropical Indo-Pacific Oceans, and in the eastern Atlantic.

Averaging four to six inches, it has two color phases: light when the fish occurs over sandy bottom or when swimming high above the corals; and dark when the fish occurs in dark crevices and especially in deep water.

Paintings by Hashime Murayama

Fish Are Aptly Named

THE rainbow parrotfish (above—*Pseudoscarus guacamaia*) is confined to the tropical Atlantic, and in American waters is found mostly from Florida throughout the West Indies.

The parrotfishes are named for their beaklike teeth, resembling those of a parrot. Food consists of algae which is bitten off the rocks and corals. Parrotfishes, usually nearly a foot in length, are used to some extent as food and are important in the diet of island peoples.

The **queen triggerfish** (right—*Balistes vetula*) is so named because the first dorsal spine can be locked erect at will by the fish. When the trigger is depressed, it releases the locking mechanism, and the first spine is then depressible. Locked erect, these spines will break off without being depressible.

The trigger is a defensive weapon for the owner. The spines are locked erect whenever the fish is disturbed. Should the triggerfish be gulped into the mouth of a predator, the latter is in serious difficulty. Usually the predator and the triggerfish die together, with one lodged in the throat of the other.

Paintings by Hashime Murayama

230

Pugnacious-looking Grunt (Above) Stay Close to the Sea's Floor

THE **bluestriped grunt** (above—*Haemulon sciurus*) ranges in the western Atlantic from Florida and the West Indies to Brazil.

It feeds by night, and during the daylight hours often occurs in great schools, which lurk among the coral growths to within a yard of the bottom.

Averaging a foot long, it is an important food fish of the West Indies.

Ranging in the western Atlantic from Woods Hole, Massachusetts, to Brazil, the **yellowtail snapper** (below—*Ocyurus chrysurus*) is one of the most abundant species around the gorgonian thickets of the reefs.

Important as both a game and a food fish, it is caught with crabs or small fishes as bait. In Cuba and elsewhere in the West Indies it is very popular and abundant. It has reached two feet in length but averages much smaller.

231

Florida Game Fish Is Appropriately Nicknamed Polka Dot or Speckled Hind

THE **rock hind** (*Epinephelus adscensionis*) belongs to the sea bass family, Serranidae. It inhabits the reefs of Florida and extends through the West Indies to Brazil.

This grouper is a game fish of importance and forms part of the West Indies commercial catch.

The rock hind is one of the smaller species of groupers, reaching a length of about 16 inches.

The **shark sucker,** or **shark pilot** (below—

Echeneis neucrates), occurs in all warm seas and may be recognized by the flexible suction disc on the dorsal surface of the head, by which they attach themselves to the sides of large predaceous fishes, usually sharks.

The shark sucker stays on its host until the larger fish makes a kill, then feeds on the floating bits of flesh bitten out by the predator but too small for the shark to eat.

Tough Spines Are Dangerous to Ungloved Hands →

IN various shades of scarlet, red, and orange, the **squirrelfish**, or **soldier fish** (right—*Holocentrus ascensionis*) occurs in all warm seas, being most abundant along coral atolls and where corals and algae growth are plentiful, ranging from Florida to Brazil.

Its large brown eyes remind one of squirrels, a fact which undoubtedly gave rise to the name squirrelfish.

Squirrelfish are largely nocturnal in their habits. During the day, a casual observer would not see even one squirrelfish. At night, if he shone a light into the waters around a growth of corals, he might see several dozen.

Although squirrelfish may be caught by hook and line, they are not popular as game or food fish and are eaten mainly in the West Indies and the Hawaiian Islands.

232

Paintings by Hashime Murayama

← **Porkfish Family Is Related to Snappers**

PORKFISH (left—*Anisotremus virginicus*) is carnivorous, feeding on crabs, shrimp, worms, and small fishes. It ranges from Florida, through the West Indies to Brazil.

The spawning season of the porkfish around Key West, Florida, is from June to August. It spawns in the channel about the shoals and may be caught in great numbers. About a month after the spawning season, the young are seen in shallow reef waters in immense numbers.

Dr. W. H. Longley states that the porkfish does not feed by day but is nocturnal in its habits.

The porkfish may be taken on hook and line, but it is not a game fish of importance. It has attained a weight of two pounds but averages only a third of a pound.

Coral Residents of Brilliance, Grace, and Beauty →

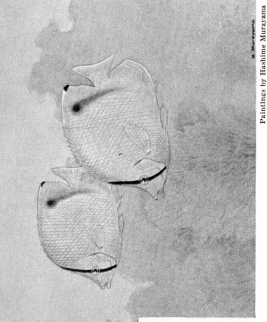

THE **four-eyed butterflyfish** (upper left—*Chaetodon capistratus*) ranges throughout the Caribbean, sometimes in the summer following the Gulf current to Cape Cod. It is carnivorous and is said to feed, at times, on the parasites attached to other fishes.

The **common butterflyfish** (pair at right—*Chaetodon ocellatus*) is the most abundant species of the genus in the Florida Keys. The naming of the family after the scalewinged insects was a well-chosen comparison.

The common butterflyfish typically feeds in pairs or in a few pairs over comparatively bare and sandy areas near the protection of coral growths. It has neither market nor game value.

Paintings by Hashime Murayama

← Six-foot Giant Eels Attack Fishermen

THE **green moray** (*Gymnothorax funebris*) inhabits coral reefs and rocky shores. It is predatory, pugnacious, and savage. Some of the species of morays hide in crevices, holes, and under coral ledges by day, venturing out at dusk and at night to feed. Others wander about the reefs during the daylight hours.

The green moray occurs in the tropical Atlantic, and, along American shores, ranges from Florida to Brazil. Large specimens brought into a skiff can be vicious, and many a fisherman has gone over the side when this happens.

The green moray reaches a length of six feet. One about five feet long weighs about 27 pounds. Other species in the Indo-Pacific Oceans probably reach 10 feet.

233

← Tentacles Paralyze Foes

THE spadefish (above—*Chaetodipterus faber*) ranges in the western Atlantic from Cape Cod to Rio de Janeiro. Close relatives occur in the eastern tropical Atlantic and in the tropical Indo-Pacific Oceans.

It is noted for the persistent occurrence in the large adults of bony tumors on the spines and the ribs. These are mentioned in ancient writings, and are found in fossil remains and in the kitchen middens of ancient Indians.

The spadefish, averaging a foot long, is of economic importance in the West Indies.

The **Portuguese man-of-war** (left—*Physalia*) ranges in tropical seas, where it floats at the surface.

It has hundreds of little organs in its tentacles, stinging mechanisms used for paralyzing prey or enemies. Touching the nematocyst, even lightly, releases automatically a coiled, springlike thread with a point containing a poison that produces instantly a severe pain like a bee sting. Swimmers have been so badly stung they have died.

The float of *Physalia* reaches several inches in length, but the tentacles may extend several feet.

Paintings by Hashime Murayama

ENCASED in a bony boxlike covering resembling a trunk, the trunkfishes (right) can move only their fins, mouths, and eyes. Their covering serves as a protection against predaceous fishes.

The 10-inch **cuckold** (top—*Lactophrys triqueter*) ranges on the western Atlantic from North Carolina to Brazil and may stray northward to Cape Cod during the summer months.

The **cowfish** (center—*Acanthostracion quadricorne*) and the **buffalo trunkfish** (lower pair—*Lactophrys trigonus*) reach a length of 12 and 9 inches respectively.

The tropical Atlantic angelfishes (below) are all spiny butterflyfishes, varied in colors and ranging in length from one to two feet.

The species here include the **blue angelfish** (lower left—*Holacanthus isabelita*); the **rock beauty** (upper left—*Holancanthus tricolor*); the **black angelfish** (upper right—*Pomacanthus aureus*); and the **French angelfish** (lower right—*Pomacanthus arcuatus*).

Angelfishes have no importance as food or game fish. The young of most angelfishes differ in color from the adults, which has led to confusion in identifying species.

Paintings by Hashime Murayama

236 Kodachrome by J. Baylor Roberts

At Key West, Fishing Is Not Limited to Any One Season

South Florida's year-round fishermen bring back a highly varied collection. Behind this girl is the barracuda, whose teeth support its reputation for ferocity. Often alleged shark attacks on bathers are made by barracudas.

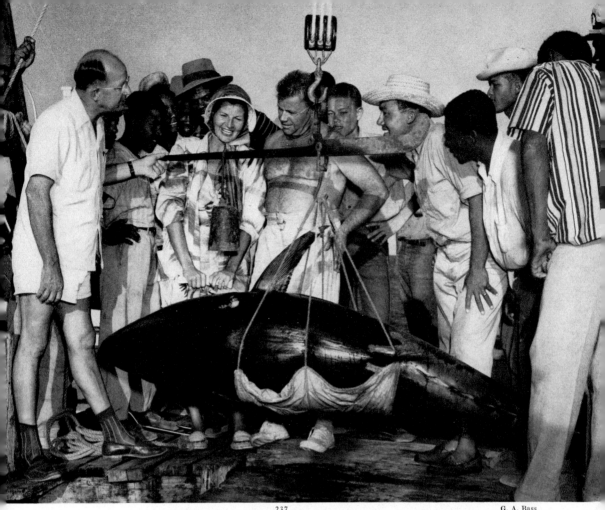

G. A. Bass

Her Bluefin Tuna Breaks a World Record

The tension ends and Mrs. G. A. Bass, a champion woman angler, smiles broadly as the scales on a Bimini dock indicate 518 pounds, an all-time world record for tuna, taken on a 45-pound test line. Mrs. Bass landed her prize after a battle in Gulf Stream waters. Capt. Tom Gifford, noted fishing guide, stands next to her and smiles his congratulations. Crowding around to see the fish and its weight are officials and natives of the tiny British colony.

others travel up the Old Bahama Channel. Sometimes in pairs or small groups, and frequently in fairly large schools, these tuna never dally along the route, but keep moving ever northward at a speed of about six to eight miles per hour. Many are caught by trolling when they wander into the shallow waters around Cat Cay and Bimini Island.

Though large, they are very lean for their size, when migrating long distances.

It is obvious that their trek takes them to the far North to feed on the glut of herring and mackerel found in Nova Scotia waters, where they remain to fatten until mid-October. Their whereabouts from then until they reappear off the Bahamas the following May is a mystery.

An occasional bluefin caught off Bermuda during December indicates the possibility of a migration southeastward past that mid-ocean island. But they have also been taken there in April, a fact which tends to complicate the matter further. This leads to the supposition that there may be two or more groups of the tuna, which migrate along separate routes. Fish-tagging experiments now under way may help solve the mystery of the bluefin.

Names of Fishes Are Revealing

Not all of the citizens of the warm seas are large game fish. Such fine fish as wahoo, kingfish, and Spanish mackerel (page 211), bonefish (page 205), and the groupers (pages 218-219) are species to be reckoned with for sport or food value. There are also many smaller varieties, such as the grunts (page 230), margate fish (page 207), mullet (page 35), the look-down, or moonfish (page 208), and many others taken on light tackle.

Most of these fish have derived their names from some characteristic pertaining to their make-up—the kingfish for its fine eating quality, the fighting bonefish for its peculiar bony structure, the groupers because they

National Geographic Photographer J. Baylor Roberts

Victor and Vanquished in a Salty Tussle

Fishing in Key West waters, a sportswoman has boated a hard fighting kingfish. Kingfish, or Cero, a close cousin to the mackerel, run in large schools in south Florida coastal waters.

group together seasonally to spawn, grunts because of the sound they make, and the lookdown because of the position of the eyes.

Commercially, the kingfish and mackerel family outstrip all the others in value, hundreds of thousands of pounds of these fish being marketed each year. However, the economic aspects of some of the less marketable fish should not be lost sight of. The bonefish,

---

David D. Duncan

← **Beside the Broadbill Sword the Marlin Bill Is Dwarfed**

The two are matched (top, left), showing the difference in size and shape. The larger weapon is flat, the smaller round and needlelike; hence the Spanish names *pez espada* (swordfish), and *pez aguia* (needlefish). Both were caught in the Humboldt current (Peru Current) off Chile.

Michael Lerner and Douglas Osborne boat a giant broadbill captured in the Humboldt off Tocopilla, Chile. Swordfish are of world distribution. In recent years their flesh has become popular in sea-food markets of the United States.

sailfish and tarpon, to mention but a few, bring thousands of persons to Florida annually, and the sale of food, rental of boats and accommodation, sale of fishing tackle and gasoline bring into circulation within that State millions of dollars annually.

We cannot pass on without special mention of the bonefish, rated by many anglers, pound for pound, as probably faster and stronger than any other. Its fighting qualities, and the fact that it is both wily and shy, are its chief appeal. Great sport may be had in stalking this wonderful scrapper on the shallow sand and grassy banks of the Tropics, where a false move or bad cast will flush the quarry from the immediate area forthwith.

The principal food of the bonefish is crab, worm, shrimp, and small fish.

It is found in all warm seas throughout the world, though in the Atlantic the largest specimens have been taken in Hawaii, Bermuda, the Bahamas, and Florida. One of the greatest of fishing thrills attainable is to fish for bone-

Robert F. Garland

Big Fish Produce Big Grins

Leonard Roy, of the National Geographic Society staff, proudly hefts a thirty-eight-pound amberjack caught
in the Gulf Stream off Morehead City, North Carolina.

fish with an artificial fly on a suitable fly rod. To date the record is a 16-pound scrapper.

Many tales have been told about the ferocious-looking great barracuda. This so-called "tiger of the sea" is indeed a savage fish, though many stories attributed to it are not true. When hungry the barracuda will attack almost any moving object. Although a swimmer would fall in this category, few substantiated facts are on record to show that humans have been attacked by them.

The largest barracuda now on record weighed 103¼ pounds, though the average size would be nearer 15 pounds. They are savage when attacking their prey and can sever in two a fish much larger than themselves. It is very deliberate in its attack, usually severing with one clash of its teeth sufficient food to satisfy itself. A fish bitten by a barracuda appears to have been cut straight across as with a knife, rather than with a crescent-shaped weapon as would be the case with a shark.

A large, though completely harmless fish is

the channel bass, or red drum. It appears to be a rather dull and stupid species, though when hooked it puts up a satisfactory battle for a short period. Surf casters off the Carolinas find them great sport, as do the followers of salt-water fly fishing on the shallow flats of Florida's Keys and the Texas-Louisiana Gulf coasts. The largest channel bass taken by game fishermen was above 80 pounds in weight.

The mouth of the channel bass is on the under side of the head, and this modification has taken place because of its habit of feeding by grubbing along the bottom. Also, the small eyes are focused downward, a characteristic which makes the observer believe that the fish is stupid.

The Dolphin's Precision Broad Jump

Channel bass will often swim right along into danger, and not until they are within a few feet of an object in front of them do they realize its presence. However, to counterbalance this nearsightedness, they react very

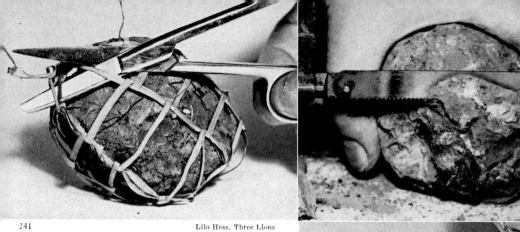

Lilo Hess, Three Lions

African Mud Ball Produces Live Fish in New York

The African lungfish must come to the surface to breathe, and it can live for long periods out of water, rolled up in mud, consuming its own body tissues. The grassbound mud ball (top left) was sent from Africa to New York. The grass was removed and the mud carefully cut away. Then the curled up fish was placed in water and 12 hours later (below) bore a faint resemblance to a fish. Completely recovered (bottom) the unlovely creature has gained its full length of ten inches.

Some lungfish attain a length of six feet. With powerful teeth, they feed on freshwater clams, whose shells they crack. In the aquarium they seem satisfied with horsemeat. They cannot be reared in captivity because they tear each other to pieces when placed together in a tank.

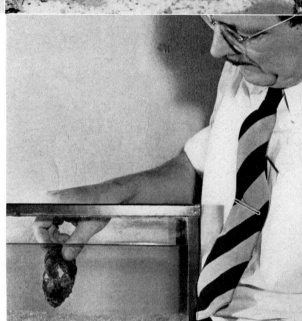

National Geographic
Photographer B. Anthony Stewart

Fish from Bikini Atoll Are Checked for Atom Bomb Effects

Dr. Leonard P. Schultz, curator of fishes at Washington's Smithsonian Institution, makes precision measurements of a parrotfish. Jars contain some 70,000 specimens collected before and after the 1946 atomic blasts. Fish that survived showed no anatomical changes, but continuing radiation from the lagoon bottom might cause sterility, destruction of red blood cells and abnormal growth in some fish.

At left a fish from the Lerner Marine Laboratories, Bimini, British West Indies, is dissected for subsequent study of special tissues in the American Museum of Natural History at New York.

American Museum of Natural History

242

Thirteen Feet of Marlin

This giant Blue, being measured at Bimini by Miss Francesca LaMonte, renowned ichthyologist of the American Museum of Natural History, weighed 741¾ pounds, a few ounces short of the record.

Despite the dreamy expression, the burrfish "crooner" facing the microphone is not broadcasting on a network. Instead his voice is being recorded so that Navy sonar operators, probing the ocean depths by means of echoing sound waves, will not mistake it for the propellers or engines of a submarine.

Luis Marden,
National Geographic Staff

243

Lilo Hess, Three Lions

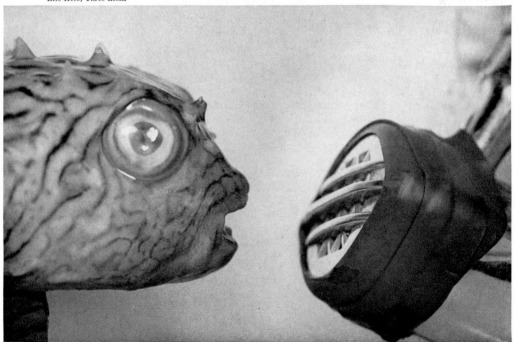

244

rapidly to a change in light, a moving shadow, or splash on the surface and beat a hasty retreat.

Of all the game fish, the dolphin (page 221) I consider the most beautiful. The brilliant blue-and-gold coloring is an eye-filling sight, and the almost continuous changes of color which take place when the fish is dying are a sight which no angler can forget. This fish is equally notable for its great speed and its ability to leap many feet into the air when approaching or attacking its prey. The keen judgment shown by the dolphin when it jumps from 20 feet away and lands directly on a fast-moving bait has to be seen to be believed.

Dolphins are very susceptible to a moving object and therefore seldom refuse to hit at a trolled lure. They often travel in schools. It is a well-known fact among fishing guides that, if one dolphin in a school is hooked and allowed to continue to swim around the boat, the entire school can usually be caught with the other lines.

Because of the dolphin's habit of resting or sheltering under driftwood or other flotsam, the experienced angler will look for such floating objects and troll his line past with every likelihood of success in getting his quarry. These beauties are fish of the open ocean and seldom stray over shallow waters.

Groupers come by their name quite rightly. Ordinarily solitary in habit, at the spawning season they come from miles around to gather on a common ground. Because of the fact that they will appear on the same dates and places each year, the commercial fishermen catch vast quantities seasonally in some countries of the Caribbean area.

Mammals and Reptiles of the Sea

Of course, not all of the inhabitants of the seas are fish. There are mammals such as whales and porpoises, and reptiles such as the turtles. All have some commercial value and, because of it, have become increasingly scarce in many areas. In former years there were sufficient whales in the North Atlantic to sustain a large industry, but not so today.

The green turtle (page 226), that great favorite of the table, had been nearly fished

Net and Camera Snare Flying Fish

Flying fish are considered a delicacy in Barbados, British West Indies, particularly when served in pie. At left one man dangles a basket of well-seasoned bait over the side while his mate scoops up the catch. A good day's haul may bring in 8,000 to 10,000 fish.

 The fish "fly" by gathering speed on the surface with their tail fin and then glide into the air, using their tremendous fins as glider wings. In this picture, taken with stroboscopic light by Dr. Harold E. Edgerton of Massachusetts Institute of Technology, the bottom fish with his tail in the water is taxiing, but is almost clear. His wings are spread. The fish above is about three feet over the surface and is gliding. Flying fish have been seen to make ten taxies without the body entering the water.

Harold E. Edgerton

245

James A. Allison

↑ Sawfish Is an Accurate Name

The female (above) was taken alive in a net and displayed for several weeks in a 36-foot tank at a former Miami Beach aquarium. While in the tank she gave birth to nine young, the only known record of sawfish being born in captivity.

Sawfish are sharklike rays, most often found in Florida waters and the Gulf of Mexico but sometimes wandering north to New Jersey. The record catch weighed 736 pounds and was 14 feet 7 inches long. Smaller sawfish are good pan fish but have never become popular.

← Channel Bass Jackpot

Zack J. Walters, Jr., 15, of Salisbury, Maryland, landed this 83-pound channel bass in eight minutes off Cape Charles, Virginia. The fish broke all records for the species taken on rod and reel. For his feat the 104-pound youth won a new automobile, an extra set of tires and $50 in merchandise.

The channel bass is more strictly called the red drum, since it belongs to the drum and croaker group of fishes. It has an unusually long range along the Atlantic coast, extending from New York to Mexico. It is very apt to be much heavier in weight in the northerly reaches of its range.

Popular throughout its range as a game fish for its tough, consistent fighting, only in its southern run is it favored as a food fish.

Wide World

246

John Oliver La Gorce

Birds Eat Fish and Fish Eat Fish, Too

As a rule, where there are birds diving, there are fish schooling, and conversely, when the birds stay ashore the angling is not too good. Gulls and frigate birds have come miles from shore to snatch up sardines jumping from the waters of the Gulf Stream trying to escape from a school of hungry tuna. The tuna are so hungry they break water in their efforts to gulp sardines. Jumping to escape the tuna, many sardines fall prey to the birds.

The methods employed by birds in fishing are almost as varied as those of men. The gull swoops down in bomber fashion to snatch his prey with his bill. The heron is an angler, staying in one place and waiting for the fish to swim by him. The kingfisher uses a swifter dive-bombing tactic than the gull. The penguin follows the tactics of the submarine and stalks its victims under water. The white pelicans group in squads and wading inward in the form of a crescent chase their prey into shallow water. The brown pelicans hunt from the air, but those living in populated areas are apt to wait for amused observers to feed them.

→ The muttonfish was bitten in two by a larger fish, probably a barracuda, after it was hooked by an angler near Miami Beach.

247

The Tiger of the Seas
Needs Bite But Once
to Deflate This Balloon

The puffer, or blowfish, held by the Cape Cod boy (left) has inflated himself as a protective device. When in danger— or when tickled on the stomach—he draws in water, air, or even sand to expand to as much as three times normal size. This makes swallowing difficult on the part of larger fish.

↘ This five-foot barracuda on the prowl was photographed over the cruiser side in crystal clear Bahama waters about eight feet below the surface. A savage, fearless hunter and rightly called the "tiger of the sea," it will attack and kill fish many times its size.

National Geographic Photographer Robert F. Sisson

John Oliver La Gorce

249 © Dr. Erl Roman

"Tail Walking"

The sailfish (page 215) above is demonstrating one of the reasons his species is a favorite with deep-sea anglers. He has left the water and is dancing along the surface on his tail in a desperate effort to shake the hook. Frequently the big fish will stand out of the water almost vertically.

The Atlantic sail and his larger cousin in the Pacific ocean are both caught by trolling a bait on or near the surface, well back of the fisherman's boat.

Nature omitted teeth but gave the sail a spearlike weapon with which it strikes and stuns its prey. For this reason anglers do not attempt to "set the hook" immediately upon a strike, but wait until the fish starts to swallow its "stunned" victim.

Of great popularity as a game fish, the sailfish is too oily and too strong in flavor to gain acceptance as a food fish. When smoked, however, its quality is excellent.

 Luis Marden, National Geographic Staff

In Clear Water Fish See Easily, Too

Triggerfishes, black angel and surgeon fishes are silhouetted against a sunken boat and the sandy bottom of a Bimini fishpen in clear West Indies water (above).

A playful dolphin flashes blue and gold in the sun as he leaps from the water in acrobatic maneuvers for a Florida cameraman (opposite, top).

Nature's miniature submarine, the four-eyed fish of Central American lakes and rivers (opposite, bottom) has twin periscopes. Each bulbous eyeball of the *Anableps dowei,* the four eyes, is divided in two. The upper part, adapted for air vision, projects from the water to scan the surface for floating food; the lower eye looks for submarine enemies. Difference in focus is compensated for by bifocal lenses. Lacking eyelids and tear glands, *Anableps* must constantly dip its eyes in water to keep them moist.

out of most of its former haunts in Florida and the West Indies. The hawksbill, or shell turtle, became very rare some years ago when "tortoise-shell" ornaments were the fashion. As the demand waned, the turtles began to increase in numbers once more, and today they are reasonably plentiful.

The well-known habits of the turtle during the breeding season are one of the causes for its depletion. In early May and June in the West Indies the turtles come close to the shores to seek a suitable beach on which to lay their eggs. For several days prior to laying, the large female turtles will remain within a hun-

dred yards or so of an isolated beach and at such times are spotted by the watchful fishermen.

They may then be netted, or watched until they actually come up on to the beach where they dig a sizable hole in which to deposit their eggs. At this time, of course, the adult turtle may be easily captured, and in addition the thoughtless or greedy hunter will usually take the eggs for food, thus destroying the potential as well. In the event that the turtle is not molested, she will return to the same beach on the fourteenth night after the first crawl to dig a second hole close to the first.

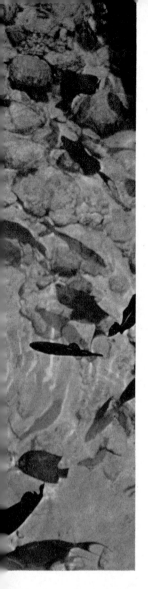

251

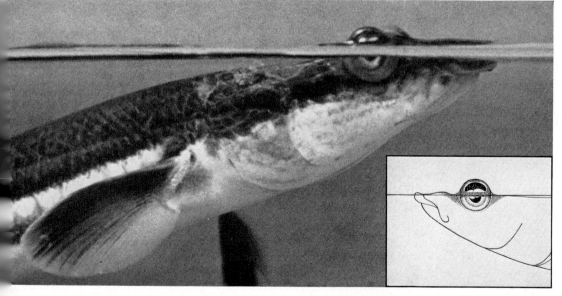

Kissing Gourami Perform Their Curious Rite

A pair of these unusual fish "kiss" in the New York aquarium. The kiss is a curious development of fish behavior and is performed when both fish extend the lips of the sharp, slightly superior mouth into broad rings and hover in the water with their lips in close contact for a considerable period. This may last as long as 25 minutes, or just a few seconds, but the longer periods are most usual. The biological significance, if any, is not understood, but observation indicates some reproductive relationship. These fish come in various light colors, sometimes almost white, frequently with pinkish or green tints. They are native to Malaya, Borneo, and Java.

A large adult female green turtle will deposit from 100 to 200 eggs in the two layings.

At the ratio of two hundred to one, it is reasonable to suppose that the survival of the species would be assured; but the fact remains that these edible creatures are on the wane. As man cannot account for all of the destruction, it will readily be seen that its natural enemies must take a heavy toll.

Such fish as the shark, barracuda, and amberjack, and birds like the pelican and man-o'-war-bird, kill hundreds of the newly hatched turtles each year, at an estimated rate of about ten for each one taken by man. The little turtles, incubated by the sun's heat, instinctively crawl to the sea immediately after hatching, where inevitably many of these rapidly moving though helpless young attract nearby surface-feeding birds and fish.

Importance of Shellfish Increases

In addition to the many strange creatures already mentioned are the several forms of shellfish which are known to most people today. Until 1949, the main shellfish catch of the Gulf and Caribbean area consisted of the spiny lobster (page 222), or crawfish. This lobster was always brought in alive and served fresh, and because of this fact it remained localized for years. With the advent of really modern quick-freeze methods and better marketing, this southern product became more in demand elsewhere. The supply could not keep up with the demand, and today a very similar form is being imported frozen from as far away as Australia and South Africa.

Another product which was difficult to market on a large scale was the shrimp. With better marketing and the resultant increased demand, experimental fishing for this little shellfish began. It was taken principally along the coasts of North and South Carolina, and most of the shrimp fishing was carried out there. Finally some large shrimps were discovered not far from the mouth of the Mississippi River, and a new ground was opened up. This trade spread along the shores of Louisiana, Texas, and Mexico.

In 1949, quite accidentally, one venturous shrimper tried setting his trawl at night over grounds which had produced nothing during the day. The result was amazing. The night hauls had produced another species of shrimp of large size, equally palatable, and apparently in unlimited quantities. A shrimping boom began with the port of Key West, Florida, as the center, and by the end of 1950 more than 300 shrimp boats were operating out of that harbor! Today, shrimp comprise the most valuable of the Gulf fisheries products and may be purchased as readily in Chicago markets as in Miami.

With this brief roundup of some of the inhabitants of the warmer seas, is there any wonder why millions of people flock south yearly to hunt them out?

253

Walter H. Chute

Hawaiian Fishes Are Colorful, Beautiful, and Fond of Coral Reefs

THE Moorish idol, or marine angelfish (middle, above—*Zanclus canescens*), is related to the butterflyfishes, but differs in its body form, long snout, elongated dorsal fins with threadlike rays, and a pair of bony projections over the eye. About eight inches in length, it inhabits the tropical Indian and Pacific Oceans.

The longfinned butterflyfish (left, above—*Heniochus acuminatus*) may be confused with the Moorish idol, but there is a definite difference in the scales. These butterflyfishes attain seven inches in length and range through the reef areas of the tropical Indo-Pacific region.

The bluestriped butterflyfish (right, above—*Chaetodon fremblii*) is known only from the Hawaiian Islands. Only six inches long, its pale yellow color and blue lines distinguish it from all other butterflyfishes.

The lazy fish, or redlined wrasse (middle, below—*Coris gaimard*), belongs to the wrasse family (page 256). Over a foot in length, they inhabit the tropical Indo-Pacific Oceans.

The birdfish (left, below—*Gomphosus tricolor*) is a species (page 256) of the same region.

The blue parrotfish (right, below—*Scarus forsteri*) is abundant on the reefs throughout the tropical Pacific Ocean. Blue to blue-gray in color, it attains a length of about 14 inches.

254 Walter H. Chute

Two Hundred Kinds of Butterflyfish Inhabit Tropical Waters

BUTTERFLYFISHES, family Chaetodontidae, are largely known in the Hawaiian language under the names kikikapu or kapuhili. Sometimes the name lauhau is given to certain species such as (top) *Chaetodon lunula*. The other species illustrated are (middle left) *C. vagabundus*, (middle center) *C. auriga*, and (lower) *C. trifasciata*.

There are so many kinds of closely related butterflyfishes that common names are not well fixed on many species.

Altogether, about 10 genera of butterflyfishes and nearly 200 species are known. Of these 66 have been reported from the area known as Oceania, and 29 occur in the Hawaiian Islands. The largest number of kinds occur in the East Indies. In the Atlantic the family is represented by not over a dozen and a half species, only five of which reach the eastern tropical Atlantic.

Among the four species illustrated, all range from the Hawaiian Islands and Johnston Island, westward through the tropical Pacific and Indian Oceans to the east coast of Africa, except *C. vagabundus*, which has not been observed in the Hawaiian Islands or at Johnston Island.

The butterflyfishes are an interesting group of reef-inhabiting species. They live in the intertidal zone of rocky reefs and coral reefs down to moderate depths of a couple of hundred feet or more.

Some prefer barren sandy bottoms; others, abundant coral and algal gardens. Since the colors of this group of fishes are as showy as butterflies and birds, they make very attractive exhibits in aquariums.

On the reefs they may be seen swimming in and out of crevices, through the interspaces of coral heads, sometimes sideways or upside down. In no one spot do they occur in large schools; instead, they appear to occur singly, in pairs, or in small groups. Their food consists of small animals such as crabs, shrimps, and worms.

With a small hook baited with bits of crabs or shrimp it is possible to capture butterflyfishes, but more may be caught by spearing. This latter method is very popular on the reefs and in lagoons of coral atolls.

The diver uses a steel rod, about three to five feet long, with a barbed tip. He shoots it through a bamboo tube by means of strips of rubber cut from old automobile tubes. This method is effective for 10 to 30 feet by experienced divers who are able to reach depths not exceeding 45 feet. Those equipped with diving gear may go much deeper.

Butterflyfishes do not reach a large size. Those illustrated seldom exceed six or eight inches in length. They occur in the markets at Honolulu.

Young butterflyfishes are very much different from the adults, with greatly developed membranes and spines forming sheaths and collars about the head.

Walter H. Chute

Colorful Spines of the Scorpion Fish Can Be Fatal to Handle

THE lionfish, tigerfish, or turkeyfish (*Pterois volitans*) belongs to the very large scorpion fish family, Scorpaenidae, whose members occur in subarctic, temperate to tropical seas.

They live chiefly around rocky shores and to depths of a few hundred feet. All are carnivorous and predaceous, feeding mostly on small fishes, crabs, shrimp, and such other animals as can be found.

The lionfish occurs from the Polynesian region in tropical seas on coral reefs westward to eastern Africa, including the Red Sea.

It belongs to a small group of highly specialized scorpion fishes usually called lion or tigerfishes in reference to the bushylike tentacles or the stripes. Sometimes the popular names turkeyfish and featherfish are used because of the resemblance to the plumage of a bird.

This group of scorpion fishes is adorned with beautiful and strikingly colored long, attenuated fin rays, long spines, and silky and bushy dermal tentacles on the head, body, and fins.

The colors usually consist of rich reddish-brown vertical bars, margined with white, with the interspaces light pink. The fins are barred with reddish brown and white, these colors sharply contrasting.

The lionfish is a stately creature when swimming. It seems to know that it is well equipped for defense, so takes its time to move through open water. Movements are slow and deliberate. The long, brilliant streamers wave in the flickering light among the corals where it lives.

Its spines are erect, protruding notably beyond the fin membranes, always ready to deliver a venomous poison if touched even lightly.

Each of the dorsal fin spines has a groove along its rear edge from base to tip. At the base of each spine is a poison gland.

The venom produced flows along the groove into a victim who is so unfortunate as to step on or grasp the beautifully decorated lionfish, for beneath such gorgeousness, death lurks.

There are records of small Polynesian children grasping a lionfish and receiving the venom in their hand. Death occurred in a day or so, the symptoms being much like those from a venomous snakebite.

Most specimens of lionfishes are only a few inches long, but *P. volitans* reaches a length of at least 10 inches.

The lionfish is not the only venomous scorpion fish. Many, but not all, of the members of the family have poisonous spines. The most notable exceptions are the rockfishes (pages 55, 87) of the North Pacific and Atlantic Oceans.

Of no economic use, the lionfish is a remarkably exquisite aquarium attraction. Transferring it from its native habitat to the aquarium, however, is a delicate job that involves carefully controlled tanks.

256

The Tropical Wrasse Family Ranges among Coral Islands of the Pacific

VARYING in color from blue to green, the hinalea iiwi, or birdfish (top, above—*Gomphosus tricolor*) is distinguished by its long tubular snout and small jaws. Reaching 12 inches, the birdfish is common among Pacific coral heads.

The **malamalama**, or **bluelined wrasse** (above, lower right—*Coris ballieui*), a market fish occurring only among the Hawaiian Islands and Johnston Island, reaches 12 to 15 inches in length.

The fish at lower left above is apparently a young redlined wrasse (page 253).

When adult, the **orangelined wrasse** of the Pacific corals (middle, below—*Thalassoma lutescens*) has a green body with vertical orange lines

on the scales and a reddish area in the pectoral fin, although, above, its drab gray body has not yet acquired these markings.

Originally described from the Red Sea, the **poou** (lower left, below—*Cheilinus unifasciatus*) lives among the coral reefs from east Africa to Polynesia in deep water. It can be captured by hook and line and reaches a length of 12 inches. The poou is distinguished from all other wrasses by a white bar on the caudal peduncle.

The **saddle wrasse** (lower right—*Thalassoma duperrey*) is one of the commonest species in the Hawaiian Islands and Johnston Island, inhabiting coral reefs and averaging a foot in length.

257 Walter H. Chute

Surgeonfishes (Above) Have Lancet-sharp Spines for Protection

THE tangs, popularly called surgeonfishes, are equipped with sharp spines which are normally sheathed in the skin. But when the tangs are frightened, the spines are erected to wound the enemy. The 10-inch **black tang, or black surgeonfish** (middle, above—*Acanthurus nigricans*) ranges from the Hawaiian Islands to Mauritius and the Red Sea.

The **orange-spot tang** (lower right, above—*Acanthurus olivaceous*) reaching a length of a foot, is a market fish in the tropical islands.

The **striped tang** (lower left—*Ctenochaetus striatus*) is one of the most abundant species on the reefs of coral atolls. It is a valuable market fish, reaching a length of about 11 inches.

The **pinktailed triggerfish** (upper right, below—*Balistes vidua*) is spectacularly colored, with dark fin margins and pink tail. Reaching 10 inches in length, it ranges from the Hawaiian Islands and Polynesia to the East Indies.

The **whiteline triggerfish** (lower left, below—*Balistes bursa*) ranges from the Polynesian area westward to the east African coast. It reaches a length of eight inches, but is not used as food because its flesh is reported to be poisonous.

The 15-inch **black triggerfish** (lower right, below—*Melichthys radula*) ranges from the East Indies to our American waters.

258 Walter H. Chute

Flying Gurnard (Top) Is Grounded by Its Heavy Body

THE Pacific flying gurnard, or loloau, as it is known in the Hawaiian Islands, carries the scientific name *Dactyloptena orientalis*.

Remarkable creatures, these fish have the first few rays of the pectoral fin free and use them as legs to propel themselves over the bottom sands, to feel about for food, or to hold them off the bottom. The enlarged pectoral fins or wings are beautifully colored.

Although it is reported to fly, its boxlike body of 14 to 15 inches long probably is too heavy for it to sail through the air! The long black spine over the head is a prominent and distinguishing characteristic of the "flying" gurnard.

The threadfish (middle—*Alectis ciliaris*) ranges in the warm seas of the Pacific and Indian Oceans.

This species, when young, has the dorsal and anal rays greatly extended and threadlike, several times longer than the body. When it reaches a length of nearly a foot, the rays are much shorter and the body becomes less deep. The long "streamers" on the fins make it a beautiful aquarium exhibit.

The foot-long sandfish (bottom—*Malacanthus hoedtii*) occurs in the Indo-Pacific Oceans, ranging from the east African coast to the Hawaiian Islands.

259 Walter H. Chute

The Triggerfish (Top Left and Top Center) Has a Built-in Locking Mechanism

THE triggerfish, or humu-humu nuku-nuku a-puaa (top, left—*Rhinecanthus aculeatus*), is a very close relative of the rectangular triggerfish (page 266).

It ranges through the warm seas of the Indian and Pacific Oceans, but does not reach the American shores. It lives among the corals on the reefs, in shallow water, where at low tide, it may be seen trapped in small tidal pools.

Like the **orangestriped triggerfish** (top, center—*Balistapus undulatus*), all triggerfishes have the locking mechanism described on page 266. They reach a length of 10 inches and are reported to be poisonous to eat.

The **brownspotted grouper** of the genus *Epinephelus* (top, right) belongs to the sea bass family. It is confined to the tropical central Pacific, where it occurs in some abundance on the coral atolls. The largest of this valuable food fish is 15 to 18 inches.

The **bluespotted grouper** (lower, right—*Cephalopholis argus*) is one of the commonest species in the Indian and Pacific Oceans, but does not occur in Hawaiian and American waters.

This beautiful 2½-foot sea bass varies from purple and brownish to blackish, always with brilliant blue spots.

Lower left is a **lionfish** (page 255).

260

The Smaller Reef Fishes Make Decorative Aquarium Exhibits

SOMETIMES not more than two or three inches long, the tiny but colorful fishes of the tropical central Pacific and Indian Oceans are imported for exhibition in public and private aquariums.

The 3-inch **bluegreen damselfish** (top, above —*Chromis caeruleus*) is a common inhabitant of coral reefs, where it may be seen flashing its brilliant blue color.

When frightened, **blackbanded damselfish** (left center, above—*Dascyllus aruanus*) swim among the interspaces of coral heads, where they will remain, even after the coral head is broken off and carried on shore. They reach a length of about three inches.

The **anemone fish** (right center, above—*Amphiprion percula*) is so named because it lives symbiotically with the sea anemone, and is not stung by the latter's battery of stinging cells. Instead, it attracts other small fishes, which are promptly paralyzed by the sea anemone. Then the two partners share the banquet. It reaches a length of three inches.

The **clown goby** (lower right, above—*Gobiodon hypselopterus*) ranges among the interspaces of the branching corals, where it builds small nests. The eggs are adhesive and cling to the base of a coral branch, protected by one of the parents until hatching occurs. This goby may reach a length of two inches.

The **blackstriped cardinal fish** (lower middle, above—*Apogon novemfasciata*) is abundant on coral reefs of the central and western Pacific and Indian Oceans. The male of this delicate little fish uses its mouth for the incubation of eggs. It reaches a length of about three inches.

The **polkadot moray** (second from left, above —*Gymnothorax meleagris*), partially concealed in a piece of coral, reaches a length of about one and a half feet.

The **orange anthiid** (far left, above—*Odontanthias elizabethae*), known only from the Hawaiian Islands, is related to the sea basses, but differs in having each lobe of the tail fin greatly elongated. It may reach a total length of eight inches.

The **redspotted tang** (top pair, upper right— *Acanthurus achilles*) is a surgeonfish, which inhabits the shallow areas of coral reefs. Feeding on algal growths, it occurs in the central and western tropical Pacific Ocean and reaches a length of 11 inches.

The **whitespotted wrasse** (lower figure, upper right—*Anampses cuvier*) is known only from the Hawaiian Islands.

Its teeth are peculiar. The pair of canines at the tip of the lower jaw extend straight forward and curve a little downward, whereas the pair at the tip of the upper jaw extend forward and are flattish with a wide, straight "cutting edge" along their outer margins. When the mouth closes, the pair in the lower jaw fit between the upper pair, which are widely spaced. This species reaches a length of a foot.

261

Hawaiian Oddity →

AVERAGING six inches in length, the **fantail filefish** *(Pervagor spilosoma)* is found on the reefs in the Hawaiian Islands. The single long spine, with its rough, file-like edges, gives the fish its common name.

The fantail filefish expands its tail at times until the front edges are nearly at right angles to its body.

Many of the filefishes are edible, but some are reported poisonous, so that care must be taken in using them as food.

Hawaiian fishes make bright aquarium exhibits, although their colors often fade in captivity. The average life of the fish in an aquarium is only about 10 months, and new specimens are continually required.

Walter H. Chute

Walter H. Chute

The Convict Tang (Lower Right) Is Named for Its Stripes but Can Also Wield a Knife

KNOWN by its giant fins, the **sailfin tang** (top—*Zebrasoma veliferum*) ranges throughout the tropical Indian and Pacific Oceans except in American waters.

Exceeding a foot in length, sailfin tangs occur on the shallow parts of coral reefs, sometimes in large schools. They feed on the algae growing on the reefs, gorging themselves on sea lettuce.

The **convict tang** (lower right, pair—*Acanthurus sandvicensis*) is easily distinguished from other tangs by its five or six narrow bars. Like the sailfin, it likes shallow reefs and feeds on algae.

It reaches a length of about 10 inches and is used as food in many of the Pacific and Indian islands.

Although it is smaller than the sailfin, it must be handled carefully because of the knifelike spine on each side at the base of the tail fin. Deep cuts may result if the fish gives a powerful strike with its tail, but the spine is not venomous.

The **red goatfish** (lower left—*Parupeneus pleurostigma*) and the **yellow-spot** or **whitespot goatfish** (left center—*Parupeneus porphyreus*) may be recognized by the pair of long barbels that hang downward from the tip of the chin like the beard of a goat. There are more than 30 kinds of closely related goatfishes in the tropical Pacific. They are mostly bottom feeders, living on small crustaceans and other animals. Some species attain 20 inches in length and are important market fishes in tropical Pacific islands.

The Carnivorous Jack (Top) Is Noted All Over the Pacific as a Food Fish

THE **ulua**, or **jack** (upper right—*Caranx melampygus*), ranges from the east African coast in tropical seas eastward to the Hawaiian Islands and the eastern American Pacific.

There is a considerable change in color pattern as the ulua reaches the adult size. Beginning at a length of nine to eleven inches, small dark spots form on the body, first only a few as shown in the illustration. At lengths over 15 inches, it is profusely spotted. It reaches a length of 3 feet.

Also a market fish, the **blackbarred jack**, **ulua pauu** (upper left—*Gnathanodon speciosus*), is of the same family and range.

Another fish of the same range is the carnivorous **red bigeye**, **aweoweo** in the Hawaiian language (lower left—*Priacanthus cruentatus*).

The **scorpion fish**, or **nohu** (lower right—*Scorpaenopsis cacopsis*), occurs only in the Hawaiian Islands. The dorsal spines have poison glands at their bases and deliver a very potent venom, dangerous to man.

Walter H. Chute

263

Walter H. Chute

Inhabitants of Polynesian Waters Differ in Color, Shape, and Temperament

THE only thing that all these fish have in common is their habitat among Pacific coral reefs. The **unicorn fish**, or **umaumalei**, in the Hawaiian Islands (top, right) is scientifically named *Naso litturatus*. A reef dweller from Polynesia to Africa, it differs from some of the other surgeon-fishes in having two blunt spines on the caudal peduncle instead of a single sharp, knifelike erectile spine. The common name, unicorn fish, is derived from a close relative, *N. brevirostris*, the adult male of which has a long hornlike projection that develops on its forehead.

The **black-banded wrasse** (top, left—*Coris flavovittatus*) is called **hilu** in the Hawaiian language. It occurs on the coral reefs of the Hawaiian and Philippine Islands and at Guam. The hilu is a valuable food fish in the Hawaiian Islands, where it occurs in the markets. A length of at least 16 inches is reached.

The physical contortions of the wrasse at the right in the middle picture give it its nickname, "acrobat of the seas." Equally applicable is its common name, the **clown wrasse** (*Xyrichthys taeniourus*), occurring from Polynesia to the east African coast. Studies made this year indicate that between lengths of two to three inches, the clown fish changes its color pattern radically. The adults reach a length of about 10 inches.

The **black-spot wrasse** (middle, left), or **aawa** in the Hawaiian tongue (*Bodianus bilunulatus*), of the same range is 14 inches long and a valuable market fish in Honolulu.

The **moray eels** (bottom) occur in all tropical and subtropical seas on the rocky shores, and especially around coral reefs to depths of a few hundred feet. Largely nocturnal in habit, hiding by day, they are carnivorous and predacious. Some species are savage, malicious and dangerous. The **brown moray** (right—*Gymnothorax undulatus*) occurs on coral and rocky reefs from Polynesia westward to the east African coast. Specimens 6½ feet long have been captured, weighing 34 pounds. Other specimens have been reported between 9 and 10 feet long.

Vernon Brock, director of the Division of Fish and Game in Hawaii, was diving and spearing fishes on the coral reefs of Johnston Island, an atoll south of the Hawaiian chain. He saw a large brown moray eel, 20 feet down, resting along a ledge. He estimated an unusual length of 10 feet. Diving down, Brock put a spear squarely through its head. The eel never moved, so after 15 or 20 minutes, he revisited the eel. Assuming it was dead, Brock dived down, grasped the spear and started to swim back to a small boat. The eel started directly for him, reared its head high and struck viciously at Brock's head. Brock raised his arm for protection, and the eel savagely grasped his entire arm, biting it terribly. The eel let loose at once, and Brock made the boat, where his companions stopped the blood flow with a tourniquet. After three months he recovered the use of his arm. Only his remarkable swimming skill had saved his life.

The other eels illustrated are: **yellow-spotted eel** (second from right—*Echidna nebulosa*), ranging from the American tropical Pacific to the east African coast; **black-speckled moray** (second from left—*Gymnothorax picta*), ranging from Polynesia to the east African coast and abundant in the shallow waters of coral reefs; and **brown-marbled moray** (left foreground—*Gymnothorax thalassopterus*), occurring in the Hawaiian Islands. All the species reach a usual length of about two or three feet.

266 Walter H. Chute

Pacific Fish Are Well Named for Familiar Characteristics

THE **longnosed butterflyfish** (top, upper left—*Forcipiger longirostris*) is distinguished by the long tubular snout, with the jaws at the tip. Seven inches in length, it ranges from the Hawaiian Islands to the eastern coast of tropical Africa and the Red Sea.

The **rectangular triggerfish** (top, lower left—*Rhinecanthus rectangulus*) lives among coral heads throughout the tropical central Pacific westward to the western Indian Ocean and Red Sea.

Triggerfishes are reported to have poisonous flesh, and all have the trigger mechanism described on page 229.

The **yellow tang,** or **yellow surgeonfish** (top, upper right—*Zebrasoma flavescens*), has two color phases—one bright chrome yellow, and the other blackish or dark brown. The yellow is predominant in the Hawaiian Islands, whereas the dark is predominant elsewhere. This species ranges from the tropical central Pacific westward to the east coast of Africa.

The six- to eight-inch yellow surgeonfish is so named because the spine resembles a surgical knife.

The **whitelined squirrelfish** (top, lower right—*Holocentrus diadema*) is also called soldierfish, in reference to its strong armorlike spines or spears.

The **longfinned razorfish** (bottom, center—*Iniistius pavoninus*) is a member of the wrasse family. It occurs in tropical seas from the east coast of Africa to Hawaii. It is recognized by its compressed, knife-shaped body. Used for food in Hawaii, it reaches a length of about 15 inches.

The **spotted hawkfish** (bottom, lower left—*Cirrhitus pinnulatus*) is found only in Polynesian waters and the western Pacific Ocean. It prefers the coral reefs where the surf beats and breaks over corals and algae.

The six-inch **squirrelfish** (bottom, lower right—*Myripristis berndti*) is noctural in its habits, hiding in crevices among the reefs by day.

267

Most Vicious of the South American Tigerfishes, the Piranha Is World-famous

ALTHOUGH not very large and seldom over a foot and a half in length, the **piranha** (*Serrasalmus rhombeus*) is the most feared fish in the basins of the Orinoco and the Amazon. Explorers of the region have returned with well-authenticated stories of its fierce aggressiveness.

The piranhas, which attack in groups, have appetites of giant proportions and equally bad tempers. They are instantly and indiscriminately destructive of any animal life they encounter. Other fish, birds, cattle, sheep, horses, or human beings who venture in tropical rivers within its habitat are exposed to swift skeletonizing. In 1819 an entire army fording a South American river was attacked by piranhas.

Only constant vigilance can save other fish in the piranha's habitat. Wading birds have had their legs amputated. Sheep have been stripped of all flesh in a matter of minutes. Careless native canoeists, allowing a hand to drift through the water, have had it torn to shreds.

The piranha's size is more than compensated for by sharklike teeth and one of the most powerful sets of jaws in all animal life. A valued food fish, it responds readily to almost any bait. But members of Amazon expeditions have had to use wire between hook and line. Otherwise the piranha bit through the line. Three strands of wire have been reported as necessary to hold the fish.

When pulled out of the water, the piranha makes a low, grunting noise and sometimes closes its jaws so forcefully on the sides of a knife blade that it crushes its own teeth.

Particularly dangerous away from the main currents of the rivers, such as in the calm and shallow waters along the edges or in placid estuaries, they travel in schools of hundreds or even thousands and can quickly devour animals of any size.

What looks like a deformed eye in the specimen illustrated is really a nostril.

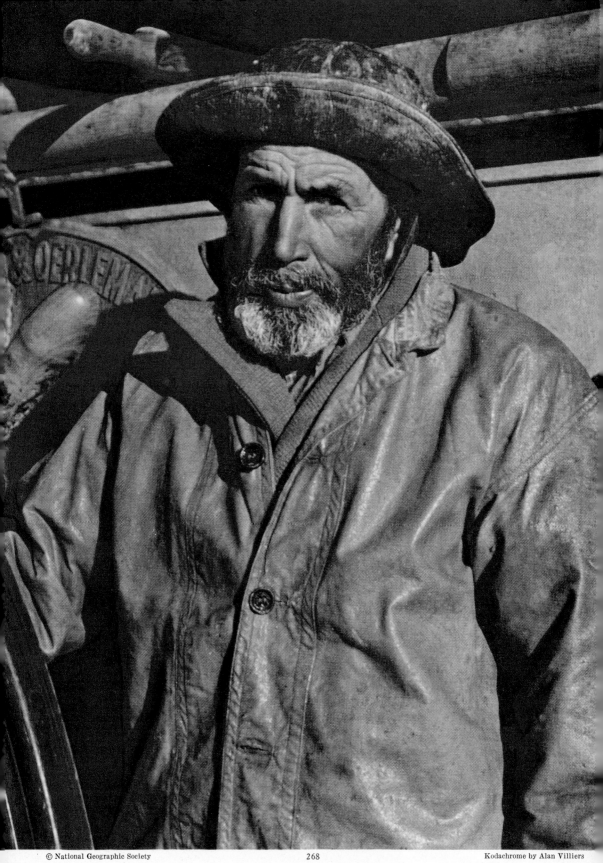

268

A Heritage of Four and a Half Centuries Backs the Portuguese Fisherman of the Grand Banks

For the forty-third time in his 63 years, this weather-hardened mariner has sailed across the Atlantic with 2,000 countrymen to catch cod off Newfoundland. They still use sailing ships primarily.

Portugal's Captains Courageous

By Alan Villiers

FOUR hundred and fifty years ago, Portuguese in sturdy sailing ships were crossing the Atlantic on the spring east wind to fish the Grand Banks off Newfoundland, 2,000 miles away. They fished with hook and line, filled their holds with cod, and raced for home before the fierce northern winter began.

In the 1950's, a fleet of Portuguese sailing ships still sets out each spring for the Grand Banks. Though time has brought changes in the size, shape, and gear of the ships, the 2,000 hardy fishermen who man the fleet face most of the same hazards their ancestors did.

Early in a recent spring, I shipped out with the Portuguese fishing fleet of 32 sailing vessels in the graceful steel four-master *Argus*, built in 1938-39, queen of the banking ships.

The sailing vessels, I learned, still depend mainly on the wind, though they now have Diesel engines to help out when necessary. They also have electric lights, steam heat, and refrigeration. Power winches, within the memory of some of the older fishermen, have done away with the backbreaking job of raising and lowering sails and anchors.

But the fishing itself, the sea, and the danger are unchanged. The men still fish in the classic way: in the morning each sets out alone in his small one-man dory, pitting himself, his skill, and his luck against the ocean.

I picked up the *Argus* in the broad River Tagus, or Tejo, where the fleet of hand-liners was assembling for the blessing service. Aboard the *Argus* all was activity. Throaty calls of the dorymen sailors mingled now with the clank of the windlass bringing the cables home and the creak of blocks as high white sails piled aloft.

Three other schooners were sailing with us, for the bankers like to go in company. This has been traditional since the days when pirates roamed the North Atlantic, but it has still another purpose: in early spring when the ships sail, and in autumn when they return, sudden gales blow up and old ships may founder. If there are others near by, they can rescue the crew.

The longer I was aboard the *Argus,* the more I marveled at her. She was a sailing ship, but she was fitted with every modern device that was of use. The Portuguese are not old-fashioned; they stick to the schooner rig because it is ideal for fishing on the Banks, where a ship must be at sea for months, and a powered vessel might run out of fuel.

We got to St. John's and there was still no bait, for it was a bad ice season, and the Newfoundlanders could not get at the herring. It was early April, and cold. We passed 17 days in the harbor, just waiting until we took on bait. Then we fished for cod on the Grand Banks off Newfoundland for six cold and foggy weeks, while we waited for the summer sun to melt the ice in Davis Strait and clear the way to Greenland. But there wasn't any sun and there wasn't any summer, either.

The *Argus* and her consorts just anchored on the Banks, choosing a place where the rocky bottom prevented the horde of trawlers from working because the rocks would rip their costly trawls. Her 53 dorymen went over the side at 4 o'clock every morning they possibly could, fog or fine—and it was rarely fine.

They'd streak away under their tiny oiled sails for the horizon, lay their long-lines, and fish all day. While the 600-hook long-lines were down, they'd fish by hand with lead jiggers, shaped like a herring and fitted with two large hooks.

When we'd used up the St. John's bait, we went into North Sydney, Nova Scotia, for more herring and fresh mackerel to take along to the Greenland grounds. As soon as the bait was aboard, off we went again, north through the Strait of Belle Isle toward Greenland.

There was continuous daylight from the midnight sun for the first two and a half months. The dorymen worked and worked, often putting in a 20-hour day, fishing from 4 a.m. and cleaning and salting until midnight.

At last there came a day when even Captain Adolfo thought that we had cod enough, though not a full cargo, mark you!

For a hundred days we had eaten the midnight soup of codfish faces. The dorymen call it the "soup of sorrow," for they say that, once having eaten it, you are bound to come back to the Banks again. One hundred days of the soup of sorrow were enough for me.

Yet it was not until we had sailed past the Danas Bank that the dorymen dared smile. Danas was the last large bank. The course now was southeast toward the Azores—the Azores, and sunshine, and good Portugal!

Kodachrome by Alan Villiers

With a Gale on the Way, Crewmen Stow *Gazela Primeiro's* Foresail. She Is the Last Square-rigger in Portugal's Fleet

Once barkentines like *Gazela* were common on the Banks; now most have been replaced by easier-to-handle schooners. The furry-looking stay at left is covered with woven yarn to prevent its chafing the sail. Opposite: Sailors hang on as a North Atlantic comber breaks over *Argus's* low rail.

In Davis Strait: Sails Speed Dories to Cod. Oars Double as Rudders

Each doryman chooses his own rig. Most *Argus* boats carry small jib-headed mainsails (above, center). Inset: This man prefers a gaff-and-boom rig. The Cross of Christ was stitched on the sail by his wife.

Kodachromes by Alan Villiers

Unless the Schooner Signals Them Back, Dories Won't Return Until They Are Filled

A full dory, in the hands of an expert, will hold up to a ton of cod; if overloaded, it may founder. These men may
sail five miles off in search of fish. If a storm threatens, *Argus* will fly a recall flag.

Kodachromes by Alan Villiers

274

After They're Caught, Cod Must Be Cleaned, Salted, and De-livered

When a full dory comes alongside *Argus*, the cod are gaffed up on deck into boxed-off compartments along the rail. Gangs of three then slit and clean the fish. Livers are carefully saved and taken forward to a pressure plant, which removes the valuable oil.

Cod themselves are thrown into the hold, where a skilled crew salts each fish carefully and stows it. Careless salting can spoil a whole cargo.

Almost every man aboard lends a hand when the load is in, sometimes working a 20-hour day. Above: The chief engineer splits cod with one stroke. Right: A deck boy pulls up more fish from the dory below.

Portugal's Champion Fisher Passes a Big One over the Side

Francisco Emilio Battista is the *Argus's*—and the fleet's—First Fisher. For the past several seasons he has averaged between 90 and 100 tons of cod, caught entirely with hooks. While he gaffs up his catch, his dory is held alongside the schooner with a boat hook and a long painter. The gaff itself resembles a pitchfork with two steel prongs. The coiled rope is the doryman's 1,000-hook long-line; a cod's mouth gapes beside it.

Cod, Gear, and Rigging Crowd Every Inch of a Dory

Dories contain no lifesaving equipment. If one capsizes away from the mother ship, a fisherman's only hope is to hang on and pray that help comes before he freezes. This *Argus* fisherman is coming in with a full load caught off Greenland. Behind him, besides cod, are his bait basket, his long-line, and a small grapnel.

Kodachromes by Alan Villiers

275

276 Painting by Walter A. Weber, National Geographic Staff Artist

The Tarpon's Large Scales Glisten as It Fights the Hook Defiantly

OFTEN admiringly called the "silver king" by sportsmen, the **tarpon** (*Tarpon atlanticus*) is one of the most coveted of all marine game fishes (pages 277-283). Although its range extends from Brazil and the West Indies northward to Cape Hatteras and occasionally even to Cape Cod, its chief habitat is the Caribbean and the Gulf of Mexico. Usually the tarpon is about 5 feet long, but it is known to reach 8 feet or more and to attain a weight of more than 300 pounds. The record size taken on rod and reel was 7 feet 5½ inches in length and 247 pounds in weight.

The popularity of the tarpon among anglers stems less from its speed, which is very limited, than from its strength, endurance, and agility when hooked. It dashes and jumps and puts up a spectacular if sometimes brief fight. Its flesh is dry and coarse and popular as food largely among the Central American Indians. The tarpon's food consists chiefly of smaller fishes and of crawfish, crabs, and shrimp. It is readily available to anglers, frequenting in considerable numbers the passes between reefs and islands, channel banks, estuaries, and river mouths. It may be caught both from shore and from boats.

The Lordly Tarpon—Angler's Delight

By Van Campen Heilner

Field Representative, Department of Ichthyology, American Museum of Natural History

THE tarpon, or *sabalo* (*Tarpon atlanticus*), has often been called the angler's delight. He is one of the best known and most spectacular of the fighting fishes. His stuffed skin adorns the walls of countless clubs and sportsmen's retreats, and his portrait in oils has graced the cover of many a magazine.

Although few realize it, to him is due no small amount of credit for the development of Florida, though he is by no means confined to that peninsula. He is the original big game fish, anglers having come from each of the five continents in search of him long before sailfish, marlin, or tuna were heard of as game fish.

Tarpon as Far North as Long Island

Largest of the herring family, the tarpon is more or less common from offshore Long Island (summer) to Brazil. Occasional tarpon wander north along the Atlantic seaboard every summer and are frequently caught in nets, infrequently by anglers. At Hatteras, North Carolina, the fish are present throughout the warm months, no doubt because of the close proximity of the Gulf Stream edge, which at this point is about ten miles offshore. Breder mentions that off Cape Hatteras exists the greatest concentration of flying fish on the entire Atlantic coast, and undoubtedly sailfish and marlin are there as well. Although the writer has seen and caught very small tarpon up the rivers of the west coast of Florida, he does not believe that they breed north of Cuba, or if so, rarely.

Wherever they occur, tarpon are eagerly sought by anglers. As a food fish they leave much to be desired, although in Cuba the natives salt and smoke all they can get. But as furnishers of spectacular sport, when taken on the proper tackle, they have few equals.

Most of the tarpon clubs are in Florida, though a number flourish in Texas and Mexico and there is a famous club in the Canal Zone. Here where the great Gatun Dam spans the Chagres River is to be found some of the finest tarpon fishing known.

I see no reason why the tarpon should not flourish in the Pacific, especially on the west coast of Central America, if introduced into those waters from the Atlantic side. Other fish have been transplanted from the Atlantic to the Pacific with success, notably the striped bass (*Roccus saxatilis*) from the Shrewsbury and Navesink Rivers, New Jersey, in 1879 to California, where it is now more abundant than on the Atlantic coast.

The tarpon loves to frequent passes, channels, and cuts through the banks. Here he lies in wait for whatever small fishes the tides will bring him. He can be caught either by trolling or still-fishing, and the writer has taken young tarpon on salmon flies.

Angling for the Big Fellows

In trolling, a baited hook or artificial bait is trailed slowly from a launch or skiff back and forth through the passes known to be used by the fish. In still-fishing, a hook baited with crab or cut bait is lowered to the bottom and sufficient time given the tarpon to swallow that bait before setting the hook.

The instant the fish feels the point of the hook he rushes to the surface and hurls himself into the air in an amazing and sensational series of leaps in a frequently successful effort to free himself. So violent and furious are these jumps that he finally exhausts himself and, if he does not throw the hook or break the line, is brought to boat.

There are, however, exceptions to this rule of battle. One of the largest tarpon of which I have any record, taken by the late L. P. Schutt of the Long Key Florida Fishing Camp, jumped only once during the entire fight. At the end, as the fish was almost to boat, a large shark rushed up and bit it in two just behind the dorsal fin. The part remaining, which weighed more than 200 pounds, was mounted and exhibited for years until the building was destroyed in the hurricane of 1935.

In Florida the best tarpon fishing occurs in May and June. Earlier in the season the fish are frequently caught along the viaducts of the Overseas Highway to Key West and in the ship channel at Miami Beach. At that time of year they seem to strike best at night.

Curiously enough, in many trips to Cuba I found that tarpon take the bait best between

278

The Silver King Fights for Life

Enraged by the hook in his bony mouth, a big tarpon surges up in a gallant try to shake the barb, and he may do it! One of the hardest fighting fishes known, the Silver King always gives a spectacular battle, and many more are hooked than landed. Prize battlers, they sometimes reach eight feet in length and weigh more than 200 pounds.

Dr. Thomas W. McKnew

Tackle Replaces Scalpel; a Doctor Shows His Catch

Dr. William A. Morgan, prominent Washington, D. C., surgeon, relaxes after boating 215 pounds of tarpon in the Gulf of Mexico off South Boca Grande, Florida. The larger silver king weighed 125 pounds and measured six feet, three inches from nose to tail. The smaller fish weighed 90 pounds.

9 in the morning and 4 in the afternoon. Later or earlier than that it was almost impossible to get a strike.

I have seen the tarpon around Florida's Cape Sable lying all over the shallow flats and banks like shoals of bait, and in the harbor mouth at Bimini in the Bahamas, about 55 miles across the Gulf Stream from Miami Beach, there are at all times large numbers of young tarpon weighing from 30 to 50 pounds. These, which are clearly visible through a waterglass, lie on the bottom.

I first became interested in the tarpon through the enthusiasm of my late friend Anthony W. Dimock, father of Julian Dimock. Father and son, great sportsmen and students of marine life, took the finest photographs of leaping tarpon ever made.

Biggest Thrill—the First Fish

My first tarpon weighed only 20 pounds, but if he had weighed 200 my excitement and delight could not have been greater.

The circumstances remain engraved upon my memory. A moonlight night, the ghostly arches of the Florida Keys viaduct, the putt-putt of the tiny launch that carried me crosswise to the rushing tide; then the strike and the flash of silver, dripping diamonds of spray from its flanks as it catapulted into the air again and again, and yet again.

A lot of water has flowed through those arches of the then Florida East Coast railroad since that time and many a tarpon has leaped at the end of my line, but that first one I shall never forget.

I remember one blazing hot day toward the end of March on the vast miles of banks off the southern tip of Florida. The tide had turned to the flood about 3 in the afternoon, and all along the vast shoal from Sandy Key eastward to Snake Bight tarpon were rolling. The mullet were "in," and the water was discolored a milky white.

As we slid across the flats in our little skiff propelled by an outboard motor, we could see the long plumes of tarpon wavering for an instant on the surface. The sun had just set in

Top: A. W. & Julian A. Dimock   280   Bottom: © Venice Tarpon Club

A Tarpon and a Half, Both in Florida Air

The fighting hundred-pound tarpon in the upper picture takes to the air. If he lands in the boat (as sometimes happens), men and fish will probably be in the tarpon's natural element! Shark or barracuda beat this angler to it (bottom). Well-hooked, the tarpon was being played when a hungry, underwater pirate claimed half of him for his dinner.

a great ball of red fire as we started up a long blue-green channel that wound between the banks. I was fishing with an extra-light outfit, a rod that weighed only four and a half ounces over all and was more suitable for fresh water gamesters than for tarpon.

We came to the end of the channel and turned to retrace our wake. Suddenly there was a swift surge on my line. I struck, and into the air bounded a tarpon.

I could hear the tinkle of the spoon as he twisted his head from side to side in an effort to dislodge the hook. But it held, and this seemed to increase his frenzy, for he was in

and out of the water so fast that I wondered if I was bound to some great sea bird or a fish that preferred air to its natural element.

The skiff drifted with the tide, and the fish continued its mad leaping. Half the time I did not know whether I had him on or not. But then the line would straighten out and the dead weight would come at the end, and I knew the fight was not yet finished. The tackle was so light that I could not easily force the fighting, and it was more than half an hour before I had him alongside.

He was worn out from his terrific exertions. We tipped the skiff down on one side and slid

The Silver King Reaches →
for the Sky

Hooked with artificial lure and bait rod, a 40-pound tarpon leaps ten feet from the water of Tarpon Bay, Shark River, Florida. A 40-pounder on light tackle is a match for any angler.

John Oliver La Gorce

© Dr. Erl Roman

← The Angler Has Won a
Battle Royal down the
Florida Keys

The fighting tarpon, together with the marlin, sail, tuna, and of late years, the bonefish, and numerous others, have done much to establish both coasts of south Florida as a Mecca for fishermen from all over the world. Many sportsmen, successful in boating gamesters like this, release them unless they were so injured in the fight that they would be prey to everpresent sharks or barracuda, or are to be mounted.

A. W. and Julian A. Dimock

Free!

In a magnificent leap this lordly gamester has shaken the hook and is free to swim away. Because of his horny mouth, the tarpon's efforts to escape are very often successful. The thrown hook and line can be seen to the right of the fish.

him over the edge into the boat. He weighed 56 pounds and even today adorns the walls of my studio, one of my proudest achievements with rod and line. For thrills aplenty, try the "silver king" on bait-casting tackle!

Tarpon Are Caught and Released

I remember another day in June on the west coast of Florida. We were still-fishing in a pass. Tarpon had been rolling all around us, but we could not tempt them to bite. I was drowsing in my seat at the stern of the skiff when suddenly I noticed the line, which I had stripped from my reel and laid on one of the thwarts, start to uncoil and slide over the edge into the sea. For several seconds I watched, fascinated; when it had almost reached the end, I let it come taut and struck, once—twice. Immediately a tarpon shot skyward astern and a little to one side, and the battle was on.

From then on, tarpon bit at anything and everything offered, and in a brief time we boated and released seven.

So it goes. A friend, B. W. Crowninshield, brought to boat 25 tarpon between sunup and sundown at Boca Grande, the famous Florida west coast resort of these mighty fish. Off Cuba we have hooked and jumped as many as 104 fish in one day, of course releasing them if uninjured.

About three out of every four tarpon throw the hook on their first leap.

As a rule, they run from 30 to 80 pounds. Many are caught weighing from 120 to 170 pounds. These are large fish. A specimen of 200 pounds is exceptional.

The present world's record was taken in 1938 by H. W. Sedgwick in the Pánuco River, Mexico. It tipped the beam at 247 pounds, topping by five pounds the record previously held by J. M. Cowden with a fish taken in the same locality. We have a mounted tarpon in the Museum, details of capture unknown, which from appearances must have been close to 300 pounds. This I should think is about the limit of heft for this species.

Tarpon May Spawn in Florida Rivers

Tarpon probably spawn somewhere in the Caribbean, possibly up brackish or fresh-water rivers from which they descend to the sea and wander all over. I have always felt, though I could never prove, that some must spawn up the rivers of the west coast of Florida; I

A Battler's Days Are Ended

Caught on light bait-casting tackle in Florida's Shark River, this big tarpon is pulled from the water to pose for his picture and later to be mounted as a trophy. The proud angler, left, surveys his catch, whose weight almost pulls the gunwales of the small boat under.

have seen countless baby tarpon in these streams and in the ditches along the Tamiami Trail. Very tiny tarpon, only a few inches long, have been taken off Puerto Rico and Cuba, and the chances are that the main spawning grounds are below the Tropic of Cancer.

There is no doubt that the majority of tarpon seen run from 30 to 80 pounds. Where the big ones keep themselves is a question. It occurs to the writer that as tarpon grow larger and older they lose some of their agility and more easily fall prey to sharks.

Of course there are plenty of big tarpon still left, but the smaller ones outnumber them five and six to one. The shark theory is at least plausible.

For several years the writer carried on exploratory work in the swamps and rivers of southern Cuba. This country was well-nigh inaccessible and could be reached only after arduous travel on horseback and afoot through almost impenetrable swamps. Many of the rivers literally swarmed with tarpon which had never even seen man. They would strike at any moving object.

The rivers were dark and narrow, and the mangrove bushes crowded them closely on both sides. The water extended in under the bushes for some distance, and, as one passed, the tarpon (or sabalo, as they are called there) would rush out from beneath the overhanging branches and seize the lure.

One Might Land in the Boat!

Quite frequently their first leap landed them in the trees, from which they fell with a great crashing and breaking of branches into the water, leaving the angler's line a tangled mass above. Though no sabalo ever actually landed in the boat, two or three of them came mighty close to it. If a fish should actually land in a fishing boat—the accident has occurred on one or two occasions—the results might easily prove disastrous.

If you love angling and want some of the most spectacular sport to be found, pack your tackle and make your plans next spring to slip down the coast to Florida, Texas, Mexico, Panama, or to any one of countless other places that fringe the Caribbean. There you may try your mettle on one of Nature's grandest gifts to fisherman, that bow of flashing silver, that master of aerial acrobatics, the leaping tarpon.

National Geographic Photographer Willard R. Culver

"What's This One, Grandma? I Found It All by Myself!"

The young, sunbonneted conchologist triumphantly holds up a valve of the Calico Scallop she has picked up on a Sanibel Island beach, off Florida's west coast. Overflowing the basket is a chain of egg cases of the Left-Handed Whelk, or Conch, of which a specimen is at the right. A giant Band Shell, or Horse Conch, thrusts out its white spire at the left, and under the farther end of the handle is a Tulip Band shell.

Sea Creatures of Our Atlantic Shores

By Roy Waldo Miner

Curator Emeritus of Marine Life, American Museum of Natural History

VOYAGING southward from New York toward tropic waters on a midwinter day, we gaze out over a leaden sea of dull-green color, lashed by the stiff, chilling wind. But the next morning we awaken to a balmy air and go on deck to behold the ocean miraculously changed to ultramarine blue.

We are in the Gulf Stream, that marvelous river in the ocean, which gives the North Atlantic its unique character and profoundly affects its temperature even as far as the North Sea, bestowing upon the British Isles and Scandinavia the inestimable boon of a chastened climate.

The Gulf Stream exerts an influence on the spread and distribution of the marine life of the Atlantic which cannot be overestimated.

The main current warms the whole North Atlantic, and spurs setting in toward the coast have a striking effect on the distribution of floating life off the Middle Atlantic States and southern New England. Here, however, the warm stream is separated from shore by colder waters forming what is known as the "Cold Wall." South of the Grand Banks of Newfoundland it meets the icy Labrador Current which flows down from the north, bringing a northern fauna and making its influence felt along the shore, particularly north of Cape Cod.

Cape Cod and the Labrador Current together form an efficient barrier which prevents the more southern species from reaching the northern New England region, though some may be carried far north of this latitude toward Europe.

On the other hand, Cape Cod, because of its somewhat barren and sandy character, also acts as a barrier to the northern shore fauna, keeping it confined to the gulf of Maine, Nova Scotia, and Labrador.

Nevertheless, in recent years, such species of mollusks as the indefatigable periwinkle, dog whelk, and "buckie" have slowly surmounted this obstacle and are now found on the coast of southern New England and Long Island Sound.

Warm and cold currents determine the spread of floating sea life, while barren stretches of shifting sand are difficult for many of the creeping animals of shallow waters, and only those survive that are particularly adapted to such conditions.

To emphasize the contrast between the barren shore just south of New York and the teeming life of the tropical Florida shallows, let us visit a part of the southern New Jersey coast toward dusk.

Ghost Crabs Are Fleeting

A sandy beach extends into the distance until hidden by the curve of the shore. It is bounded inland by the sand dunes, their snowy sides diversified by beach grass and stunted vegetation. Long lines of beach wrack brought in by the tides parallel the water's edge. The sands seem empty of life and movement except for the wash of the sea.

But not quite!

There is a shadowy stir by the dead seaweeds—and another like a fleeting wraith farther up the sands. We blink our eyes, for it has vanished. Now there is a start directly in front of us and a ghostlike creature materializes before our very eyes, only to disappear apparently into thin air. We focus our gaze more carefully and, at the next sign of movement, follow it eagerly.

Now at last we identify a swift, silently moving form, a set of scampering legs, and a pair of shining black eyes erected on upright stalks. We have stumbled on a community of ghost crabs (*Ocypode albicans*), and well do they deserve their name.

Their pale, yellowish-gray carapaces match the beach so exactly that when they are stationary it is almost impossible to see them. They are betrayed only by their swift movements as they glide over to the beach wrack to snatch a sand hopper or two, and quickly dart back to their homes when alarmed.

Their abodes are burrows dug deep into the sand above the high-tide line. The entrance is a round hole flanked by a sand heap, where they stand guard or retreat until only partly visible in their doorways.

If we approach, they vanish inside in a twinkling. It is difficult to catch them, so fleet are their movements. We secure a few specimens only by flinging a hand net over them from a distance as they dart across the beach.

National Geographic Photographer Robert F. Sisson

Crabmeat "On the Hoof"

Anna Mae Goodwin proudly grins over the fine crab she helped her father take on his crab line off the South Carolina coast. The crab lines are taken in daily and crabbers sell their catch to the market "buy boat" that makes regular rounds.

Apparently the cold winters prevent the adults from becoming established north of New Jersey. To the south they range with increasing abundance to Florida and the West Indies, while on our New Jersey beach they have merely established their venturesome outposts.

Contrast this bleak barrenness with the balmy and prolific region from which they have migrated in the south. It is, of course, a sea abounding in coral reefs, with an amazing undersea life. But we shall speak of the interesting creatures of the quiet lagoons enclosed between the reefs and the shore, as well as of those that have invaded the low-lying beaches and the extensive shallow mangrove swamps that abound here.

Water Almost as Clear as Air

The sea is very transparent, and on quiet days the boat seems to be floating in air, while the sandy bottom with its denizens shows with the utmost clearness.

If cut off from their homes, they will take refuge in the sea, but it is apparent that they do not enjoy a watery environment, for at the first opportunity they dart out and make for their burrows.

They seem veritable creatures of the sand, being adapted to it by their concealing coloration, burrowing habits, agility, and speed, as well as by their custom of feeding upon the small crustaceans living in the jetsam of the sea.

But even these dwellers on the barren beach are invaders from the south, for this is the northern limit of their range. There are a few doubtful records of their having reached Long Island, and their free-swimming larvae often have been found as far east as Block Island and Martha's Vineyard.

Huge sea stars (*Oreaster reticulatus*) slowly crawl about looking for mollusks. They vary in color from red to blue or purple and are marked with an intricate network of raised ridges forming a pattern of triangles decorated with small knobs. They are the largest of the West Indian sea stars.

Conchs of two species are especially abundant. One, the queen conch (*Strombus gigas*), is the largest sea snail found in American waters, some specimens growing to a foot or more in length.

The thick shell has a coiled spire nearly obscured by the flange of the broadly flaring lip, its lining a brilliant rosy pink.

When the creature is alive, the narrow foot of the thick-skinned, muscular body projects from the aperture, armed with a horny, hook-

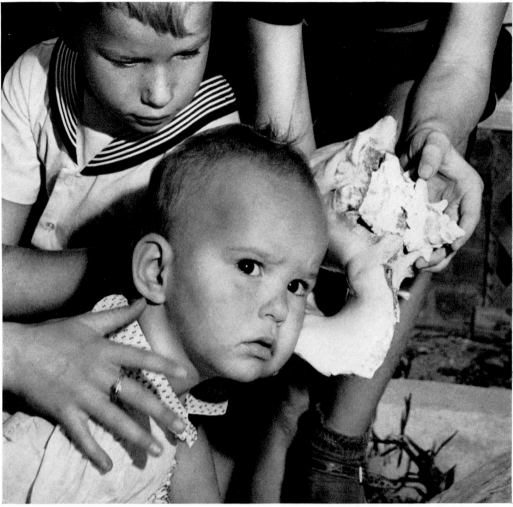

"What Is the Sea Doing in That Big Shell?"

Children all over the world listen to mysterious "sound of the sea" in sea shells. This one is the shell of the Giant Conch, common on the Florida Keys and the West Indies. Conchs are prized not only for their beautiful shells, popular as souvenirs, but for their delicious flesh, which makes fine Conch chowder.

like spine. By means of this, the conch pulls itself actively about on the sea floor, digging the hook into the sand and moving in irregular hops and jumps. It causes the heavy shell to rock wildly from side to side in its haste to escape pursuers. This interesting creature is a scavenger, its food consisting of dead and decaying animal life.

One of the occupations of the Bahama negroes is "diving conchs." As our launch lies anchored in a lagoon at Andros Island, we see the homemade sailboats of the natives drifting about slowly, while the occupants scan the bottom through a water glass.

Suddenly there is a splash as a negro dives overboard. Soon reappearing, his dripping body gleaming like polished mahogany, he hands up a conch over the gunwale, then drops back to get another.

Sometimes conchs are baited with meat, the odor of which attracts them in large numbers, and thus more may be caught in a short time by diving.

Conchs form an important article of food for the native islanders. In fact, the divers themselves are often termed "conchs" to distinguish them from persons not born in the islands.

Conch shells are sold for ornamental purposes and are familiar everywhere, especially in country districts in the United States, as parlor ornaments, doorstops, and borders for garden walks. They sometimes secrete "conch pearls" of a beautiful rose color, which are mounted as jewelry and have a moderate value. The shells, with the tips of their spires sawed off, are sometimes used as dinner horns by the Bahama Island natives.

National Geographic Photographer Willard R. Culver

Shells as a Decorative Motif for the Seaside Home

Between two rooms of her Miami Beach winter residence porch, Mrs. John Oliver La Gorce has fitted a number of glass shelves for her collection. A polished Chambered Nautilus is at the center near her right shoulder. At the top to the right of the coral are: a Partridge Tun Shell, a Measled Cowry, and a *Trochus niloticus*. Two Helmet Shells are to the left of the starfish above her head, and to the right are the Fighting Conch and the Triton's Trumpet. Below her right hand, to the left, are two Left-Handed Whelks. On the bottom shelf two Queen Conchs flank the coral.

The helmet shell (*Cassis madagascariensis*) is another conch common in the West Indies and often associated with the queen conch on sandy lagoon bottoms. It almost equals the latter in size.

This huge snail creeps about on a flat foot, searching for the bivalve mollusks on which it feeds.

The shell is indeed shaped like a white helmet, with a broad, flat, cream-colored lip, blotched and striped with a deep chocolate brown. It is quite thick and of fine texture, composed of layers of white shell over the deep brown.

Since about 1820 it has been exported to Italy and France for making cameos, and has practically superseded the more expensive semiprecious stones formerly used for that purpose. Beautifully delicate carvings are made, standing out in white bas-relief against the brown background. Rome, Genoa, and Paris are the most noted centers for cameo cutting.

The queen conch is also used for this purpose, but not so extensively. Cameos made from it show a rose-colored carving against a white background, but because the rose tint tends to fade upon too great exposure to light, eventually these cameos lose much of their contrast, and those made from the helmet shell are more highly favored.

Land Crabs Scuttle About at Dusk

We step off an outcropping of rock onto a white beach of calcareous sand. Thickets of sea grape grow along its upper margin under the coconut palms, diversified with low, flat clumps of beach lavender, the pale-green leaf clusters of which are covered with a whitish bloom, like dusty miller. Even here animal life is abundant. Large land crabs of two species—the red mountain crab (*Gecarcinus ruricola*), purplish red with pale-yellow markings, and the great white land crab (*Cardisoma guanhumi*) with shell of bluish gray to yellowish white—dig extensive burrows in the sand with their powerful claws.

These huge crabs scuttle about awkwardly, but with considerable speed. They come out in large numbers at dusk, and if we are walking along the beach in the darkness, they are likely to come bumping against our legs. Both species dig their homes not only near the shore, but also on the low wooded hills.

H. S. Jennings

Trapped by a Sea Star, the Mojarra Will Never Get Away

Caught in the maw of the starfish, the fish struggles helplessly, but it cannot escape the hundreds of tiny feet equipped with suckers. The starfish will have a leisurely meal, digesting its prey little by little, tail first. Just how a sluggish sea star captures lively fish is unknown, but one theory is that any small creature touching its arms is anesthetized by poison and becomes easy prey.

The "pearl necklace with rosette" below is a giant *Synapta,* a genus of holothurians, or sea cucumbers. The knobs on its body are soft and pliable, and aid the animal in creeping. The "rosette" on the head is made up of highly sensitive petal-like tentacles or feelers that locate and entangle food particles. This creature, taken off Andros Island, largest of the Bahama Islands, is a relative of the sea stars and sea urchins.

R. E. Dahlgren

Without Benefit of Hollywood

No stage director was present when the remarkable picture was made of the pair of sea horses (left), and the squid below need no imagination or camera tricks to make a "horror picture." The smaller squid in the mouth of the nightmare (below, left) had taken a bait when the larger one snapped at it in time to be gaffed and landed, at considerable risk to the captor. In the picture at lower right, a squid is being pulled into the boat in the Humboldt Current (Peru Current) off Chile, with its vicious, parrot-like beak aimed directly at the camera. A slip by the hooded fisherman could mean serious injury or loss of fingers to toothy tentacles or beak. The pillowcase hood is worn to protect clothes from the squid's inky fluid.

290

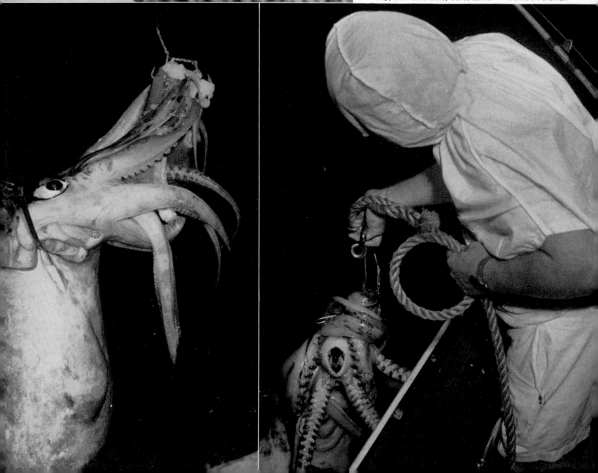

Each year they migrate to the sea in immense armies. There the females enter the surf to wash off the eggs clinging to the undersides of their abdomens, and thus allow them to hatch. Then the adults return to their abodes in the hills, to be followed about two weeks later by the migration of their newly hatched young.

Red mountain crabs have a delicious flavor when boiled, stewed, or baked in the shell.

The land hermit crabs (*Coenobita diogenes*) run along the beach, foraging among the dead leaves and the decaying trunks of fallen coconut palms. Their spiny pincer claws are brightly colored red and blue, and, like our northern hermits, when disturbed they quickly withdraw into their shells, blocking the entrance with expanded pincers.

They utilize empty mollusk shells for homes, and, when they outgrow them, promptly investigate all new possibilities, alternately trying various shells and popping back into the old one for comparison. Finally they select the most comfortable abode, though they may walk off with the original shell, after all.

Apparently they are willing to try anything that at all resembles a shell, for one of our expeditions from the American Museum discovered a hermit crab on a Bahama beach that had adopted the bowl of an old clay pipe for its abode! This specimen, pipe and all, is now on exhibition in the Museum.

Coral reefs and sand bars are typical of the eastern, or windward, side of the Florida coast and the Bahama Islands. On the westward, or sheltered, side of the larger bodies of land, coral reefs are practically nonexistent, and the sea is floored with a very soft calcareous mud.

This is true especially of the Great Bahama Bank between the Straits of Florida and Andros Island. A curious spreading seaweed known as "old man's beard" grows over the muddy bottom, and here and there are outcrops and ledges of old limestone rock. These are the great sponge banks. Here and on the Gulf coast of Florida most of the commercial sponges of American waters are harvested for the market.

True commercial sponges, however, when alive, probably never would be recognized by one not familiar with them in this condition. They are of very somber colors, from yellowish gray through various shades of brown to coal black. In fact, some of the finest and most valuable varieties resemble masses of coal-black leather or rubber.

The commercial sponge, as seen in the market, is merely the skeletal network by which the gelatinous animal tissues of the sponge are supported and held in shape. Of silken texture, it is composed of a fibrous, somewhat elastic substance known as spongin.

The finest commercial sponges are those of the Mediterranean, but certain varieties fished on the Bahama and Florida banks are of excellent quality. The best American sponges are the sheep's-wool, velvet, and Florida yellow. Fleets of sponging schooners carry the fishermen out to the banks, and the sponges are obtained by diving or "hooking."

The latter method, used generally on the Bahama banks, consists of spotting the sponges through a water glass, then lowering a long-handled hook with two or three prongs to dislodge the sponge. The boats are filled with them, and as much of the animal material as possible is beaten off against the gunwales of the boat with wooden bats. The sponges are then allowed to decay in the sun, and more of the ill-smelling soft tissue is beaten away.

They are then heaped in "crawls," wicker enclosures built in the edge of the water near the shore. The macerating process is advanced and cleansing completed by more beating and rinsing. The catch is dried aboard the boat while it is returning to the sponge market. In the market it is sorted and spread out in long sheds to be auctioned off to sponge merchants. It is then taken to sponge houses to be shaped, trimmed, and sorted for sale to the trade throughout the country.

Undersea Battle for Survival

These are only a few examples of the multitudinous forms of life that swarm in the shallow waters along the ocean margin.

In the more southern waters, genial temperatures the year round allow continuous development of myriad creatures not adapted to northern seas, while an abundance of lime-producing organisms makes possible the construction of skeletal substances and protective shells to a degree not attainable elsewhere. Consequently, coral reefs abound, and the shell-building mollusks have reached an unusual degree of development.

Nevertheless, the same fundamental principle of interdependent relationship of all life remains. Conditions of temperature, essential chemical elements, and sunlight determine the abundance of plant life, whether microscopic or of larger growth.

In describing the constant warfare of species in the world under the sea, one might apply in reverse the principle of the old bit of doggerel: Great fleas have little fleas upon their backs to bite 'em; and little fleas have lesser fleas, and so *ad infinitum*.

The basic submarine pasturage feeds hosts of the smaller animals, which in turn serve as food for larger forms. The process goes on endlessly in obedience to the sea's inexorable law that the strong shall prey on the weak and the fittest shall survive.

Men Who Go Down to the Sea—in Aqualungs

By Commandant Jacques-Yves Cousteau, French Navy

THE best way to observe fish is to become a fish. And the most practical means of becoming a fish is to don "gills" that permit one to roam, unhurried and unharmed, the reefs and dusky caverns of the fish's world.

One device which enables a diver to do just that is the Aqualung—a lightweight breathing apparatus that feeds the swimmer compressed air automatically regulated to equalize the pressure within his body with the pressure of the sea without. No cables or hoses connect him with the surface. Under water the air tanks on his back weigh only three pounds when full, nothing when empty. In almost perfect equilibrium, the diver can glide face down through the water, roll over, or turn on his side, propelled along by flippered feet.

It took many years to develop the Aqualung. For me, those years began on a morning in 1936 when I first put on a pair of sea goggles and looked beneath the surface. A naval officer, I had sailed in many waters and swum at every opportunity. But I had been a blind man; the goggles opened my eyes upon a new, neglected kingdom.

Then and there, I took out citizenship in the sea. With my companions, Frédéric Dumas and Philippe Tailliez, I dived the year 'round in shallow water and deep, in warm and icy areas.

Always, however, I rebelled against the limits imposed by a single lungful of air. I wanted to go deeper and stay longer. My friends and I began to experiment with oxygen rebreathing devices (such as the Momsen lung) and then with compressed-air cylinders and masks. Our stumbling block was a regulator. In December, 1942, I took our problem to a brilliant Parisian engineer, Emile Gagnan.

"What we need," I told him, "is some kind of gadget that will adjust the flow of compressed air in ratio to depth—automatically."

Gagnan grinned and reached up to a shelf behind his desk. He brought down a small plastic object. "Something like this?" he asked.

"Perhaps. What is it?"

"A valve I designed for these infernal natural-gas tanks we've had to put on our cars. Same kind of problem, you know."

I agreed. We went to work. In three short weeks we had designed and built a "lung" which utilized an adaptation of Gagnan's automatic regulator. By June we were ready for sea tests.

Cautiously we descended into the depths, a little farther each day. It took us 500 dives and the balance of the summer to attain 130 feet. Then in October, Dumas, in one carefully planned and attested plunge, dropped to 220 feet.

Quick to grasp the Aqualung's advantages, the French Navy requested me, after the Liberation, to organize and train a team of divers. This Undersea Research Group combed the mine-infested waters around Sète, detonated (at a safe distance) dozens of hidden Nazi mines, reconnoitered the scuttled French Fleet, and located in the harbor of Toulon a sunken bargeload of armed magnetic mines capable of almost demolishing the city itself.

None of these martial achievements by the Aqualung, however, were to please me quite as much as the role it soon played in making possible the first extensive color photography of the deep sea. Like most scientists and divers, I had assumed that the color band 50 to 100 feet below the surface was narrow and pallid. Then in 1948 I dived by Aqualung down to the wreck of an ancient Roman galley, sunk in 130 feet of water off Tunisia. From its deck I brought up a fragment of a marble column—part of Sulla's Grecian loot. Though daylight had appeared to illuminate it well enough on the sea bottom, where it seemed a dull gray and brown, I was astounded to find at the surface that it actually glowed with violent reds and oranges.

Determined to defeat this capacity of deep water to screen out the more brilliant colors, I started at once to improvise means of bringing adequate artificial light below. We proved off Tunisia that it could be done. Then we set about the organizing of full-scale, ship-borne voyages, aided by the National Geographic Society, to photograph in methodical and scientific fashion the watery realm of the Mediterranean and the Red Seas.

The photographs that follow tell something of the life we found beneath the sea. You will see it in its true color—as no men, prior to the Aqualung, have ever seen it before.

293

A Man-made Lung Gives This Diver an Hour's Permit to Explore the Twilit Sea

At 132 feet below the surface, atmospheric pressure on the body is 73.5 pounds per square inch—five times as great as at sea level. But to diver Frédéric Dumas, skimming past coral branches in his special breathing apparatus, pressure is no problem.

From the tanks strapped to his back, compressed air flows by tube to his rubber mouthpiece. Inhaled and absorbed into his blood stream, it raises the pressure within his body to that of the surrounding sea. Result: He feels the atmospheric pressure no more than a fish. If he stays down too long, however, or comes up too quickly, he may incur the "bends" as the nitrogen he has absorbed rushes out of the solution and bubbles within his body's fatty tissues. Usual precaution is to pause for decompression at 20 feet and again at 10 feet below surface.

His tanks will last him for about an hour. As they empty, he will weigh some three pounds less. Except for this slight tendency to rise, he will remain in perfect balance, able to float, turn over, or glide ahead with the languid ease of a dolphin.

A slow crawl beat with foot flippers produces a top speed of two knots; against heavily resistant water, more violent motion only defeats itself. Hands act as rudders.

For work below the Mediterranean, divers with "Expedition Flash" usually wear a brief tunic of foam rubber, sufficient to insulate them in waters that dropped at some depths to 43°. When separated by several hundred yards, divers communicated with each other by blowing into their mouthpieces—an underwater Bronx cheer. Close up, they managed to convey simple phrases by careful enunciation.

Dumas, exploring a reef a half-mile off France's La Ciotat, gathers here an armload of giant gorgonians for examination above. Their strong pigmentation, dimmed at this depth, will stain his hands a bright red.

Over the Stern Go Aqualunged Divers and Cameras

→ Captain Cousteau in white shirt looks on as Dumas, at ladder's lower rungs, dons his goggles. Waiting above him is Wladimir Nesteroff of the Sorbonne, his geologist's hammer and specimen bag hung at his belt. Third to go will be Dr. Haroun Tazieff, expert on volcanoes from the University of Brussels.

Recognized now as one of the greatest of contemporary diving theorists, Dumas, the son of an eminent physics professor, used to play hooky at every opportunity. His complaint: "They don't hold school in the water."

→ Disguised by mask and breathing tubes, Cousteau receives his still camera. It will weigh nothing in the water, thanks to its built-in air ballast. An attached Aqualung will keep its internal pressure constantly adjusted. Cable trailing from camera leads to watertight flash-bulb reflector which Cousteau will use to bring out the color of the depths below.

294

Ektachromes by Jacques Ertaud

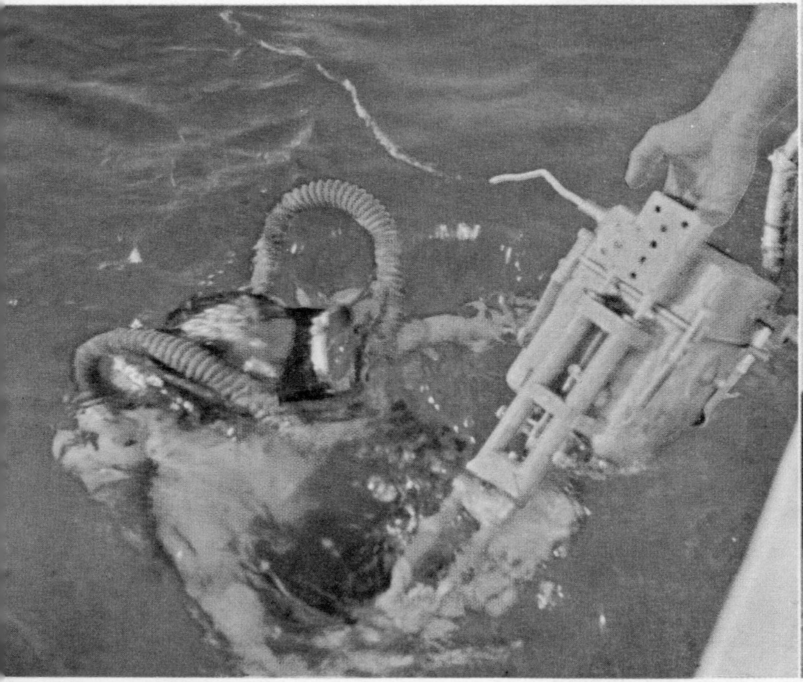

Sharks Constantly Prowled Around Divers, but Accepted Them Guardedly as Strange, Bubble-blowing, Two-tailed Fish

Swimmers near the surface, like the Aqualunger here descending ladder with his reflector, risked sudden attacks by sharks. These fish apparently assumed any bodies floating in upper waters were fair game. Farther down, however, they became cautious to the point of cowardice. Divers saw a 4-pound triggerfish chase one big shark.

© National Geographic Society

Ektachromes by Jacques-Yves Cousteau

296

A Cloud of Pastel Fish Drifts Through This Shallow Forest of Red Sea Coral

Chief zoological explorer with the expedition was Prof. Pierre Drach of the Sorbonne. At 55, he took a course in diving. Emerging a qualified Aqualunger, he eventually reached 220 feet on the Red Sea trip. His customary equipment for work below included a housewife's string shopping bag, a depth meter, a compass, a watertight watch, a white board and indelible pencil, and a burglar's jimmy. On this reef, only 25 feet down, natural and artificial light combine to bring out the delicate shades of coral clusters and their inhabitants.

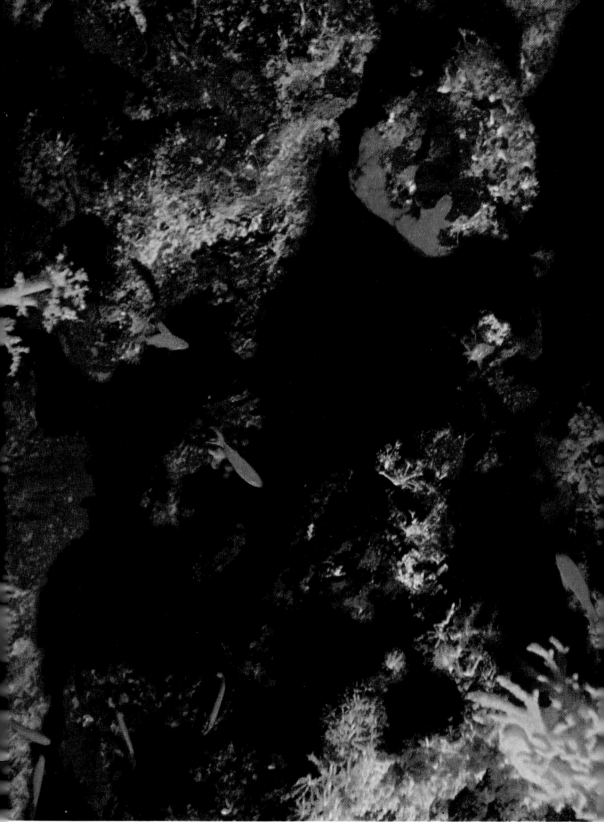

297

Same Reef, 110 Feet Deeper, Reveals Hues Which Only Powerful Bulbs Can Illuminate

For the marine biologist, one advantage of deep diving in the Red Sea was that water below 20 feet was virtually immobile, with no perceptible currents to stir up sediment. Aqualungers at this level detected wave action only by a barely noticeable increase in pressure as water far above them rose and fell. Until a photoflash went off in front of this sea wall, divers could dimly glimpse only dark blues and greens. Reds and russets were completely absorbed by the intervening sea water.

Rosy Damsels Swim Past Sea Wall Dense with Marine Life

Explosives detonated in the crevices of this Mediterranean cliff, 130 feet below Cap Sicié, revealed a biological blanket of living and dead organic matter more than six feet thick. Little damselfish, brightly hued at this depth, are cousins to the drab, brown variety found near the surface.

Filtered sunlight was sufficient for black-and-white movie film, but to make color photographs in the dense twilight sea, with its quintillions of suspended minerals and microscopic organisms, only the most powerful flash bulbs sufficed. Cousteau's men used the "slow peak" type. Though each bulb gave off more than 5,000,000 lumens (equivalent to 400,000 candlepower), it could light up only a 5-foot radius. With an 8-bulb simultaneous flash the camera's color range was extended to a scant 12 feet.

These lemon-sized bulbs could resist pressure down to 300 feet, but water seeped into their sockets. Varnishes proved useless as insulation; shoemaker's wax worked, but gummed up hands, feet, the reflectors, the deck, and even the ship's dachshund. Finally Cousteau designed several watertight reflectors to house the bulbs and attached miniature Aqualungs to pressurize the containers.

A Second Later, Alarmed Fish Vanished into a Hundred Crevices

Dumas, studying this reef's outgrowth of supple gorgonian coral, lolls without effort at 100 feet down. Regarded by the rest of the expedition as half-fish, Dumas has made more than 3,000 dives. When a diver ventures below 100 or 150 feet, he begins to feel increasingly intoxicated. Life appears wonderful. Danger reactions fade. If he continues down to 300 or 400 feet, he may pass out, lose his mouthpiece, and drown. But if he confines himself to a moderate depth and then returns to the surface, the exhilaration departs—and with no avenging "hangover."

Scientists describe this process as narcosis and liken it to a gradual anesthesia.

Scraggy "wire" at upper right is actually a whiplike horny coral.

Ektachrome by Jacques-Yves Cousteau

300

Gogglers Don Rubber Fins to Kick Themselves Down to Eerie Deep-sea Hunting Grounds

The man in background churns the surface of a rock-walled pool, ready to dive when he sights his quarry off La Jolla, California. Fishermen, wearing rubber-and-glass face plates, carry five-tined spears. With prying irons (right) they dislodge abalone from rocks. Bottom Scratchers Club candidates must capture two sharks, barehanded, in 20-foot dives.

Goggle Fishing in California Waters

By David Hellyer

A S I slipped from the reef into deep, clear water off La Jolla for my first goggle-fishing adventure, my diving companion shouted a friendly warning.

"Prepare for a shock," he cautioned, swimming alongside. "Your first look at the ocean's innards will give you a jolt!"

My nose was tightly encased in the rubber housing of an unfamiliar face plate. I tried to inhale before submerging. This created a strong suction which pressed the mask against my cheekbones but gave me no air at all.

"Breathe through your mouth," my colleague advised.

Swimming breast stroke, I gingerly submerged my head until the cool water lapped my ears. Instinctively, I kept my eyes shut. Half dreading what came next, I opened my eyes and—wonder of wonders! My goggle-fishing friend was right—my first impulse was to paddle for shore as fast as possible!

A Submarine Wonderland

Even Alice, fresh from Wonderland, would have gasped at the landscape spread below me. Long, brown tentacles of kelp, waving weirdly in submarine currents, appeared to clutch at me. Eelgrass danced on the ocean's floor; every grain of crystal sand, each little animal and fish stood forth boldly like images in a stereoscope. First I was amazed, then enchanted; the spell never has been broken.

Color abounds along these reefs. Incredibly orange garibaldies, the goldfish of the sea, dart from rocky holes on the bottom. This inquisitive denizen frequently will swim to within arm's length of a goggler, his comical face gaping into the diver's face plate. Perhaps the goggler appears as ridiculous to the garibaldi as vice versa!

Acres of sea urchins carpet rocks and reefs, their purple and red spines at stiff attention like hatpins in grandma's pincushion. Sand dollars dot the ocean floor, partially buried and standing vertically like wheels from some abandoned prairie schooner.

Countless sea anemones blanket the reef walls, their tentacles waving a fatal invitation to small marine animals on which they feed. Spider crabs dart in and out of dark crevices, and pink and white starfish cling to rocks like decorations on a Christmas tree.

Occasionally a diver discovers a group of strange, cone-shaped objects, like leather corkscrews four inches long, lying on the bottom. These are eggs of the ugly bullhead shark.

Tide-pool blennies swim jerkily from rock to rock, looking for a fight, for this pugnacious, eellike little fish always has a chip on his scaly shoulder. Sea hares, fantastic, sluggish specimens which look like animated puddings, slither over the rocks. An occasional long-jawed goby swims by. This mudsuckerlike fish will live out of water for a day or longer if kept covered with damp seaweed. Fishermen covet them for bait.

Anchovies Flash Like Mercury

We were swimming in a narrow channel, walled in by reefs, in water perhaps 15 feet deep. A school of anchovies flashed by, their scales sparkling in the morning sun. In tight formation they cut through the blue water like an errant river of mercury. Suddenly their ranks were shattered by a lightning-quick flash of white.

"Halibut feeding," my friend called, as he took a deep breath to dive. Down, down he swam, almost to the bottom of our private pool. Over a sandy patch in the weeds he poised his spear, then lunged the five-tined weapon into the sand.

A cloud of roiled water muddied his spearhead, and when the sand settled I saw that he had transfixed a beautiful California halibut, much prized by anglers and gogglers alike as table fare.

This species, a member of the flounder family, is frequently taken by divers. One recently speared at La Jolla weighed 30 pounds, though commercial fishermen have taken specimens weighing up to 60 pounds. Pacific halibut may weigh 500 pounds!

My only equipment for this underwater adventure was a face plate and a pair of swimming trunks. But my experienced companion wore swim fins—black rubber "feet" somewhat suggestive of a duck's.

"Fins allow us to utilize the tremendous driving power in our legs," he explained. "The human foot is very inefficient in water because its area is so small in proportion to the muscle power of the leg. Wearing fins, a good 'skin diver' can travel 70 to 100 feet under water in half a minute! And even a dub wearing them can outdistance an Olympic champion."

These men who "live with fish" form a fast-growing group. Ten years ago the sport was virtually unknown, save to a few hardy individuals who made their own crude goggles and broomstick spears and explored the surf alone. By 1949 more than 8,000 enthusiasts had joined the ranks in southern California alone, with other groups forming on Gulf and Atlantic coasts and in inland waters.

Most experienced gogglers have their own favorite fishing holes, secret spots in reef or surf where granddaddy lobsters lie, or where abalone or fish are especially large and abundant. A good skin diver can keep his family well fed on his submarine efforts. During depression times one goggler supported his family for two years in this fashion.

The Bottom Scratchers Club

Seasoned divers are the men comprising San Diego's unique Bottom Scratchers Club. Each is a veteran of several years' underwater fishing; each has passed rigorous tests. So difficult are these trials that only nine men qualified for membership in the first 15 years of the group's history.

As a starter, you must swim alone through the heavy surf, navigating your way over a treacherous reef covered with razor-sharp coral and white with foaming combers.

Later you must dive in 30 feet of water, bringing up three abalone in one dive. If your wind holds out, you then go down 20 feet for a spiny lobster—and they have been known to measure three feet in length!

Surely your prowess has been proved by now? Wrong. A final test challenges. You must seek bottom at 20 feet and bring up two sharks, one at a time! That test doesn't sound too formidable until you learn that said sharks are to be captured by the tail, *barehanded!*

At least a few women divers have done it. Admittedly, the captives were harmless pointed-nosed guitarfish, frequently called shovel-nose sharks. They attain a length of four feet.

"I once grabbed one of these four-footers by the tail," said Jack Prodanovich, veteran goggler. "He was lying in eelgrass when I cinched onto him. He gave me a swell ride, jerking me through the weeds for about 10 feet before shaking me off!"

This same diver also made goggling history by spearing and landing single-handed what was credited with being the largest fish ever taken by a goggler at the time.

"Several years ago, Wally Potts and I took our wives out fishing near the La Jolla caves," Jack related. "We were swimming 'battle formation,' about 50 feet apart, and I held the inside position nearest the cliffs. From experience, I knew we would swim over a channel where we usually found good fish.

A 500-pounder Lurks in Depths

"Suddenly I spotted a reef I knew didn't exist. The 'reef' moved, and I backed water and yelled for Wally. Together we peeked into the depths and spotted a monster—a black sea bass, or jewfish, that must have weighed 500 pounds!"

The boys held counsel of war. Armed only with five-pronged spears on short shafts, they must have felt like Don Quixote in his classic encounter with the windmills. Undaunted, they decided to take a stab at the jewfish.

"Wally was to hit him on the right side, while I smacked him on the left," Jack told me. "We took deep breaths and dove. We had to swim farther than we anticipated, and Wally ran out of air, leaving me alone with this deep-sea citizen. I speared him just back of the head. Three prongs penetrated, and I saw them bend over at right angles.

"Mr. Jewfish suddenly remembered an appointment in deeper water and tore out of that channel like a PT boat, his tail whipping up a froth of sand and kelp en route. Our wives reported that the spear shaft went past them like a sub's periscope, bound for Japan. We didn't see big boy any more that year."

For two years they experimented and failed in attempts to capture one of the giant fish. Finally they built a slip-point spear, powered with a high-tension spring, and prepared for the showdown.

In September, 1945, Prodanovich was cruising the waters off La Jolla on his paddleboard; by his side lay his new spear, not yet tried in battle. Searching the depths, he suddenly caught his breath as a monster swam into view below him.

With his spear cocked for action, he dove. Within range, he struck, his spear entering the fish squarely between the ribs and completely penetrating its body. The goggler quickly surfaced, then mounted his paddleboard as the fishline from board to spearhead whipped the water to froth.

"He towed my heavy paddleboard as though it was a piece of driftwood," Jack related. "Sometimes both board and I were completely submerged. Finally the fish wore itself out, and I started the long tow to the beach. But every time I thought the sailing was smooth, he'd take off for Honolulu again!"

Finally the huge fish was beached. It weighed in at 207 pounds. The catch caused excitement among local marine biologists, who identified it as the first broom-tailed grouper

 Luis Marden, National Geographic Staff

Sharpshooting under Handicaps

A goggle fisherman draws a pretended bead on a channel bass in the circular tank at Florida's Marine Studios.

known to have been taken in California waters.

Since then, Prodanovich has speared and landed several of these monsters, though none outweighed his first.

One of his catches provided a dramatic reverse twist to the old "big one that got away" story. Not far off La Jolla he spotted a deepsea behemoth lolling under a weed-covered shelf.

Another Big One

Aiming carefully, he drove his powerful, spring-driven spearhead into the creature. The line sang and zipped through the water as the fish took off. To his dismay, Prodano-vich realized that the bass was taking his line *under* the reef—almost sure death for any line. And so it proved; the line soon parted, probably neatly cut in two by a jagged piece of coral.

Sadly the champion spear fisherman returned to shore, with nothing but a broken line to testify to the big one that got away.

But he who laughs last sometimes is a good fisherman. One month later, Prodanovich again spied a big one. He knew that these big bass sometimes like to lie in kelp beds. Skirting one bed, he saw the tail of a giant protruding from the forest of brown weeds. Quickly he drove home his spear, aiming through the kelp at the fish's concealed body.

One of Mankind's Oldest Weapons Captures a Fish for Dinner

Jack Dorsett, member of a Miami goggle fishermen's club, emerges from the waters of Biscayne Bay with a fat sheepshead he has speared.

Then began a fight which ended one hour later with Prodanovich the victor.

As he dragged the 112-pound gulf grouper onto the beach, Prodanovich gasped with surprise. *Two* spear points were embedded in the giant's back. From one hung the remains of the spear he had lost the month before, a remnant bent and twisted by the efforts of the grouper to dislodge the barb. Prodanovich had the last laugh with his "big one that got away"—almost.

Many jewfish, or black sea bass, have been caught by gogglers and hook-and-line sportsmen in the area. An inventory of the stomach of one specimen recently caught revealed five fishhooks, several feet of line, leaders, and a six-ounce sinker!

Abalone, a mollusk much prized for its meat, must be taken by surprise, for once warned of danger it clamps itself firmly to the rock and is very difficult to pry loose. One diver nearly drowned when an "ab" clamped down on his prying iron, which the goggler had carelessly tied to his wrist with a leather thong. Thereafter, he followed the usual custom of fastening the iron loosely to his wrist with a strip of innertube rubber.

Knowing that abalone clamp down when

touched, one waggish diver played a trick on his fellow gogglers. Finding a good bed of the mollusks, he tapped each abalone with his iron. When his companions tried to pry them loose, they couldn't dislodge a single one! Noting the location of his private stock, the practical joker later returned to reap a rich harvest.

Many fish are weird. An example is the "horned" bullhead shark.

"I spotted one of these ugly fellows under a reef," reported Lamar Boren, one of the Bottom Scratchers. "All I could see was a big red mouth and two long, white horns. I shouted for Jack, who was hunting near by. He dove, and came up laughing with the report that it was only a bullhead shark.

"Jack has always wanted to catch one with his bare hands. So he handed me his spear and dove, surfacing a minute later with the brute thrashing around in his hands. He was holding it by the tail and one flipper. We put a stick in his mouth when we got him ashore, and you could hear him crunch down on it with those strong teeth 20 feet away!"

Moray eels are vicious, too. Specimens up to six feet long have been taken. These salt-water horrors are especially fond of abalone meat, and often mistake the hand of a diver for their favorite food. One goggler had just pried an abalone loose when an eel darted from its crevice and snatched the meat right out of his hand, leaving the diver with an empty shell!

"Eels will follow you with their teeth bared if you threaten them," one diver disclosed. "We always check carefully when diving for abalone. Some day one of these submarine bulldogs may strike and clamp onto an arm, hand, or leg, and we'll have to come ashore to pry him loose!"

Other dangers lurk in the underwater world. Contrary to popular notion, however, octopuses, sharks, and rays are not considered perils by divers in these waters.

"Our worst enemy is carelessness or misjudgment," explained one veteran. "Hunting abalone or lobster, we sometimes dive under ledges or into crevices. A strong current could catch a man in such a position and keep him there until he drowned."

305   David Hellyer

Only Another Guitarfish Could Admire Such a Face

Gogglers find these harmless nightmarish creatures half buried in the Pacific floor off La Jolla, California. From the lower body of the fish, held in hand, is the thick, powerful tail.

Like aviators flying in rarefied air, divers must beware that they do not run out of oxygen. Once a pair of gogglers were diving in kelp beds, in search of grouper. As customary, one man mounted watch on the paddleboard while his companion dove.

Submerged Almost Four Minutes

"My friend had been down nearly four minutes before I sensed danger," related the watcher. "Most of us can manage a two-minute dive, but even the best of us is no four-minute man. I was just getting ready to go down after him when I saw him floating to the surface, face down and arms outstretched.

"Somehow I managed to get my friend's body across the paddleboard. By beating him mercilessly on the back, I finally got him to take a deep breath of air. He gasped and gulped for several minutes before regaining consciousness."

The unfortunate goggler afterward related his recollection of the incident.

"I had spotted a good fish and followed him into the weeds. I knew my oxygen was running low, but thought I had a few seconds more to go. But I didn't reckon with the fact that 25 feet of water lay between me and the surface. On the way up I suddenly blacked out. It was very peaceful!"

Most gogglers bear the scars of encounters with coral. Frequently a diver will be swept against coralline reefs by a strong wave or current and emerge from the engagement badly cut and bleeding.

Encounters with sea lions are not uncommon. One pioneer diver was prying abalone from a reef when something hit him in the back.

"The pain was so terrific it bent me double,"

David Hellyer

A Trophy of His Spear

Off La Jolla, this king-size black sea bass or jewfish was stunned by a thrust of the goggler's spear. Jack Prodanovich then paddled his prize ashore. Beached, the fish revived and struggled furiously until again subdued. Its captor's spear has a detachable point with a long line for playing fish.

he recounted. "I thought a moray eel had hit me. But my enemy soon made another pass at me, and I saw then that it was a large seal, probably a mother with young. It took several stitches to close the wound."

Sometimes big seals just feel playful!

Swimming with a Seal

"One afternoon, after fishing all day, I decided to take a swim, for the exercise," related one diver. "I dove in without any weapons, wearing only face plate and fins. I submerged several times for the scenery, and each time I surfaced I noticed a crowd had gathered on the breakwater. This was not unusual, so I kept on diving."

What he did not know was that a big seal cavorted beside him, submerging and surfacing with him like a shadow.

"Finally I spotted the monster streaking along under me like a torpedo. I decided this was no place for me and headed for shore, with Mr. Seal swimming alongside. Then he dove, and surfaced right in front of

me, between me and salvation. He stopped me cold, his beady-eyed face so close to mine I could count his whiskers!

"I lived and died fifty times during the next few seconds, remembering what had happened to another goggler in similar circumstances. But just as I was about to double up and kick him in the face out of sheer desperation, he took off."

These underwater sportsmen make important contributions to marine biology and frequently contribute specimens of interest to experts at Scripps Institution of Oceanography, located at La Jolla.

"According to the textbooks, certain fish grow to certain maximum lengths and weights," one goggler observed. "We have helped correct many of these ideas. For example, one manual says sheepshead attain a maximum weight of 25 pounds. I personally speared one weighing 27 pounds and have seen many larger specimens. And the texts tell us that moray eels grow to five feet. We know of a goggler who caught a six-footer!"

Gogglers have learned to relate certain fish to specific types of bottom, much as hunters seek their quarry in definite kinds of cover. California halibut, for example, most frequently are taken in sandy patches surrounded by eelgrass or other weed. Sheepshead inhabit rocky bottoms where plenty of crevices and holes provide protection.

Lobsters Hide in Crevices

Lobsters seldom venture into the open and are found only where cracks and crevices furnish safe hiding places. They do come out at night, however, to prowl the bottom for food.

Black sea bass, or jewfish, lie in kelp beds, while croakers often are found feeding in a few inches of surf, right on shore. Game fish sought by deep-sea anglers—the barracuda, bonito, tuna, yellowtail, and other rod-and-reel favorites—seldom ranging out of deep water, are not often taken by gogglers.

Because of their delicious flavor, California halibut are prized catches, and divers have perfected halibut spearing to a high degree. Hard to spot as it lies on sandy bottom, the California halibut has a chameleonlike capacity for changing color to suit his surroundings. On clean sand he adopts a sandy hue; near rocks his coloring becomes mottled. But his underside always is snow white. Oftentimes the fish buries itself completely in the sand and can be detected only by its outline.

Not gifted with the rakish lines of some of his underwater brethren, the halibut appears sluggish, an appearance which proves very deceptive. Actually this fish is lightning-quick, capable of flashing through the water with incredible rapidity when feeding or frightened.

Several kinds of rays are common along the California coast. Many of these biological nightmares have saw-toothed barbs in their tails—a fact which an occasional bather discovers to his misfortune. Stepped on, such a ray instantly whips its tail upward, burying its tiny serrated sword in calf or ankle.

Poison glands exist in many rays and, like the earthbound rattlesnake, such rays are venomous. While the sting is very painful and may be dangerous unless cared for promptly and properly, it is rarely lethal. Cases of death from such punctures have been recorded, however.

Rays Blanket Themselves in Sand

Rays thrive on sandy bottoms. On one goggling adventure I swam over a large sandy area in eight feet of water. Dark, dime-sized spots covered the sand. Curious, I prodded one with my spear. A sting ray shook off its blanket of sand and swam away.

There were literally hundreds of such spots within an acre or two of sandy bottom, and each marked the bed of a sleeping ray!

Once I noted a curious, diamond-shaped outline in the sand, measuring nearly two feet across. Prying with my spear, I dislodged a sluggish guitarfish, which reluctantly swam off.

Gogglers frequently find "treasure" in their underwater adventures. Tackle boxes, rods and reels, all sizes of anchors, rings, bracelets and other jewelry, knives, and tools are among their booty.

I once found a revolver on a reef. While swimming at Waikiki Beach I spotted a beautiful ring sparkling in the coral. Retrieving it, I found it to be a class ring of a famous eastern academy. I wrote the academy, disclosing the initials and year engraved on the ring, and was given the name of its owner. The ring was then sent from Honolulu to Rhode Island, and another friendship was born!

During the war special teams of gogglers were formed by the Navy to scout reefs and beaches for anti-invasion obstacles. The Underwater Demolition Teams, recruited in part from peacetime sportsmen, are credited with saving the lives of thousands of Allied soldiers and sailors by removing barriers in the face of heavy enemy fire.

UDT Performs Underwater Miracles

Units operating off Guam destroyed more than 1,000 large obstacles, making troop landings possible. Frequently these divers, equipped only with face plates, fins, and steel courage, worked right in the wake of Jap divers who were installing obstacles. When our boys had set their high-explosive charges, they retired to safety while time fuses blew obstacles and Japs into oblivion.

UDT crews performed underwater miracles on Omaha Beach in the Normandy campaign, suffering heavy casualties in action. Their mission: to slash sixteen 50-yard gaps through three principal lines of obstacles. Working under devastating machine-gun and sniper fire, they sapped over 85 percent of the German-placed traps on the beach within two days.

Until recently it was illegal to spear game fish in California's ocean waters—and it still is, for everyone except a goggler! In recognition of this new sport, and in tribute to the divers who put themselves on a par with their prey, the California legislature passed an amendment to the fish and game code making the goggler an exception to the spear-fishing rule.

"Anyone who wants a fish badly enough to hunt him out in his own element deserves to spear him," one legislator observed in voting "aye."

Don Fay

Deep Ocean Trawling Produces Some Odd Catches

A huge metal-mouthed net goes over the side of the research vessel *Atlantis* in mid-Atlantic. Lowering and raising the net in deep water sometimes takes three or four hours, and some queer creatures are brought up from the lightless depths. One rich haul was made in 1,770 fathoms (about two miles) along the side of the Atlantic Ridge, an underwater mountain range explored by a National Geographic Society, Woods Hole Oceanographic Institution and Columbia University Expedition. Some 200 species of deep-sea creatures—"shrimp, fish with long feelers, sponges . . ." were obtained.

Strange Babies of the Sea

By Hilary B. Moore

Professor of Marine Biology and Research Associate of the Marine Laboratory, University of Miami

AS APPLIED to many of the creatures of the sea, there is special truth in Shakespeare's line: "It is a wise father that knows his own child."

On land we are accustomed to young animals whose parentage is at least guessable. Among the strange and fantastic youngsters of the sea the story is very different. Though scientific study is steadily revealing fascinating facts of parentage and life history, many riddles remain.

New World of Tiny Life

Back in the middle of the last century, when Johannes Peter Müller developed the method of straining plant and animal life from sea water with a fine net, he opened up a whole new world of minute life. Some of the larger animals had been known to earlier naturalists, but most of the smaller ones were of new and strange types, often wholly unlike any known animals from land or even fresh water.

It was almost as if man had just discovered the insect kingdom, with its gorgeous butterflies, teeming termite nests, and swarms of locusts. Here was a new field to be explored, with promise of exciting discoveries. Naturalists were not slow to follow Müller's lead.

At first, collections were made in the more accessible waters near land. Then came the historic ocean-going H.M.S. *Challenger* expedition in 1872-76 and its many successors, which studied this drifting plant and animal life in oceans around the world. Eventually Victor Hensen, of Kiel, Germany, proposed a collective name for it: plankton, from a Greek word meaning "wandering."

Scientists found, too, that plankton hunting could involve them in just as much difficulty, hard work, and disappointment as hunting for bigger game.

For example, the *Challenger* had to use several miles of rope to lower its plankton-catching nets into the ocean's abysmal depths. All this rope had to be coiled down by hand each time it came back on board, for there was no winch drum capable of taking it. All the different specimens found had to be described and sketched, a work which, when completed, amounted to a quarter-ton of scientific reports.

The early workers with plankton were fully occupied in distinguishing between the various new animals they found and in classifying and describing them. The next step was to find out something about their life and habits.

Commercial Fish Live on Plankton

This undertaking was seen as especially urgent, for naturalists had come to realize that plankton is the sole food of many commercially valuable fishes. Further, it appears that plankton acts as a nursery for the young of such important food animals as the lobster and even oysters and clams.

The plankton serves the same purpose in the sea as do pastures on land. We need to know its workings if we are to understand the great fisheries dependent upon it, just as the farmer profits from research on how plants seed.

Such early workers as the Swedish botanist Carolus Linnaeus (1707-78) sometimes gave names to strange new plankton animals without realizing that they were looking at babies whose parents were already well known. So it was that the name "Zoea" was given to a queer little rounded shrimplike object, and "Megalopa" to one that looked halfway between a lobster and a crab.

Today we know that both are stages through which most young crabs pass in the course of their development.

Such an error is easy to understand. When a mother bird cares for her young, their parentage is clear. A butterfly abandons her newly laid eggs, but it is possible to keep the captive until she has produced eggs, see what kind of caterpillar hatches from them, then what kind of moth or butterfly it turns into. But matters are far less simple in the sea.

Mouths Too Small to Feed

To begin with, most plankton animals—we do not quite know why—are extremely difficult to keep alive in captivity. Accustomed as they are to the cushioning of the ocean waters, they may bruise themselves fatally when they bump into the walls of an aquarium. Or perhaps we do not yet know the right food to give them, and they starve. Many of them, it is true, have mouths so small that they

Eight Million Plankton May Not Quite Balance a 50-Pound Sinker

Dr. Moore attaches the net to the towing cable for a sweep across a stretch of the plankton-rich Gulf Stream. A guard mesh across the net's mouth rejects sargasso weed. The torpedo-shaped weight, equipped with fins, holds the towing line at the proper level.

England, seem to have "green fingers" where this process is concerned. Among them they have built up a picture of the kind of life history which is typical of most of the groups of marine animals.

As with the butterfly, we can also catch specimens of the various kinds of marine animals, wait for them to lay eggs, and see what they hatch into. Sometimes they live for only a short time, but a few have been reared until they themselves became parents. This method does not help, however, when the parents themselves live in the depths of the ocean and defy all attempts to "bring 'em back alive."

Offspring of a Living Fossil?

One way or another, we have by now learned enough to say roughly what most kinds of plankton babies will grow up into. We generally know what family they must belong to; but the day when we can be sure of the exact species of all or even most of them is still far ahead.

could not swallow anything bigger than a few thousandths of an inch across.

When you add to all this the fact that many of the most exciting animals come from deep, cold waters into which daylight never penetrates, where the pressures are tons to the square inch, you will see why so many of them are killed even before we can bring them to the surface in our nets. To keep them alive in the laboratory is a problem.

It is understandable, then, why so few of the animals found in the plankton have been watched through their whole life cycle. Sometimes, though, we have pieced together the story bit by bit, managing to keep a baby shrimp alive long enough to see it grow into the next stage, then catching a slightly older one; and so on.

A few people, such as Dr. M. V. Lebour in

Some still remain utter mysteries. One of these, with the name of *Planktosphaera*, floors us completely. Occasionally our nets bring one up from the deep ocean waters—a transparent, spherical animal about half an inch long. It just does not fit into any known group of animals, although it hints tantalizingly at relationship with several.

A possible solution to the problem, and an exciting one, if true, is that it might be a young crinoid, or sea lily, one of the living fossils of the deepest ocean floors. We hope that someday we may be able to rear one and find out. Where on land can you find an animal that still, after some fifty years, can't be classified?

The best introduction to these plankton babies is, of course, to see them for yourself.

Marine Biologists Chart a Voyage to Study Mysterious Pastures of the Sea

The National Geographic Society and the University of Miami cooperate in a long-range program to study plankton, the drifting meadows of microscopic "fodder" on which most of the fishes of the seven seas depend for existence. The plankton studied in the program are found between southern Florida and the Bahamas. Dr. F. G. Walton Smith, Director of the Marine Laboratory at the University of Miami (left) and Dr. Moore, Associate Director, chart a voyage into the plankton-country.

Alive and in their natural colors, they are things of entrancing beauty. It is no easy task to catch their delicate fragility on paper or to paint a glassy-clear animal, as transparent as the water in which it lives, revealed only by glancing reflections of light and such patches of color as it may contain.

Eyes Seemingly Without an Owner

Sometimes I have spent five minutes examining a dish of live plankton before noticing an inch-long lobster baby that was swimming right under my nose. Even then it was revealed only as a pair of dark eyes, apparently swimming around all by themselves. I had been looking right through the body without noticing it.

This transparency may make things difficult for us, but it gives us an X-ray-like ability to watch such processes as the beating of a heart. On the other hand, it must be a great advantage to a baby lobster which is

being hunted by a fish to wear a cloak of invisibility that prevents the fish from seeing its prospective meal.

It would take a whole book to describe the life found in these waters, but Craig Phillips and Jacqueline Hutton have captured the general atmosphere in their paintings (page 317-324). The emphasis in these is on the crabs, fishes, and other reef animals rather than on the corals themselves. It is these other animals which provide so many of the plankton babies which we find in the Gulf Stream as it runs northward outside the reefs off Miami.

To the many visitors to Florida who enjoy good sea food, the spiny lobster may appeal as one of the most important inhabitants of the reefs. They may debate the relative merits of Florida and Maine lobsters, but perhaps our best escape from the argument is to say that they are quite different animals.

Northern baby lobsters look rather lobster-like when a few weeks old; the southerners

312

A Plankton Net Starts Down for Samples of Abundant but Invisible Underwater Life

Mysteries lie hidden in the world of plankton that sustain sea creatures as large as whales. The name plankton from the Greek word for "wandering," was given to the minute organisms because of the drifting life they lead. This 12-foot net gathers plankton specimens for reseaches by the National Geographic Society and the University of Miami. The brass mechanism at the right closes the net.

spend the first six months of their life swimming around in the plankton and looking much more like squashed spiders (page 323). Only the hint of a lobster tail at the end of their bodies points to their future shape.

Most of the animals grow more or less continuously, but the lobster, like its relatives the crabs and shrimps, saves up its growth to expand in sudden jumps each time it molts. The armor plating which it wears will not stretch; so at intervals it has to throw this off and replace it by a size larger, changing its shape at the same time if this is necessary.

Transformation of a Baby Crab

One important result of our work in the Gulf Stream has been the tracing of the 11 stages through which the Florida lobster passes before it is ready to settle to the bottom as a lobsterling. It must have traveled far on the current during its six months afloat; wandering plankton is providing important clues to the movement of ocean currents.

We have mentioned already that the baby stages of crabs were a puzzle to early zoologists. Page 322 shows the Zoea stage of a porcelain crab similar to the one shown on the bottom on page 321. We say similar, because this is one of the many cases where we know only the approximate parentage. We are not yet sure to which of several kinds of porcelain crabs these babies belong. With long-drawn-out spines in front and behind, they look, when swimming, absurdly like medieval knights charging, lance in hand.

Later, in the Megalopa stage, the creature begins to look quite like a crab (pages 322, 323). True, its tail still sticks out behind like a lobster's, instead of being neatly tucked away underneath the body as the parent has it. On the other hand, the claws are obviously those of a crab, and, in the case of the one on page 323, the keel along the top of the claw points strongly to the box crab as parent (page 320).

These claw ridges, when the little crab set-

 Marine Laboratory, University of Miami

A Random Catch of Ocean Small Fry Resembles a Selection of Angler's Lures

Plankton includes two main divisions: zooplankton, animals; and phytoplankton, plants. Magnified four times, these tiny animals include a transparent salp (right), a lobsterlike pelagic amphipod (right center), two kite-shaped pteropod mollusks, a jellyfish (crossed ring, left), arrowworms (named from their shape), a snail-shaped heteropod mollusk, and several beady-eyed fishes.

tles to the bottom, will fit tightly against the front of its shell and help keep sand grains from its mouth and gills as it burrows into the bottom. In much the same way, the backward-hinged claw tips of the ghostly little mantis shrimp shown on page 322 foreshadow the penknife action of the claws which have earned the adult the local name of "split thumb" (page 320).

For yet another relative of the lobsters the study of plankton babies has helped solve a problem which defeated earlier zoologists. The acorn barnacle, which grows limpetlike on the rocks (page 320), and the related ship's barnacle, were first classified as mollusks. After all, they had shells, so where better could you put them? The French naturalist Georges Cuvier (1769-1832), apparently with some misgivings, so classified them in his *Animal Kingdom*, although he no longer accepted the medieval myth that they would later drop off and grow into barnacle geese!

However, when young barnacles were exam-

ined as they first swam away into the plankton from the shelter of the parent shells, they were found to have quite unmollusklike jointed legs. In fact, they belonged to the same order as the crabs and lobsters, albeit as humble relatives.

Babies Aid Study of Parents

This is just one of many cases where a study of young animals has led to a better understanding of the parents, a principle surely applicable to man himself.

Sea urchins and starfish are among the most colorful inhabitants of the reefs. The unwary diver is liable to make an all-too-close acquaintance with the spines of the black urchin shown on page 321. Each female urchin sets free thousands of minute eggs into the plankton; as they drift there, they grow into animalcules even stranger than the young lobsters and crabs.

Page 323 shows the young of both sea urchins and brittle stars—frameworks of slen-

 Marine Laboratory, University of Miami

Magnification, Making a Dime Bigger than a Dollar, Lays Bare the Teeming Sealife

Planktonic organisms dwell in lakes and rivers as readily as in oceans. They reproduce with unbelievable fecundity; for example, acorn barnacles may raise 20 tons of young a year for each mile of shore. This sample consists largely of seedlike copepods. Transparent ribbons are arrowworms; two elongated triangles are pteropods. A salp's diaphanous form (right) suggests the ectoplasm of a ghost!

der arms connected by a small body in the middle. These arms are stiffened by the most delicate of supporting skeletons, sometimes built with three lengthwise rods and connecting struts like a radio mast. These are joined in the middle to a basketlike cage which protects the body.

When these babies, looking like long-legged stools, are ready to leave the plankton some six weeks later, they change to the grown-up shape in an even weirder way than the lobsters. In the case of the starfish, a bud begins to grow out of the back of the body, and from it tiny starfish arms emerge. The bud grows away from the rest of the baby on a slender stalk, which finally breaks off. Then the little starfish settles to the bottom of the sea, while the old body and arms swim away and eventually die.

A somewhat similar trick is played by some of the planktonic baby snails. The massive shells which their parents can drag about on the bottom would be far too heavy for the babies to swim with, even in a miniature edition.

Usually the young snails get around this difficulty by forming an early shell which is exceedingly thin and delicate. But this is none too strong a foundation on which to start building the adult shell; so some relatives of the well-known cowries have two shells. The baby uses one of these, a crystal-clear spiral with rows of sawteeth around the edge and completely unlike the adult shell. Then a second shell is formed inside this one, and, as the baby grows, it sheds its old house and starts building on the new foundations.

The squids and octopuses may look far removed from cowrie shells, but they are really quite close relations. Though their young (pages 318, 324) do not usually differ as widely from the parents as do some that we have been considering, they deserve mention, notably for their beautiful coloring. The skin which covers their transparent bodies contains sacs of various colored pigments. The animals can expand or contract these, and so produce constantly changing color effects.

"Searchlight" Shines into Squid's Body

Not content with this, many of these creatures are equipped with light-producing organs, also in assorted hues, so that they can put on a most spectacular fireworks display in the deep, dark waters in which they live.

As usual, the more we study these animals the more problems they present. Why, for instance, should some of these little squids have elaborate searchlights, complete with lens and reflector, arranged so as to shine into the body instead of outward? And what strange design formed another kind which always has one eye large and the other small?

We have been fortunate to catch the young stages of another very interesting octopus, the argonaut, or paper nautilus (page 321). The adults probably live somewhere outside the reefs, because they are occasionally found washed into shallow water after a gale. Their shell, which delights the collector fortunate enough to find one, does not house the body of the animal, as it does in snails, but rather serves as a baby carriage in which the female guards her eggs until they are ready to hatch.

Page 322 portrays a planktonic baby—a female argonaut. It also shows a nearly full-grown male, and this is the real prize. The males never grow much larger than a pea and as a result rarely have been found by collectors. The difference in size between the adult male and female is relatively as great as between, say, a chipmunk and an elephant!

Many reef animals, as we have seen, cast their young adrift to fend for themselves in the plankton. For example, the shrimplike copepods shown on page 319 shed their bril-

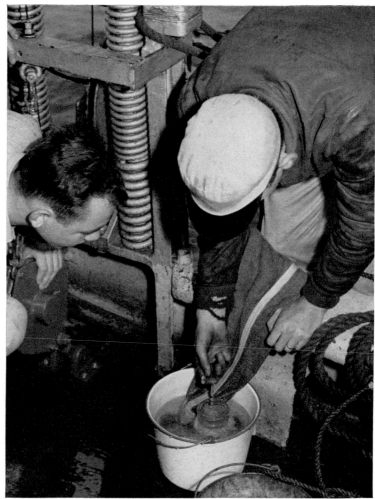

315

Each Haul of the Net Could Yield a New Species

Crew men on the research ship *Atlantis* empty a haul of plankton caught above the mid-Atlantic Ridge; the springs ease the strain on the net towing cable. Plankton is found at all depths, but especially in the upper 1,000 feet. Deep water's prodigious pressures do the tiny creatures no harm.

liantly colored eggs into the plankton to take care of themselves. These little copepods, usually a quarter of an inch or less in length when fully grown, are the grazing animals of the plankton and play the same part as the cattle and deer on land. Like these, too, they are preyed upon by carnivores, which in the sea range from big fish and whales down to the little arrowworm shown in the same plate. Though only an inch or so long, these arrowworms are a swift and long-fanged peril lying in wait for the copepods.

Plastic Nursery, Jet-propelled

Other reef animals care for the offspring in one way or another until they are well-grown replicas of their parents. At this extreme is the opossum shrimp on page 317, with its brood pouch like that of a kangaroo. Through the transparent walls of the pouch one can see the babies, which will be well-formed little shrimps before they are let loose. The Phronima shown in the same painting is even more ingenious. Since Mother Nature has not provided her with a pouch, she takes over the discarded house of another plankton animal, a Tunicate.

This house, or tunic, for which the animals are named, is a transparent barrel made, surprisingly, of cellulose. The Phronima creeps into this ready-made plastic barrel, and, by paddling water through it with her legs, achieves very effective jet propulsion. At the same time the barrel makes a splendid nursery for the babies. They are as safe from attack as human babies behind the glass windows of a hospital ward; yet the streams of water pumped in by the mother bring them a steady supply of the minute food which they need.

Plankton Study Poses Many Problems

Every time we touch on another aspect of plankton animals we run into fresh problems, and it is these which make the exploration of the plankton world so exciting. There is, for instance, the old question as to which came first, the chicken or the egg. In the plankton we meet an even more baffling question: Which is the parent and which the child?

Take the Salps (members of the Tunicate group) on page 317. When the eggs hatch and the young grow up, they are different animals from their parents—so much so, in fact, that they originally were described as a different species. What is more, this second generation does not lay eggs. Instead, it grows a long chain of buds, which finally break off to grow up into the egg-laying generation again.

The situation is about the same as if a greyhound had puppies which turned out to be dachshunds, and these dachshunds grew extremely long tails which broke off and grew into greyhounds. Absurd as it sounds, this is what happens, and which are we to call the parent of which?

Why do so many animals use the plankton as a nursery school? Why are so many of the young quite different-looking from their parents? And, for that matter, what becomes of all the surplus babies?

There is a lot to be said for turning offspring loose into the plankton. The parent does not have to expend energy looking after them or share her possibly meager food supply with the children. Instead, she can put her whole energy into getting the next brood ready to follow them.

Then, too, the young are being scattered far afield by the ocean currents, just like the windborne seeds of plants, and, like the seeds, they have the chance of finding new grounds to settle on. To an animal like a coral or sponge, which cannot walk about, this is essential; even to a lobster or crab it is extremely useful.

Just as plant seeds have to be lightly built and often have hairs or wings to help keep them airborne, so the plankton has to be specially adapted to drifting in water. Heavy shells, like those of a lobster or oyster, are obviously undesirable. They must be replaced by much more delicate structures. Air bubbles or oil droplets are helpful in keeping afloat. Above all, long projecting arms or feathery spines help to turn the creatures into living parachutes, and fins help them swim.

Add to this that the young animals may eat quite different food from that of their parents and need different mechanisms for catching and chewing it, and you see again why the two are likely to look so different.

One trouble about turning babies loose in the plankton is that they are more likely to be eaten by some carnivore than they would be if their parents mounted guard over them until they were old enough to take care of themselves. The answer to this is to produce so many babies that there are plenty to spare.

This process has been carried so far that the average egg production from each female creature in the plankton is probably about a million a year. Since most of these will be eaten before they ever grow up, this adds up to a tremendous food supply for such fishes as herring and mackerel. The little acorn barnacles that grow on our rocky coasts may produce as many as 20 tons of babies a year for each mile of shore, and the barnacle is but one of the many animals that live there.

Of course, it must be borne in mind that the plankton is not composed solely of babies or even of animal life. Plant life and tiny but adult animals compose a large percentage.

The farther we go from shore, and the deeper below the surface, the less we know about plankton. It is only natural that the more accessible places should have been explored first.

We know that fresh-water eels go to deep midocean waters to breed. We know too the story of the thousands of miles that the baby eels have to travel to return to the rivers.

But what about gamefish like marlin, wahoo, and others? They probably live their early life in the ocean plankton, but we do not know where or how.

These ocean waters come very close inshore along Florida's east coast; half an hour's sailing from Miami and you are in them. One laboratory in one year, or even in a lifetime, can begin to touch only the fringe of the problems that lie waiting in these waters. Yet we hope to continue learning more and more about the private life of the plankton.

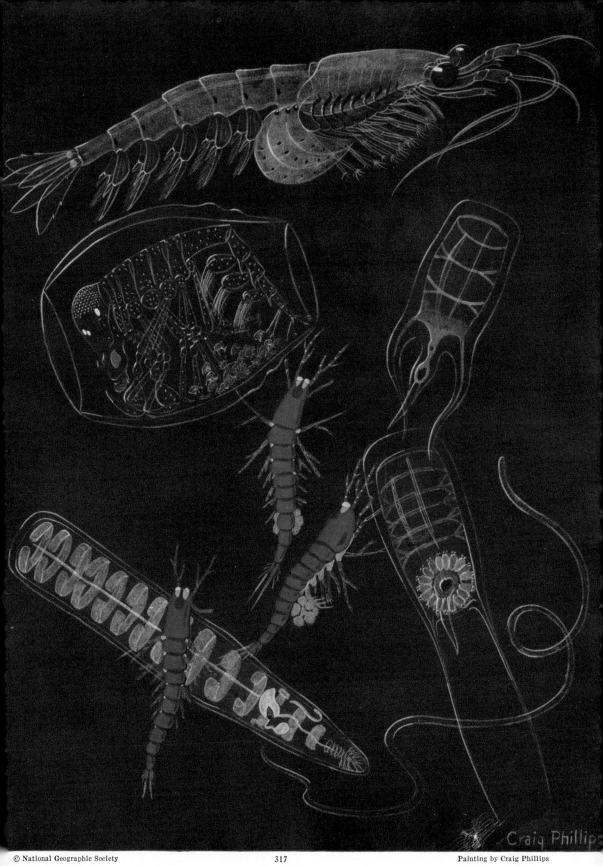

317

Glassy Plankton, Adrift in Sea Pastures, Raise Families in Strange Ways

Opossum shrimp (top) keeps its young in a pouch. **Phronima**, just below, uses the Tunicate's discarded barrel-shaped house as a nursery. Blue **copepods** wear orange aprons of eggs. **Salps** shed young by budding.

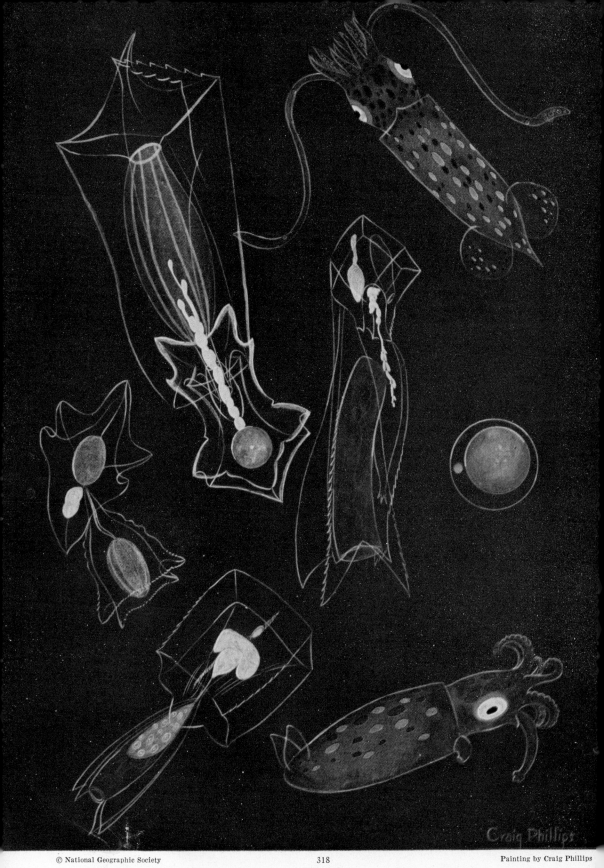

318

Painting by Craig Phillips

Transparent Bodies and Spots of Color Camouflage Nursery Life in the Plankton

Spotted baby **squids**, flanking a fish egg at right, can change color by expanding or contracting dots. **Siphonophores** (left), cousins of stinging Portuguese men-of-war, lay eggs in one generation, bud like plants in the next.

319

Life and Death Swim Side by Side. An Egg-laden Arrowworm Seizes a Copepod

Copepod, from the Greek, means "oar foot." The shrimplike creatures, which form the bulk of all animal plankton,
row with waving limbs. Arrowworms, like this marauder, resemble tiny transparent torpedoes.

320

Painting by Jacqueline Hutton

Graduates of the Plankton World Inhabit Sunlit Florida Reefs

Handle-bar feelers of the **spiny lobster** take the place of claws. **Mantis shrimps** (top) are as savage as praying mantises of the insect world. **Acorn barnacles** (foreground) wave fernlike fronds for food. **Box crab** rests beside watermelon-striped **sea urchins.** Branched sea rods, brain and lettuce corals (left) resemble plants.

321

Danger Lurks in Camouflaged Claws, Bristling Bayonets, and Waving Arms

Sponge crab crouches in portable ambush. **Green porcelain crab** rests beside three shelled cowries (right). Wary sea creatures avoid **black urchin's** stinging spines. Female **argonaut,** or **paper nautilus,** an octopus uses her shell only as an egg nest. Squirrelfish (top) and green cowfish swim among coral and weeds.

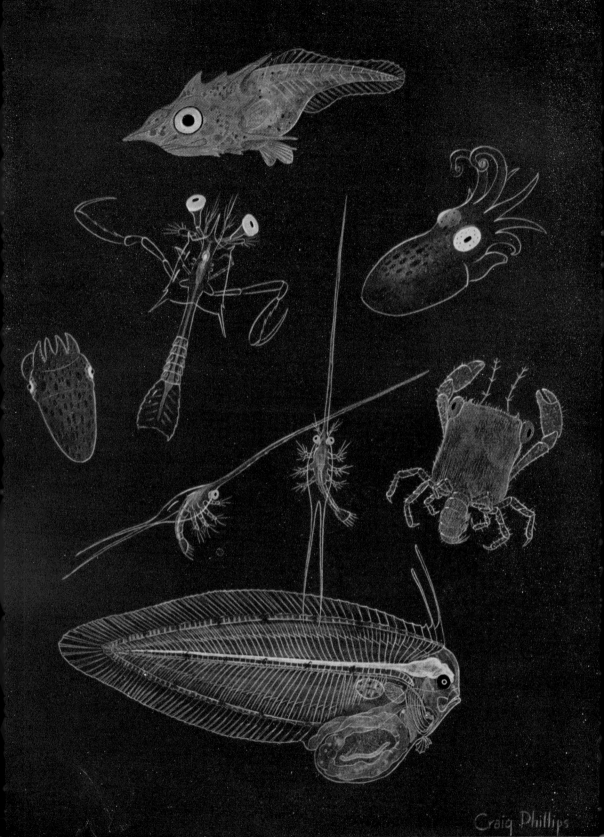

322

Children of the Reef Dwellers Leave Home in Nightmare Shapes

Needle-nosed babies are **porcelain crabs**. Male **argonaut** (left) is nearly fully grown; female (upper right) grows long arms. **Squirrelfish, mantis shrimp, sponge crab,** and **flatfish** plankton are greatly magnified.

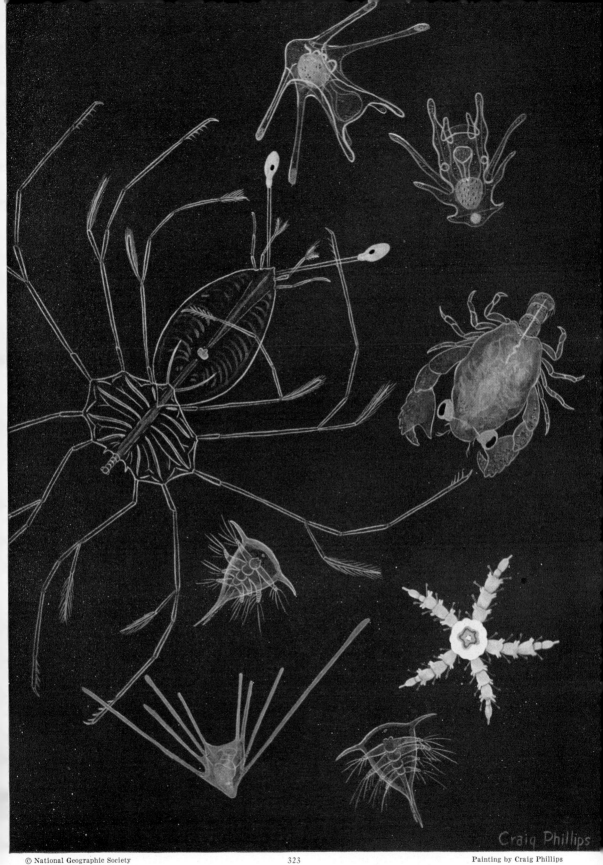

323

Spun-glass Spider (Left) Is a Spiny Lobsterling. Sea Urchins Float at Top

So transparent is the baby lobster that the eyes seem to swim by themselves. **Speckled box crab** (center, right) and
white **brittle star** soon will settle to the bottom. Jewellike baby barnacles rest beside a green star bud.

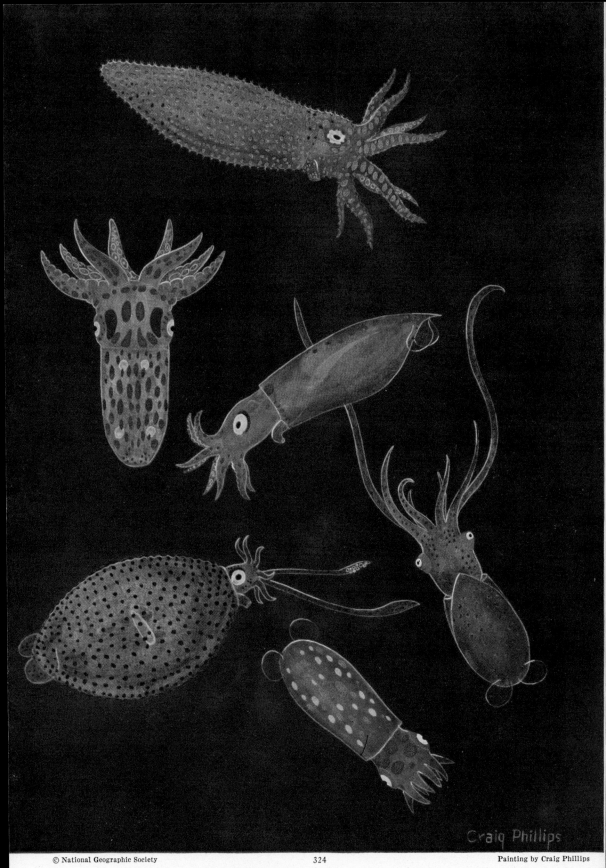

324 Painting by Craig Phillips

Little Acorns of the Sea Grow into Tentacled Squids and Octopuses

Related to the oyster and the snail, these are baby cephalopods of six different types, several of uncertain parentage.
When startled, the little **Cranchia** (lower left) pulls in its head like a timid turtle.

INDEX

Page   Page